MOOKIE

"Mookie Wilson is a legendary Met—both on the field and off. Here, in rich detail and color, is what it's like to be a New York baseball icon. A wonderful book."

—Jeff Pearlman, *New York Times* bestselling author of
The Bad Guys Won!

"We all tend to think of William Hayward Wilson not just as 'Mookie,' but as 'good old Mookie' for his effervescent persona and demeanor. In fact, Mookie is really, really good, and not nearly old, but this thoughtful, compelling book will show you a side of this all-time Mets favorite that might surprise you. His candor and honesty will undoubtedly deepen your respect and admiration for a man who is about so much more than a ground ball to first base."

—Howie Rose, New York Mets broadcaster

"Mookie Wilson is one of the most beloved figures in more than a half-century of Mets' baseball. Now, he has established himself as one of the foremost chroniclers of a baseball life. Mookie's relentlessly honest portrayal of his career and the unforgettable 1986 World Series Champions further elevates his status as a Mets icon."

—Gary Cohen, New York Mets broadcaster, SportsNet New York

"Mookie is a classy and compassionate person. Because he had feelings and respect for me as a player, I never wanted him to feel guilty about 'the play.' Instead, I wanted him to enjoy and appreciate the accomplishment of being on a World Championship team."

—Bill Buckner, member of the 1986 American League Champion
Boston Red Sox, twenty-two-year Major League veteran,
and 1980 National League Batting Champion

continued . . .

"There's nobody that I thought more highly of than Mookie Wilson on that '86 Mets team. He was respected, funny, honest, and just as solid a citizen as anyone I've ever known."

—Tim McCarver, longtime Major Leaguer, broadcaster, and recipient of the 2012 Ford C. Frick Award

"One of my favorite teammates—a class act, an even better person than the great ballplayer he was. Mookie was the moral rudder wherever he went."

—Ron Darling, former All-Star pitcher and member of the 1986 World Champion Mets, current SNY and TBS color analyst

"All the clichés you hear about Mookie are true. On a team of 'out there' characters, Mookie was mature and wise beyond his years. In a selfish, me-first business, Mookie was a great mentor and legitimately cared for others."

—Bobby Ojeda, member of the 1986 World Champion Mets, current SNY studio baseball analyst

"Mookie is, in a nutshell, an awesome man of God both inside and outside the church. His spirit of giving and his spirit of caring are an inspiration. His life speaks for him."

—Bishop Wendell B. Sumter, pastor at Zion Mill Creek Baptist Church, Columbia, South Carolina

MOOKIE

LIFE, BASEBALL, AND THE '86 METS

MOOKIE WILSON

with Erik Sherman

BERKLEY BOOKS, NEW YORK

THE BERKLEY PUBLISHING GROUP
Published by the Penguin Group
Penguin Group (USA) LLC
375 Hudson Street, New York, New York 10014

USA • Canada • UK • Ireland • Australia • New Zealand • India • South Africa • China

penguin.com

A Penguin Random House Company

Berkley trade paperback ISBN: 978-0-425-27133-9

Library of Congress Cataloging-in-Publication Data

Wilson, Mookie.
Mookie : life, baseball, and the '86 Mets / Mookie Wilson, Erik Sherman ; foreword by Keith Hernandez.
pages cm
ISBN 978-0-425-27132-2 (hardback)
1. Wilson, Mookie.   2. Baseball players—United States—Biography.
3. New York Mets (Baseball team)   I. Sherman, Erik.   II. Title.
GV865.W565A3 2014
796.357092—dc23
[B]
2014000492

PUBLISHING HISTORY
Berkley hardcover edition/May 2014
Berkley trade paperback edition/April 2015

PRINTED IN THE UNITED STATES OF AMERICA

10 9 8 7 6 5 4 3 2 1

Cover design by Richard Hasselberger.
Cover photos: Red Sox vs. Mets © T. G. Higgins/Getty Images.

*Penguin is committed to publishing works of quality and integrity.
In that spirit, we are proud to offer this book to our readers;
however, the story, the experiences, and the words
are the author's alone.*

First, I would like to thank God for the many blessings He has bestowed on me. I am grateful for the special people He has placed in my life. I thank each of them for their love and support.

To my wife, Rosa: I don't believe that behind every good man is a good woman, but I do know that beside every good man stands a loving wife.

To my children, Preston, Adesina, Ernestine, and Esthermae: Thank you for your love and respect. You make fatherhood a joy and an honor.

To my father, the late James Wilson: I pray to be the role model you always were. Your spirit and memory continue to guide me. And to my mother, Nancy Wilson: It is your strength that inspires me every day. I've been blessed by your love and support.

To my brothers, the late Richard Wilson, Stebia, Collis, Daniel, John, and Phillip: The first and best teammates I ever played with.

To my sisters, Ruth, Dorothy, the late Verdia Wilson, Vivian, and Marilyn: A loving family would not be complete without sisters to fight with.

To my in-laws, Preston Hicks and the late Jessie Hicks, a true example of a strong black woman.

To the late Judge Julius B. Ness, who confirmed what my father always taught me: *Judge every person on his own merit.* Thanks for being a true friend.

This book is the reflection of the influence all of you have had in my life as a husband, father, son, brother, and professional. May God continue to Bless you all.

—Mookie Wilson

To my double-play partner in life, Dr. Habiba Boumlik; our children, Alex and Sabrina; and Tim Neverett, whose friendship and loyalty is never taken for granted.

—Erik Sherman

CONTENTS

FOREWORD

I t was just prior to the winter meetings following the 1983 season, another last place finish for the Mets. I had begrudgingly come over to New York in a trade from St. Louis that June, even after asking my agent if I had enough money to retire from baseball instead of living in the concrete jungle and reporting to that lousy Mets team. He assured me I did not, so I packed my bags for New York.

Now it was decision time once again. Would I stay with the Mets or move on to another team?

After coming to the realization that the Mets were loaded with a plethora of tremendous prospects coming up from the farm system, I decided to sign a five-year extension and try to help the club transform itself into a winner.

At the winter meetings, there were rumors in the papers that

Mookie was on the trading block. I made a statement to the press that I was emphatically *against* any such trade. As an opposing player with the Cardinals who played against those perennially terrible Mets teams of the early eighties, I had seen how Mookie stood head-and-shoulders above anybody else on his team.

I remembered watching him and thinking, *Gosh Almighty, it's May and they're twenty games out, but this guy only knows one way to play. Just one speed. He hits a routine ground ball and sprints to first base every single time.*

———

I told the media, "Mookie's the kind of player we need. We've got all these young guys and if we're going to go forward, if we're really going to turn this thing around, then we need a veteran to set the example for them. What better example than Mookie hustling and playing it hard every single day?"

Lo and behold, they didn't trade Mookie. Thank God.

What's very ironic to me is how his leadership and hustle all came full circle when he hit that ground ball to Bill Buckner in Game Six of the 1986 World Series. A lot of guys would have run three-quarters up the first base line, thinking that since it would be a sure out, why bother running hard. But this was Mookie and he busted his butt up the line like he did *every* game he ever played in his career. It's possible that Buckner may have felt added pressure to get to the ball and the bag quicker with Mookie running hard. Of course, the ball skipped through Buckner's legs and the winning run came home to turn the series around. That play said it all about Mookie.

Two nights later, we were world champions.

Mookie was one of the more exciting players on what became an outstanding Mets club that played with a lot of gusto and grit. His teammates and fans alike loved him for his aggressive style of play. It was every bit as exciting watching Mookie leg out a triple as it was seeing Darryl Strawberry hit one of his moon shot home runs.

Mookie was one of my all-time favorite teammates, a consummate professional.

When Lenny Dykstra came up from the minors and management started platooning Mookie despite his being a productive switch-hitter, he could have sulked, moaned, or grumbled about it. Instead, he never complained even though he wanted badly to play every day. Not only did Mookie not gripe about it, he did everything he could to help Lenny get adjusted to major league life. That's the kind of teammate and individual Mookie was to everybody.

Whenever Mookie's name *was* on the lineup card, he busted his tail like he was an everyday player. That perfectly sums up the strong character that he possesses to this day.

We certainly had our share of characters that enjoyed going out after games for a few drinks. While Mookie led a straight life, he still intermingled with everybody. And just because he wasn't a drinker didn't mean he wouldn't join the guys at the hotel bar and talk baseball. He was always part of the team and enjoyed the camaraderie he had with his teammates. He was, in a sense, Mets royalty.

When manager Davey Johnson decided to name a co-captain

a year after making me the team's first in 1987, I really felt Mookie was the deserving choice. Taking nothing away from Gary Carter, who was the second-best catcher I ever played against after Johnny Bench (I never played against Carlton Fisk), Mookie had the seniority on the club and I had great admiration for the way he played the game and carried himself as a human being.

It is an honor and privilege to have played with Mookie and I consider him a dear friend. Enjoy reading the story of one of baseball's all-time class acts.

—Keith Hernandez
New York, New York

PREFACE

When most people see me, they think of one thing— the guy who hit the ball between Bill Buckner's legs to win Game Six of the 1986 World Series. But while that play defines me to so many baseball fans, most everyone doesn't know or understand what I'm all about. There were plenty of things that happened to me to get me where I am in life. While baseball is an important part of it and has been a great platform for me to achieve many things, it does not define me. It is my hope that this book is really going to let people know that I have a life outside of baseball and that I am more than just another pretty face.

I have been asked many times to write a book and always refused because the timing wasn't right. And I never wanted to write a book just about game situations. Instead, I wanted my experiences to be helpful to others.

For at least the last three years, I jotted down little notes about my life. It was during this time that I thought I'd finally be ready to write my memoirs. My days as a player were long past and it seemed like my coaching career was nearing an end. But I can honestly say I knew absolutely nothing about the publishing business and I didn't know where to start.

That was when Buddy Harrelson, a good friend from my playing and coaching days with the Mets, and a guy who has always been in my corner, came to the rescue. Buddy always seems to give very good advice. When we got into a conversation about my wanting to write a book, he said, "You really need to get someone to help and guide you in the right direction." Buddy, who had already written a book of his own, referred me to his literary agent, Rob Wilson. Rob was very helpful and introduced me to Erik Sherman, the coauthor of two previous baseball autobiographies. The result of that collaboration is the book you now hold in your hands.

In this book, I try to convey to people the realities of my life. Some people may think that because I'm an athlete, I have lived in a fantasy world, that I have gone to extraordinary places, met extraordinary people, and had access to certain opportunities and privileges nonathletes do not. While some of that is true, like most other athletes, I have had my share of difficulties and have experienced great challenges and disappointments like everyone else. Yet through it all, we find a way to survive, and if nothing else, this book will definitely prove that there is a higher power directing my life.

I really hope this book is an inspiration to others. In this day and age, when some children at age six are already "planning" to be professional athletes or deciding on what college they're going to play for, I want to stress two things I feel strongly about. The first piece of advice I give to children is have a genuine love for what you do. And if that's playing baseball, then give it everything you have. The second thing is nobody needs to be a product of their environment. If you're black, poor, and from a large family like I was, it shouldn't condemn you to a life of poverty with no expectations and no future. Instead, it should be an opportunity to display your character and show that you are worthy of success. And that's me in a nutshell. I refuse to let life situations dictate who I am and what I've become.

The experience of writing a book has been more rewarding than I ever could have even imagined. It has really inspired me to voice my opinions, to share some of my knowledge and views that I have on subjects. Whereas I didn't think my life was all that interesting before, I have a new view and perspective of it right now. And I believe that there are many life lessons that you can learn from my story, but only if I share them.

I'm older now, but I'm still an athlete at heart. I still like to be congratulated and acknowledged and accepted. It's in an athlete's blood—we can't help it. It's why we perform every day. I am very happy that I've done something that has brought a smile and a little joy to people's lives—and that includes family, friends, fans, my teammates, and even people who don't like me. Maybe I've done something that's changed their lives.

I'm flattered and humbled by all the kind things people told my coauthor Erik Sherman about me, because I never look at myself that way. I tend to only look at ways that I could be better.

And I'm always very conscious of how other people feel and think about me. I often try to adjust what I say and be as accommodating as I can to others, as long as it doesn't compromise my values.

I think a lot of people will be surprised to read I was not always a happy camper with the Mets. Many fans have a lasting image of this guy running around the bases with a big smile on his face, always cheerful. I kept hidden how I felt sometimes because I didn't want my teammates and fans to share in some of the negatives. Besides, they couldn't have helped my situation anyway, so I didn't want to bring them down.

By telling my story as honestly as I can, I think people will understand that even though I was unhappy about many situations, there was a team objective that was greater than me. But at the same time, I had to be concerned about me, because there was more than just me involved. I had my family's well-being to consider.

People may view me a little differently after reading this book. And that's okay. Because when you bring about new information—for better or worse—opinions about you are naturally going to change. And while it might be disappointing to some people, I think it's time that they understand who I am and what I've gone through. I don't want to say "endured," because that word would make it sound like I've had a really rough life in professional baseball and I haven't.

I think reactions from the Mets about my revelations will be mixed. Those in the organization now who weren't with the Mets when I was playing may think, "Wow, I didn't know that was going on." Others who have been around for a while will likely say, "It's about time someone came out and set the record straight."

Some of my former teammates who knew I was penning a book were very curious about what I planned to write and how I was going to convey the content. They *knew* it was going to be the truth, but it's perhaps the wording that they'll be paying specific attention to. The truth is not always pleasant, but it's always refreshing. And I wanted to be very transparent in this book. Everything written is exactly as it happened. Nothing has been doctored or altered to add drama. It is what it is.

This book is for those fans who cheered for me when I gave baseball everything I had. And especially for Mets fans who took in a Southern boy, born and raised in South Carolina, who came to the big city as probably the most unlikely person to be embraced by New Yorkers. The odds were stacked against me. It's a beautiful thing because growing up in the South, all I heard about New York were stories about how rude the people could be. Nothing could be farther from the truth. I've met many, many courteous, generous, and caring people in the Big Apple who have a genuine regard for me as a person. And I just wanted to make sure that now, with this book, they understand all of me, not just my baseball career. I go to a lot of places where people *see* me, but they don't truly *know* who I am inside.

Now they'll have their chance.

—Mookie Wilson
New York, New York

INTRODUCTION

On a late winter evening at the Gramercy Theatre in New York City in 2013, Mookie Wilson was part of a question and answer session along with Bill Buckner. The theme of the event, naturally, was Game Six of the 1986 World Series.

The predictable question was coming, the same one he had answered literally thousands of times before. Mookie knew it. Buckner knew it. I knew it. The rest of the audience knew it.

"Mookie, if Buckner fielded your slow roller cleanly, do you think you would have beaten him to the bag?" someone asked.

For so many other athletes, the mundane question would have caused their eyes to roll. But Mookie Wilson is not like many other athletes. Those eyes of his didn't roll or glaze over, but instead shined a little brighter as he talked enthusiastically about every detail that went through his head as he raced up the first base line on that iconic play. It was like he was answering that question for the very first time.

It was the perfect example of why Mookie Wilson is the most beloved Mets player in the history of the franchise. He was known as much for his engaging 1,000-watt smile and big, hearty, infectious laugh as he was for the hustle and flare he displayed on the playing field.

But what I learned quickly from my time with him was that behind all the laughter is a highly intelligent, deeply introspective man with a wealth of experience both inside and outside of baseball. And on many occasions during his playing career, he used that big smile of his as a façade to mask his feelings of a missed opportunity for greatness.

This was, of course, a surprise to me because, having watched hundreds of Mets games during the eighties, Mookie never let on publicly about his discontent. And here I was thinking I knew about as much as there was to know about Mookie Wilson. I couldn't have been more wrong.

I also didn't realize he was an accomplished chef, a fisherman, a licensed securities trader, a soon-to-be ordained minister, and a truck driver who goes by the nickname Night Rider.

So our typical eight-hour interview sessions never ceased to leave me amazed at how little I really knew about one of the most popular athletes in New York history. He has led a very private life, until now.

In an age of sports celebrities being very guarded with what they reveal about themselves and others, Mookie's honesty is both refreshing and welcomed. He answered every one of my countless questions—nothing was out of bounds. He relished the opportunity to go full throttle into telling the good and the bad from his time with the Mets. His voice excitedly went up three octaves when he talked about Doc Gooden's rising fastball or Keith Hernandez's Gold Glove at first base or one of Darryl Strawberry's tape measure home runs. But then his voice would drop just above a whisper when he rehashed his disappointment over how a sure Mets dynasty's hopes were dashed by the drug use of the club's two biggest stars and a front office more concerned with image than team chemistry.

I interviewed a number of Mookie's former Mets teammates in developing questions for him to address. All of them said they couldn't wait for the book to come out because they knew it would be a completely truthful depiction of their storied team without embellishment. And they couldn't have been more helpful, with one after another telling me they would give me anything I needed because it was for Mookie.

When everyone you talk to says basically the same thing about someone's virtues, you know it must be true.

It became so apparent to me that Mookie never forgot where he came from. Fame didn't change the man he is. Growing up black and poor in the then racially divided South of the sixties and seventies was never an excuse for him to not chase the American Dream. In his case, naturally, that dream was playing professional baseball. He is grateful for and understands how Jackie Robinson paved the way for his generation of African Americans to play in the major leagues.

Mookie would say a big part of the way he is stems from his

Christian roots. He is a God-fearing man who, despite living a clean life, was like Mets royalty in a veritable den of iniquity. He had the ultimate amount of respect from all of his teammates, even the "Scum Bunch." To quote his pastor, Bishop Wendell B. Sumter, "His spirit of giving and of caring is an inspiration. His life speaks for him."

Right now, his epitaph would likely read how he was the one who hit the ball that went between Buckner's legs to win Game Six. But his life continues to be so much more than just a ground ball. And this book will set the record straight.

—Erik Sherman
New Rochelle, New York

1

Behind the Bag!

We blew it. *The Mets, the best team in baseball, have just blown the World Series. All of our bravado, all of our arrogance, has finally caught up with us.*

Those were my thoughts as I sat in the Mets dugout.

On the Shea Stadium Diamond Vision screen, a premature message read, *Congratulations Red Sox!*

My stomach was in a knot. I was accustomed to being nervous. I was nervous before every game I ever played in. But this was different. I had never felt this sick over a baseball game in my entire life.

We were losing Game Six of the 1986 World Series, 5–3, in the bottom of the tenth inning with two outs and nobody on base. If Calvin Schiraldi, a Mets teammate just a season ago, could get one more out, all that we worked so hard for—the 108 regular season wins, the thrilling NLCS victory over the

Houston Astros, and the fist-pumping curtain calls—would be forgotten.

We were lifeless. Guys were leaning back, slumped on the bench. Davey Johnson, our manager who personified our care-free arrogance, was visibly despondent, nearly banging the back of his head against the wall of the dugout while he stewed.

Moments before, I followed the flight of Dave Henderson's home run as it sailed over my head from left center field toward the foul pole to give Boston a 4–3 lead. I knew it was gone right away. He hit it in the one area of the Shea outfield that was generous to fly balls.

Later in the inning, Wade Boggs doubled and Marty Barrett singled him in to make it 5–3. Despite the now two-run deficit, I didn't feel any worse than I already had after Henderson's home run. Being down one run at that point in a game is almost as bad as being down two.

I was also extremely disappointed that we didn't put the game away in the bottom of the ninth when we had the chance. After Ray Knight and I both reached base to start the inning, Davey had Howard Johnson pinch-hit for Kevin Elster to sacrifice us into scoring position. There was just one problem: HoJo was not a bunter.

After an unsuccessful first attempt, Davey had HoJo swing away. Davey wasn't a big bunting guy. He didn't like giving up outs. He probably got that philosophy from Earl Weaver, his managerial mentor in Baltimore.

I would have kept the bunt on in that spot. Getting Knight to third with less than two outs was critical. Instead, HoJo would go down swinging.

Lee Mazzilli, who replaced Darryl Strawberry in a double

switch—another move by Davey I didn't agree with because of the good chance the game might go into extra innings—hit a deep fly ball to left field that would have easily scored Knight had he been sacrificed to third by HoJo.

Of course, no one can assume Maz would have hit the pitch the same way. In fact, chances are he would have gotten a different pitch had Knight been on third. As it was, Schiraldi didn't care if Maz hit a fly ball with Knight standing on second base.

Lenny Dykstra, with a chance to win the game with a single, ended our threat with a fly ball to end the inning.

Entering that fateful bottom of the tenth inning, I didn't feel as if we had blown the World Series just yet. I knew we had our work cut out for us, but I also knew who we had coming up in our half of the inning. That gave me faith that we just might be able to stage a comeback like we had so many times during that magical season.

Wally Backman, one of our "fire starters," could always be counted on to get on base in a big spot. I wanted Wally to bunt, walk, slash, dive into first, whatever it would take to get on base for Keith Hernandez, who was as clutch a hitter as we had and would certainly keep a rally going.

Get on for "Mex" and we will have a good shot, I thought.

Instead, Wally flew out harmlessly to Red Sox left fielder Jim Rice for the first out. That really took some of the wind out of my sails.

When Keith came up to the plate, I still found myself disturbed that Wally didn't find a way to get on. But I tried to put on a positive face and encourage the guys, leaning forward on the bench instead of slumping back.

Mex followed with a fairly hard-hit liner to deep center field, but Henderson drifted over to snare it for the second out.

So here we were, down to our last out.

The other guys can say what they want, but I'd bet there wasn't a player on our team who thought, *Hey, we can still come back and win this game!*

There was no question we were the better team. That wasn't the issue. It was that we failed to do what we had done well all year long up to that point in Game Six. We gave a team the opportunity to beat us.

In my mind, I was already second-guessing Davey's questionable moves. *Why did Davey take Straw out? Why didn't he keep the sacrifice bunt on with HoJo?*

It's natural to second-guess the manager. It's what athletes do. Not surprisingly, it's only on rare occasions that an athlete asks himself, *Why didn't I do this?* That's almost unheard of.

As my stomach ached, I looked across the field to the Red Sox dugout. Their guys were standing along the top step, presumably in position to storm the field after the final out was made. That sight bothered me because it was our field. We had owned that ballpark all year. Now, at this horrible moment, the *other* team was ready to celebrate their first championship in sixty-eight years.

Still, despite everything he had going for him, Schiraldi looked scared and uncomfortable on the mound that night. The Mets had drafted Schiraldi in the first round of the 1983 amateur draft. At the time, his fastball was so good that many scouts ranked him higher on the depth charts than even Roger Clemens, his University of Texas teammate. He spent parts of the '84 and '85 seasons on our big league roster, so we knew him very well.

As a teammate, he was quiet and seemed nice enough, but his character didn't fit in with the makeup of our team at all. You could pull anyone out from that bullpen on the '86 Mets and it was like one guy was just an extension of the next—same attitude, same arrogance. But Calvin wasn't like any of our other relief pitchers. We always felt that he could be intimidated. Plus, there was a scouting report that said he was a little timid, that he could get easily rattled in a big spot, which was a major reason why we were willing to move him. It certainly had nothing to do with his fastball, which was explosive.

Gary Carter, determined not to make the last out, lined a single to left on a 2-1 count. That brought up Kevin Mitchell, who had to quickly get back into his uniform and sprint from the clubhouse to the on-deck circle, to pinch-hit for Rick Aguilera.

I was on the bench thinking, *It should be Straw up there! Boom! A two-run bomb!*

Who wasn't thinking it should have been Straw at the plate instead of Mitchell at that time? While it was true Straw hadn't hit one out yet in the Series, you knew at any moment it could happen.

Mitchell was a good hitter, but as far as matching up against a right-handed fastball pitcher, I felt Straw was the guy that we needed right there. They were different players. Straw would have tried to hit the scoreboard with a home run to tie the game. We knew that about him.

Mitchell, though not yet the power hitter he later became, gave us what he could give us—a single to center field.

Up next was Ray Knight. Moving to the on-deck circle, I was surprised I might be getting another opportunity to bat should Ray get on base. All I was thinking was, *If I get a chance to bat, I can't make the last out. I CANNOT make the last out!*

I found out later that each of our guys who reached first base that inning said the same thing to our first base coach Bill Robinson: that they, too, were determined not to make the last out. It was that *never-say-die* attitude that exemplified what our '86 team was all about. It was how we got all the way to the World Series. That grit. I saw it come back to us after that second hit in the bottom of the tenth. I could feel it. I didn't know what the end result was going to be in the game, but there was still a lot of life in us.

Believe it or not, I suddenly realized I was no longer nervous. Don't ask me when that nervousness went away, but maybe it was when I thought there was no chance.

Schiraldi quickly got two strikes on Knight. We were down to our last strike. I noticed Knight taking a deep breath before stepping back in. He still looked very confident that he could keep the rally alive. Schiraldi, though, appeared a bit rattled despite being ahead in the count.

Ray blooped Calvin's next pitch into center field for a single to score Gary to cut the lead to 5–4. Mitchell, running hard all the way and showing good, instinctive baserunning skills, moved to third, which would prove critical later in the inning.

As Carter crossed the plate, he clapped twice, pointed his right index finger at me, and slapped my right hand.

I now realized that I could be the key guy, the hero.

What kid doesn't dream about being a World Series hero while playing ball in their backyard? I had a chance to do something really, really great here. Even the humblest of ballplayers still have that little bit of vanity in them. I was no different.

But I had to bring myself back to earth and think, *Okay, don't try to do too much. Don't worry about hitting a double or a home run. Just don't make the last out.*

Trying to think about anything other than not making the last out can make a hitter too anxious. And Lord knows I didn't need that. I was an aggressive enough batter as it was. It wasn't too far-fetched for me to go up there and swing at the first three pitches no matter where they were thrown. However, I knew I had to focus; I wanted this to be the best at-bat I ever had.

In my mind, like a mantra, I continued, *Don't make the last out.*

I wasn't nervous at all, even though I knew the World Series rested squarely on my shoulders. I can't explain it. I had only one intent. I didn't make it complicated. I wasn't the type of hitter who thought to hit it hard on the ground or in the air. If it's out there, hit it there. I wasn't worried about that. I just wanted to be sure I hit it.

Red Sox manager John McNamara slowly walked to the mound to take the ball from Schiraldi, perhaps sensing that Calvin would be relieved to exit this pressure cooker. Johnny Mac also may have thought Schiraldi had had enough after giving up the three straight hits.

In either case, I thought it was a good move by Mac at the time.

As I watched Bob Stanley jog in from the bullpen, I was thinking I would have rather faced Schiraldi. I didn't know much about Stanley at all. But I did know that aside from his signature pitch, the palm ball, he threw a little sinker, and it was clearly their hope that he would get me to hit the ball on the ground. I had a little power and I guess they thought I might be able to catch a Schiraldi fastball and smoke one down the line. I was a much better fastball than breaking-ball hitter. I prided myself on hitting the fastball well.

My approach would be the same no matter what was pitched my way. It didn't matter. I came up, looked fastball every pitch, and adjusted to everything else. I looked fastball even with knuckleballers. I never even moved up or back in the batter's box. I picked the same space no matter who was pitching. If it was a curveball pitcher and he saw me move up in the box, I figured he would see that and adjust. I never liked to guess what was coming, because too many times I guessed wrong.

As I dug into my space in the batter's box, Shea Stadium was rocking, but I didn't hear a thing. I was so locked into what I was doing. It was just me and Stanley and I had no idea what was going on around us. I only realized how raucously loud it was when I watched the game on tape many years later on an MLB Network special with Bob Costas. I initially could only feel the vibrations from the crowd noise, though even that would disappear once the at-bat began.

At no point did I give any thought to the enormity of the moment, because I knew if I had, it would have hurt me. The idea that there were more than sixty million people watching my every movement on television and another 55,078 fans at Shea Stadium never entered my mind. There might as well have been three people watching me at that point.

The duel about to begin between Stanley and me would be an

epic sequence of ten pitches, the longest at-bat of my life. I had never had an at-bat that lasted ten pitches—not in high school, college, the minors, or even my backyard! Usually, within three pitches, I was either putting the ball in play or jogging back to the dugout. It's why this would be the greatest at-bat I ever had.

There is an old phrase you hear in church that goes: "Thou shall not pass without offering." It's used for making sure everyone in the congregation puts an offering into the collection plate. I have adopted that phrase for baseball use because it's just *so* me. I always believed I could put the bat on every pitch.

True to my approach, I swung at and fouled the first pitch off. I wasn't looking to take a pitch, even though I didn't know what kind of stuff Stanley had. It wasn't like the bases were loaded and taking a pitch would have been the prudent thing to do. Even in that case, I would have had to think about actually taking a pitch!

The next two pitches were high to give me a 2-1 count. As always, I was still looking fastball, middle in.

I would get my wish on the next pitch from Stanley, a pitch down and middle in, but I fouled it straight into the dirt. *Man, I wish I had that one back*, I thought. It didn't matter that it was a little low. It was the kind of pitch I often pulled into the right field corner when I batted left-handed. It could have been a game-winning hit as Knight, despite being a slow runner, would have been running on contact from first base and likely would have scored. While I was always looking fastball, middle in, a part of me was still aware that Stanley would try to keep the ball more on the outside of the plate. That cost me. I shouldn't have been thinking about that at all. Now, for the second time in the game, we were down to our last strike. My approach was to not take a pitch. I was not going to let home plate umpire Dale Ford decide that game.

I fouled the next two pitches off, both pitches away and up in the zone. I think Stanley knew not to give me anything good to hit because of my aggressiveness. He probably felt he didn't have to throw me a strike. He had enough control to stay just off the plate. Despite the pitches being away, I put two pretty good swings on them.

Based on those last two pitches away that I didn't put into play, I was 100 percent sure Stanley was going to keep the ball on the outside edge of the plate. As the next pitch came in, I leaned toward the outside corner a little bit. To my utter shock, a sinker was coming in toward me, at least five inches off the plate inside. Initially, I thought the ball was going to hit me. I thought, *Why would he throw the ball in there?*

I saw the ball being run right into my knees. I was jumping, man! I made a pretty good move getting out of the way.

When I look back at the replay of the pitch, the ball wasn't that far inside. I think I was more reactive than I normally would have been on an inside pitch because I was expecting something outside.

As I began to fall forward to the ground, I saw the pitch get by catcher Rich Gedman! I hit the dirt, popped back up on one knee, and waved wildly for Mitchell to come home. I didn't know for sure if Mitchell could score easily or not. I was waving for him to slide. I was shouting at him, "C'mon! C'mon! C'mon!" I didn't want to take any chances. I didn't know how far away the ball was or anything of that nature, I just wanted him to come home and get down.

As it turned out, Mitchell scored easily without a throw to tie the game! I would hear later that Gedman had called for a sinker outside, but Stanley mistakenly thought he wanted one inside. With the width of home plate being seventeen inches and with the pitch being about five or six inches off the plate in the other direction, Rich had to try to cover nearly two feet to stop that ball from getting by. Add the fact that Gedman was crossed up and you can easily understand why the ball got by him. I've seen catchers catch balls even more inside than that particular pitch was, but if you're looking someplace else, it's going to be even tougher to catch that pitch. To this day, Stanley calls it a passed ball, while Gedman calls it a wild pitch. Either way, the score was tied.

Now there was bedlam. After Mitchell scored, all I heard was this piercing noise. In all my years as a Met, it was the loudest I had ever heard Shea Stadium. We had won some big games during the year, but that moment was like none other in terms of crowd reaction. I couldn't hear myself think. One of those planes that flies over Shea could have landed on the field and it wouldn't have been as loud and booming. It kind of took me out of my quiet zone and back into the reality of what was happening around me.

With the score now tied, I had two thoughts. The first was, *I came up to hit, down a run, it's now tied, and I'm still at the plate. I've done pretty good so far!* More strategically, my second thought was, *Now I'm off the hook. The score's tied. Just don't strike out! If you hit it and they get you out, okay, fine, we're good. But just don't strike out!*

The second thought was somewhat comforting. I knew at that point it was impossible for me to make the last out to lose the game, so there was absolutely no pressure in that regard. If the inning ended in a tie, it would already be a comeback for the ages. However, I still had a job to do. I still wanted to win it right then and there.

With a full count, I was now seven pitches into the at-bat, uncharted waters for me. It seemed like an eternity. I was locked in and once again could no longer hear the roar of the crowd. My only thought outside of my confrontation with Stanley was that Knight was on second base representing the winning run, and I wanted to drive him in.

After I fouled the next pitch off, Ray, in the chaos of the moment, took a huge lead off second—far too big—to give himself the best chance to score on a hit.

Marty Barrett, the Red Sox second baseman, took notice and gave the pickoff sign to Gedman to relay back to Stanley. Bob didn't pick up the sign, leaving Barrett way out of position as the next pitch came in to me. I didn't realize it at the time, but the miscommunication left a gaping hole on the right side of the infield. Although Buckner shaded more toward second with the pickoff play on to cover more of Barrett's ground, it wouldn't have made a difference. Anything hit in that direction surely would have been an easy single to potentially win the game. But I fouled the next pitch off and the Red Sox temporarily had dodged a bullet.

If Stanley had seen the pickoff sign and fired to Barrett, the inning likely would have ended in a tie. Instead, the legacy of two veteran players, not to mention what years from now could be written on our tombstones, would be altered forever by what was about to come next.

I dug in for the tenth and what was to be the final pitch of the at-bat. I was going to swing at pretty much anything in the same zip code. With the count full, he didn't have a pitch to burn. He was likely going to give me something good to hit.

My intuition was right. It was a pitch right down the middle, but instead of driving it somewhere, I hit a slow roller just to the left of the first base line. As I'm running hard up the line, my initial thought was, *Ugh! I should have done more with that pitch!* I also uttered a few other choice words in the heat of the moment. I may be a Christian but, hey, I'm human, too!

While hustling toward first base, I noticed how Stanley had hesitated before running to cover the bag to take what likely would have been a toss from Buckner. I didn't think Bob would get there in time.

As a result, I put my legs into high gear. It was going to be a footrace between Billy Buck and me. His ankle injury, which necessitated the need to have specially designed Nike high-top spikes made for him, never entered my mind. I did what I always did, which was run as hard as I could. That was the only way I knew how to play the game.

If that slow roller to Buckner proved anything, it is that you should always run hard. Hustling up the first base line without question forced Buck to rush the play more than he would have liked.

As Billy hobbled over to his left, I noticed that he didn't plant his feet in time to properly field the ball. When I saw the ball go through Buck's legs, once again caught up in the moment, I shouted, "Holy s**t!"

As the ball rolled into short right field, I knew Knight would easily cross the plate with the winning run. Ray's run was all that mattered. Still, perhaps instinctively, I rounded first and ran hard halfway toward second base. I don't know why I did that because the greatest comeback in World Series history was already in the books! I was in another world.

I didn't run into the madhouse that greeted Ray at home plate. Instead, I headed straight to the dugout. I don't recall who I saw or who I hugged. I just remember thinking, *What just happened?!*

In the clubhouse, the celebration made it feel like we had already won the World Series because, in our minds, we already had. I'm serious about that. We overcame our worst enemy, the one thing that could beat us—ourselves.

The question I have been asked literally thousands of times is whether I would have beaten Billy Buck to first base had he fielded the ball cleanly. My feeling is that I would have, for several reasons. The ball wasn't hit real hard, I was busting it up the line, Buck had to get in front of the ball and didn't have any momentum going toward the bag, and he was playing on a really bad ankle.

In fact, I will take it a step further. Considering where Buck was positioned and how slowly the ball was hit, I liked my chances of beating *any* first baseman to the bag on that play. With my speed, it wouldn't have made a difference who was out there.

I am also convinced that, had I made an out in that situation, we would have won the game anyway. I glanced at that Boston dugout during our rally and there were some defeated faces over there. Considering their history of heartbreaking defeats prior to their three championships in recent years, maybe they were thinking, *Here we go again.*

I don't believe in fate. I think that you create your own opportunities. And that's what we did. And if you call that luck, well, luck is when preparation meets opportunity. We had the right people, at the right place, at the right time. What happened in the tenth inning of Game Six was that the arrogance that we had all year long, but lost in the World Series to that point, was given back to us courtesy of the Boston Red Sox. We didn't take it; they gave it back to us.

Look at everything that happened in that game that shouldn't have happened: the moves and non-moves by McNamara; some of the questionable pitches their pitchers made; not using Don Baylor to pinch-hit for Buckner late in the game with left-hander Jesse Orosco pitching; the missed pickoff play; the miscommunication between Stanley and Gedman in two critical situations; the wild pitch; not inserting Dave Stapleton late in the game to replace the hobbling Buckner for defensive purposes; Stanley not covering first base on my slow roller; Buckner's error at first; and, perhaps the biggest mistake of all, McNamara taking Roger Clemens out of the game after seven innings of four-hit ball.

It wasn't like we beat them into submission. They let us win. If there was one thing we learned in that game it was humility, because our winning wasn't from anything so great that we did. What did we do so great to win that ball game? We actually won in spite of our own failings and questionable decisions. Davey took Straw out. HoJo couldn't get down a bunt. Our vaunted bullpen finally gave up some runs. By any standard of baseball you look at, we had no business winning that ball game. I might be the only person alive that would admit it, but as good as we were, we weren't *that* good to pull off what we did in Game Six without a lot of help from the Red Sox.

Back in the clubhouse after the wild celebration on the field, I sat down, stunned, and asked myself over and over again, *How did we actually win that game?*

We had come back from behind and won plenty of ball games in the regular season and even against Houston in the playoffs, but this one was different. If it sounds like there was some doubt on our part that we could come back to win Game Six, there certainly was. There was a lot of doubt. I can't believe they let us win that game.

Don't get me wrong, I am thrilled that we won and just as happy that I was an integral part of World Series history that night. I never get tired of talking with people about Game Six, because whenever I do, fans offer their own take on the game, which I find interesting.

For the most part, people ask about the relationship between Buckner and me or what I was thinking at the very moment when I hit the slow roller. I can't really tell them much about the latter because I put that foul language behind me a long time ago. I just tell them my initial reaction after hitting the little roller toward first wasn't very nice. I'm not so holier-than-thou that I can't admit my shortcomings. I'm an athlete and in the spur of the moment, athletes say and do things at times that don't portray who they are. It was just the moment. I said what I said. I'm not denying it. I just won't go around repeating some of the colorful language I sometimes used in the past.

More and more, I get asked about the legendary game-winning baseball itself. After the ball rolled through Buckner's legs, right field umpire Ed Montague picked it up and, shortly thereafter, gave it to our traveling secretary Arthur Richman. Arthur then came by my locker and offered it to me as a memento of our historic game. But I was just so much in the moment and, truth be told, was never big on personal memorabilia. I thought, *It's just a baseball. I hit a 27-hopper down the first base line. If I had hit a home run, I might have kept it.* But at the time I didn't see the value, personally or monetarily. So I told Arthur he could keep it and signed it for him as follows: "To Arthur, the ball won it for us, Mookie Wilson, 10/25/86."

Well, I guess I would never make it as a sports memorabilia appraiser because the ball last sold at auction in May of 2012 for $418,250! That ball just keeps increasing in value. It's amazing.

It all started in 1992 when Arthur called me and said, "Look, Mookie, I have the ball. I want to put it up for auction and donate the proceeds to charity. What do you think?"

I said, "Thank you for letting me know, Arthur, but I gave you the ball. It's yours. Do what you want with it."

Actor Charlie Sheen would be the proud owner of the baseball with a winning bid of $93,500.

Initally, I didn't feel any remorse because Arthur did exactly what I did with all of my stuff from the World Series—donated it to charity.

But I must admit, a few years later I started to wish I had accepted the ball. It would have been a nice thing to have. I would have loved to have had that ball, not so much for the value of it, but rather for what it means to Mets fans. It's a piece of history that everyone would want to have. There's only one. You see a number of sluggers who keep all of their milestone home runs throughout their career. But this was different.

Some people might think, *Oh, sure, now that you know how much it's worth, of course you would want to have it.* But they would be missing the point. The monetary value would have been something I never would have known because I would never have put it up for sale.

I do a lot of signings and a couple of people have asked me to sign their baseball with the same inscription I wrote for Arthur. I won't do it. I think that's a terrible request, not to mention fraudulent. I look at them and say, "Are you crazy?"

I have thought many times about what it would have been like if I had hit a game-winning home run in my at-bat instead of avoiding a wild pitch and hitting a slow roller to first. I don't know if a home run could have had more drama than what occurred in that ten-pitch at-bat. The way I see it, if I had hit a game-winning home run on the first or second pitch, all of that suspense leading up to us winning the game would never have happened. In my at-bat, there were two dramatic moments—the wild pitch and the error—as opposed to one.

Some have said it was the greatest single at-bat in World Series history because of everything that happened. It was almost like a game within a game.

I can't say I disagree.

2

An Unlikely Bond

I t had been nearly three years since my famous slow roller found its way under Billy Buck's legs. I had been a Toronto Blue Jay for less than two weeks, still familiarizing myself with not just my new teammates after the trade from the Mets, but also the American League.

Before a series opener at Kauffman Stadium in Kansas City, I was down the left field line stretching with some of the other Blue Jays. A few of the Royals walked by us to make their way to the batting cages under the stands. I may have been new to the league, but there was no mistaking Bo Jackson, one of the greatest athletes who ever lived. But then, out of the blue, here comes Buckner! I had completely forgotten he was with them! I knew I couldn't avoid seeing him forever, but I had been successful in doing so for three years.

As Buck approached, I'm thinking, *Oh, God, he's going to walk right by me!*

I had nothing against Buck, but we hadn't spoken since the "Buckner play" and I just didn't know what to say to him. But it was too late. As I was still lying there and stretching, Buck walked up to me, bat in hand, and with a slight grin, said, "Hey, Mook, you wanna hit me some ground balls?"

It was the last thing I expected him to say and the perfect icebreaker. At first, I smiled and kind of chuckled, but then I exhaled deeply because he had just lifted a tremendous weight off my shoulders. I had no idea what to say. In reality, what could I say? *"Hey, Buck, better you than me"*? No attempt to lighten the moment on my side would have worked. So I remained speechless. But his gesture made me feel a lot better.

So Buck smiled and chuckled back at me, nothing else was said, and he made his way to the batting cage to do some hitting.

Billy's short quip really helped me out a lot. He has no idea how much it helped me to move on and to be able to speak to him now. I simply will never forget that moment for the rest of my life. His coming over to me like that, after all he had gone through since Game Six, taught me a lot about Bill Buckner. He would later tell me that he knew I felt badly for him and he didn't want me to feel any guilt over what my ground ball ended up doing to his life. He just wanted me to enjoy being a world champion and not worry about something I had no control over.

He was right about the fact that I felt sorry for what the media was writing and how some people heckled him and his family in the months following the '86 World Series. Nobody should ever have to go through any of that.

Little did I realize that our encounter in left field at Kauffman Stadium was to be the beginning of a great friendship between two players who will forever be linked by one ground ball.

Several years after we had both retired, Steiner Sports, a memorabilia company, contacted us to sign copies of the iconic photo of me running up the first base line as the famous ground ball rolled past Billy. Initially, we would do the signings in a private room, but several years later we started to do them in the middle of card shows among hundreds of fans.

At first, I wasn't thrilled with the idea of teaming up with Buck because I didn't know how he would take it. I only casually knew him at the time and didn't want people to think I was taking advantage of a situation. If I had ever felt that Buck got that impression, I would have stopped signing with him.

Buck didn't like the idea at first, either. He was still bitter and sensitive about the so-called Buckner Game. He is really honest about why he went ahead and agreed to the signings. Buck was so tortured by the game that he thought he deserved to be rewarded financially by signing the iconic photo of the moment that tarnished an otherwise outstanding baseball career. In fact, Buck says that all those copies of that photograph that he signed with me pretty much paid to put his three kids through college.

I am very happy that he was able to come to grips with the whole thing. I thought he was treated very unfairly. That's why

I would never have faulted him if he hadn't wanted anything to do with the signings. I would have understood.

However, a private setting with no fans around, at the start of our signings together, helped put us more at ease. Steiner Sports did a very good job of making us feel comfortable.

At the time Steiner reached out to me, I was working as a truck driver. Because I was raised on a farm, I learned to drive trucks and tractors really early in life. Besides, I always had a fascination with trucks. The bigger the better! I love driving them and when I had the opportunity before I even started playing pro ball, I drove a truck for the McMillan Logging company. I was just out of high school and had a little bit of experience driving trucks even without having a commercial driver's license.

After retiring from baseball, driving a truck was something I really wanted to get back into. I didn't want to make it a full-time job, so I lucked out when I found this company named TMC that was hiring part-time seasonal drivers. This time, though, I went through the Truck Driver Institute and got certified to drive one. But I did lie a little bit about one thing. When the Institute asked me what my previous profession was, I told them I was a professor. I didn't want my being a former major league baseball player to cause any distractions in the class. In fact, my first CB radio handle was "The Professor."

But then one day I was driving with my trainer and got a phone call. It was the Mets. My "cover" was blown. They said they needed me to come to New York for some PR work. After hanging up, I told my trainer I had to go home. When he asked me why, I finally let the cat out of the bag and said, "Okay, this is the story . . ."

He was shocked and said, "I was wondering why you've been to every city we've driven through. Every city, you kept telling me, I've been there, I've been there."

Up to that moment, I was using my given name, William Wilson. When I told him I was better known as Mookie Wilson, he knew who I was and called the dispatcher to tell him about it.

I worked for TMC for six months before getting back into baseball as a minor league coach in 1995, though I still drove for them a little bit during the off-season. When I reported to spring training that March, Steve Phillips, then the minor league director, asked all of his coaches to introduce themselves in a conference room meeting and tell the other guys something about themselves that nobody knew. When it was my turn, I said, "I'll bet nobody here knows that I'm a truck driver." And I was right. This raised a few eyebrows, but everyone was interested and started asking me all these questions, like if I drove an 18-wheeler and how much money you can make. I was more than happy to tell them about the life of a truck driver.

Buck had been coaching for six years—four years with Toronto and two with the White Sox—when Steiner came calling. We never discussed the Steiner offer with one another before agreeing to do it. But once we got into it, we became true business partners. In fact, after the Steiner agreement became less exclusive, we started doing side events together—appearances in stores, some card shows. But I refused plenty of opportunities to do paid events I felt were inappropriate for Buck. I wouldn't ever do anything that would hurt him. We would only do signings for other people besides Steiner when it felt right, when we could trust that the organizer would not put either of us in an awkward situation.

It still amazes me to see the hundreds of people that, after all these years, line up for our autographs at the shows. Buck and I sometimes look at one another and one of us says, "Do people still want this same photo signed?"

But what's starting to happen now is that we see fathers bringing their kids and introducing us to them, saying things like, "This is the man who hit the ground ball on the video." So it's like the older generation is passing down their enthusiasm for the play to their children!

Another change in the dynamic of the signings has been that people started bringing things other than the iconic photo to get signed. It's neat to see some of the unique stuff they bring. But by and large, that photo is still the main thing that people ask us to autograph.

I know it baffles both me and Buck that his error in Game Six is where all the focus goes instead of the way the Mets rallied back from two runs down, with two outs and nobody on base. Plus, there were some truly questionable decisions and miscues by Boston in that game that hurt them just as much as the error. There is simply too much emphasis put on that one play.

I suppose with the years of autograph signings, Buck and I have been the beneficiaries of the fans' misperception so, in that regard, I'm not complaining. But if people go back and look at the video of Game Six and dissect it, they should come to the same conclusion as I have about it. But I guess it's easier to talk about that one play, that one moment. Maybe it's more dramatic. Since we started signing at memorabilia shows, there have been a few occasions when some of the autograph seekers and fans have done or said things that were inappropriate toward Buck. One time a nun who was a Mets fan actually thanked Buckner for helping the Mets win the World Series! He's handled those situations with as much grace as anyone can imagine. I'll tell you, he's a better man than I am in this respect. I may be a Christian minister, but a guy can only take so much. I probably would have punched some of these people. But the problems have never been excessive. It's always just that one idiot here and there.

A few years ago, we were signing autographs at a fund-raiser in upstate New York and this obnoxious guy got really out of line with Billy Buck. He wanted him to write some stupid phrase on his photo and Buck said, "I can't write that."

Usually, Buck signs and writes almost anything, but this request was way out of line.

The guy, who claimed to be a lawyer, got really upset and started yelling, "I paid my money! You have to sign what I want!"

Then he started leaning over the table toward Buck.

Buck told him to take his photo and leave.

The guy then started baiting Buck and dared him to hit him. Fortunately, the people who were running the show came by and gave the guy his money back and told him that he had to leave. Everybody started apologizing to Buck for this clown, but Billy was so gracious about the whole episode and told them not to worry.

Stuff like that is bound to happen when you consider we have signed close to 100,000 photos over the years. Take away the one or two unfortunate incidents that were really nasty, and the shows have gone extremely well.

In fairness, some of the insensitive comments to Buck are unintentional. Some fans say things to make light of the Buckner error and it just comes out wrong or falls flat. Others just feel like they have to say something, anything, about the play. But I know Buck has come to really appreciate the fans in New York, where most of our signings take place.

I have to admit that the first time Buck and I started signing in public I was a little on edge. I just knew something bad could happen because I know how fans can get sometimes. Plus, right from the beginning, we have always left ourselves vulnerable by interacting with the fans we sign for. A lot of ballplayers just sign and never look up at the person who is requesting their signature. They just want the people to get their autograph and move along. To Buck and me, that's not why fans come to signings. All they want is a small comment from us like, "How are you doing?" or "I like that shirt you've got on." Anything at all. Billy, in particular, is really good at giving small talk like that. And I think I can speak for both of us when I say that our interactions are heartfelt and genuine. We really appreciate our fans and never take them for granted. They are the ones keeping the memories alive.

As for Buck, I sensed he had some remorse and awkwardness the first time we signed together at a show. I would have felt the same way. As it was, I felt a little uneasy *for* him. Part of my hesitation in doing this in the first place was due to how it might affect him. But once he got past that initial feeling, he was fine.

Billy never had a problem with making that error in Game Six because he understands that errors are just a part of baseball. The thing that bothered him was all the emphasis put on that one ill-fated play. He now has come to grips with the reality that the perception of so many will probably never go away. But at least he's at peace with it now.

This may be surprising, but I also have some regrets about the error. Like Buck, I strongly believe that the play has over-shadowed what we *both* were all about. People have referred to me as "Mookie '86." Or they'll stop me and say, "You're the guy that hit that ball through Buckner's legs." I played twelve years. I know I accomplished quite a bit more than hitting a slow roller to first in a World Series game!

Thus, I understand a lot of what Buck goes through, how this one negative thing can overshadow a career like his, which produced 2,715 regular season hits (285 hits from being a lock for the Hall of Fame), a batting title, and a better fielding percentage than Lou Gehrig.

But on the flip side, I believe Buck's getting out in public and being forced to deal with the error has been therapeutic for him. Following my playing days, I was a psychology major with a con-centration in behavioral science at Mercy College, and I believe that a person has to face their issues in order to get over them. Denying them doesn't make them go away. And I think it's been really good for not just Buck, but for me as well, to sign the pho-tos, talk with the fans, and get support from the knowledgeable baseball enthusiasts at the shows. We both had to accept the fact that the play was part of baseball history. No one will ever remember our first hit, our first stolen base, or our first spectacular catch. But they're certainly going to remember Buck's error.

Billy and I talk all the time about how the error affected our lives. We've become so close over the years that we really can be very candid about anything that we talk about.

At some point, the signings will run their course and some new historical event in baseball history, like maybe the Cubs finally winning a World Series again, will come along to overshadow us. After all, before the Buckner Game, there was the so-called Shot Heard Round the World game, that historic playoff matchup between the Brooklyn Dodgers and the New York Giants in 1951. The central figures in that game, Ralph Branca, the Dodgers pitcher who surrendered the game-winning home run, and Bobby Thomson, the player who hit it, became so entwined in that important event in baseball history that they, too, signed countless photos of their own iconic play. Then again, the signings Buck and I were doing didn't seem to take anything away from the demand for the Branca and Thomson shows. Theirs was a different and, perhaps, older fan base. Buck and I did a couple of dual signings with them where we were on one side of a room and they were on the other. I thought that was so neat. I never talked with either one of them directly about the phenomenon of teaming up with a past adversary and becoming partners at autograph shows, but I did become friendly with Ralph because he's Bobby Valentine's father-in-law and we have some history together. I also refrained from asking them about the Shot Heard Round the World game, because, understanding how Buck and I have answered the same questions about our own historic game many times over the years, I never wanted to sound like a "casual fan" to those gentlemen. But at least until there is that next "big thing," Buck and I will remain partners in one of the most celebrated moments in the history of baseball.

The public's interest in me and Buck has extended beyond the autograph shows. In 2013, we did a show at the Gramercy Theatre in Manhattan, which was unique. We had done Q&A sessions before, including one with Bob Costas on the MLB Network, but this one at the Gramercy Theatre was different. Instead of having only a moderator ask us questions, they allowed members of the audience to do so as well. I was happy with the setting and how it all went. While neither Buck nor I knew exactly what to expect going in, the best thing about it was that it allowed us the opportunity to speak freely. We were provided with as much time as we needed to answer the questions; there were no time restrictions. Unlike the Costas program, we didn't feel like we had to shorten our responses to fit in commercial breaks.

I think fans' questions are the ones you want to have because they are always off-the-cuff. They didn't come to the Gramercy Theatre event with prepared questions like a reporter would. The media has ready-prepared questions that they fire off at you because they are looking for a specific answer to kind of lead the direction of a television show or feature story. Fans don't. They just hear you talking and then, all of a sudden, come up with a question.

I personally enjoy the Q&As more than just signing autographs at events. They both have their purpose, but I think Q&As give fans an opportunity to hear what we have to say.

The autographs are great—fans get them from us and take them home—but did they get the opportunity to speak with us or express their views? That's a big difference and a better experience for the fan.

The first time either Billy or I watched a tape of Game Six was twenty-five years after the fact on the aforementioned MLB Network's *20 Greatest Games* series with Bob Costas. While I understand why Buck didn't watch it before then, I have no idea why I waited so long, because I had the tape sitting in my house since shortly after that World Series ended. I guess I felt that I already knew what happened in the game and everything that was important about it. I also fell into the same kind of thinking as a lot of fans, that since the game ended with Buck's infamous error, everything else before it didn't seem as interesting. For that reason, even though it would have been fun, I wasn't in a rush to watch it. After all, I *played* in the game. But up until seeing it on Costas's show, if someone had asked me specific questions about what happened in the game before that last inning, I probably couldn't have answered them all.

When I finally did watch it on videotape, it gave me a new perspective. It reminded me just how great that game was from beginning to the end. It revealed all of the flaws, the breaks, the non-breaks, the managerial moves, the non-moves, and how everything that could go wrong for both teams did go wrong. Most fans don't realize that, because they didn't know what was *supposed* to happen in certain situations. But while sitting on the bench, standing in the batter's box, or manning left field, I knew.

One of the things I had forgotten all about was Straw being

taken out late in the game. That was critical because I was normally the one taken out of games based on the normal double-switch routine we had. Think about how pulling me instead of Straw would have changed history.

Buck said watching the video reinforced what he already knew: that the error had little to do with the outcome of Game Six and the World Series as a whole. He was also reminded about how he absolutely crushed a couple of balls off Ojeda in both the second and fourth innings that could have easily been home runs in most ballparks other than Shea. He's right. The second laser he hit, at minimum, required all six feet six inches of Straw's frame to haul it in and keep two Sox runners from scoring. If one or both of those balls had either left the yard or sailed over Straw's head for extra bases, Buck would have been a hero instead of the perceived goat.

There were at least three other what-ifs in that game that would have either made Buck's error insignificant or eliminated the possibility of it ever happening.

For example, in that fateful last inning, if Stanley and Gedman didn't get crossed up on the location of the sinker, the wild pitch that tied the game and moved Knight into scoring position would never have happened. Then, moments later, if Stanley had seen the pickoff sign relayed from Barrett, they would have nailed Ray at second to end the tenth inning in a tie.

But the third most significant what-if is something that, to this day, Buck and I disagree on.

The Red Sox had the bases loaded with two outs in the top of the eighth with a great chance to increase their one-run lead.

Davey brought in the lefty Orosco to face Buck. It would have been the ideal situation for McNamara to use Don Baylor to pinch-hit for Billy and then insert Dave Stapleton at first base for defensive purposes with Buck hobbling on that bad Achilles.

But Buck told Mac he wanted to stay in the game because he felt he was the best first baseman on the team—injury or no injury. Plus, Billy felt he was moving around better in Game Six than he had earlier in the series when Mac did indeed replace Buck with Stapleton in the late innings.

I understand Billy's thinking, but when you have an injury as bad as his, it has to have some effect on how you play your position. Now, whether that injury was a factor in his missing the ball, I'm not sure. There was no question he got to the ball in time, but my question would be what condition was he in when he got there? That I don't know.

Buck also said he had no problem reaching down for the ball, but was he hurting? That we also don't know. But I think it would be very ill-advised to think Buck could be playing hurt without his injury having an impact on his ability to make that play.

Having played against Stapleton in AAA, I knew of his playing abilities very well. When healthy, Buckner was clearly the superior defensive first baseman of the two. But Buckner clearly wasn't the same player, because of his physical condition, in that World Series.

Personally, I wouldn't have taken out Buck for defensive purposes, either. However, I *would* have replaced him for offensive reasons, opting to go with Baylor to pinch-hit against Orosco.

So there were a number of miscues, mental errors, and questionable moves that preceded Buck's error that aren't given near the amount of scrutiny and attention they deserve. But no one cares. It's easier for the media and the casual fan to just have a "hero" or a "goat" to define a given game. I don't think perception will ever change for them. Some in Boston will always say, "Buckner missed the ball. He lost it for us." Or if they're a New Yorker, they'll say, "Buckner won it for us."

But the intelligent baseball fans know the truth. And they know there was still a Game Seven to be played. So the play certainly didn't cost Boston the championship. Buck's got to be a little sick of the whole thing. I know he's amazed at how relevant it still is after all these years.

There's no escaping the Buckner play, either. Every October, Game Six is shown everywhere. People come up to me and say, "I saw you on TV last night." It was just one of those moments in time that everyone knew where they were and what they were doing. You had two teams in two major cities that had their issues. It truly was a perfect storm. I think if it had been two less iconic teams, in smaller markets, the game probably wouldn't have been replayed and discussed as much as it is today.

Would I be bitter if I were Buck? Yes, I would. I would probably feel even worse than I do now when I get introduced at an event with something like, "And now here's Mookie Wilson, the guy who hit the *famous* ball between Bill Buckner's legs." I'll think, *Geez. I'm playing second fiddle to a baseball now!*

Like Buck, I also sometimes feel underappreciated for my body of work as a player, so I understand a little of what Billy

Buck goes through. It leaves room for some regrets. However, unlike Buck, if given the chance to reverse history, I wouldn't dream of it. I am still glad the play happened because, if it hadn't, what would the alternative have been? We may have lost that game.

Also, and maybe this is a little extreme, without the play I probably would have ended up like so many other "good" ballplayers, with fans saying, "Yeah, Mookie was a nice guy, a good little ballplayer who hustled all the time and had great speed." But I think everyone has to have a moment that defines them. And I won't say the word *greatness*, because that would be overstating it. But if you take that moment away and just look at my career numbers, there's nothing that jumps out at you.

So while there may be some regrets over how the play has become the focal point of my career, I wouldn't trade it for anything in the world. I just wish people would look at the rest of my career sometimes, too.

Another angle to the story of the Buckner Game has been wildly distorted by the media. A lot has been reported about Buck being "chased" out of Boston. Let me make something clear. No one chased that man out of anywhere. He lives in Idaho now because he loves the outdoors and has long owned a ranch out there. It's only another example of how some of the stuff you read is written just to sell papers. It makes for good copy. I've known Buck for years and I have never heard him say a bad thing about Boston. But the media plays the story up like it does because it's not an interesting story otherwise. Nobody wants to hear the real reason he left Boston. Many media outlets have tried to set the whole Buckner record straight, from how insignificant his error was to the big picture of the '86 World Series to his moving to Idaho, but they always seem to go the more sensational route in the end.

Now, it wasn't always smooth sailing for Buck in Boston. In our Q&A sessions, he sometimes recounts the story of when, two weeks after the '86 World Series ended, a guy honked at him at a stop sign while he was running some errands. The guy noticed who he was and started mocking him. Buck got out of his car and grabbed him by the throat as he tried to drive away. He held on to him all the way up the street until the guy's car started picking up speed and Billy finally had to let go. I once asked Buck what he was possibly thinking in doing that. He answered that he doesn't know what came over him that morning. He just lost it. Buck definitely had a temper and could be a little bit of a hothead if someone pushed the right buttons.

That temper of his occasionally flared up on the ball field, too.

One time, when Buck was with the Cubs and Carter was with the Expos, Gary kicked Buck's bat out of the way on a pop-up behind home plate. The next time Buck came up to hit, he popped the ball up again behind home plate. Buck picked up Kid's catcher's mask that he had tossed on the ground, beat it with his bat, and ended up bending it pretty good. Oh, Billy Buck!

Regarding everything that Buck had to endure after the error, the one thing we tend to mislead ourselves about is that if we always do what we're supposed to do and always try our best, then things will always work out in our favor. We also tend to believe that everything that happens to us that is bad is the result of something we didn't do.

Well, neither is the case.

It's not all about us all the time but, as athletes, we're results-oriented. We want to see positive results from everything we put into the game. But sometimes it just doesn't work out that way.

Does Billy Buck deserve more credit for his great career? Of course he does.

Did he need something else in his life that baseball was getting in the way of? Perhaps so, because Buck has told me the challenges he has had to endure from the fallout of Game Six have strengthened his faith in God. He understands that some things we have to go through are not because of anything we've done wrong, but happen to make us stronger.

In a sense, I can relate to Billy. I feel as if I've been mistreated by an organization that I spent most of my adult life with. But maybe there was something more for me, something different that I'm supposed to be getting out of life than just baseball. Maybe I was starting to put too much emphasis on myself and less on the things that are most important. I'm beginning to understand that life still goes on after baseball, that there's a reason for things that happen, and I'm as happy as I've ever been. While I still haven't totally given up baseball, I have something else now with the ministry. And maybe that was the direction God wanted me to go in.

Donnie Moore blew a save opportunity against Boston in

that same 1986 postseason that would have advanced the California Angels to the World Series instead of the Red Sox. He never overcame it and took his own life less than three years later, soon after his career ended.

The lesson learned is that if we focus too much on our possessions and our status as athletes, we are as vulnerable to feelings of low self-esteem and hopelessness as anybody. And once our careers end or get crushed like Donnie's, we have nothing else that we can draw from because baseball was our entire life. Baseball was all Donnie lived for, so when it was taken away, what else did he have?

As ballplayers, it's so easy to get wrapped up in our own little illusion. I understand how what happened to Donnie can occur because I've been in the profession a long time and I've met a lot of ballplayers whose lives revolved around the game. There is probably more depression in former ballplayers than people might think. They do other things, but they don't get that same satisfaction and buzz that baseball gave them.

As much as I love baseball, I never wanted to be in that position. That's why I've done so many other things. Life's got to be interesting.

Besides his strengthening faith, I believe Billy Buck's sense of humor has been another factor helping him get past the unfairness of all the blame he has had to deal with since Game Six. A few years ago, the Buckner Game became a part of pop culture when we both took part in an episode of *Curb Your Enthusiasm*. I was actually amazed and happy when the HBO comedy show contacted us, especially after finding out that Billy Buck was going to be the main focus in the episode. I had the time of my life watching them tape this thing in New York. I may have had a small part, but they still gave me my own trailer! It was the big time, Hollywood-style!

I just thought it was *so* New York to do a skit revolving around the ground ball in the Buckner Game, because that play was as big a part of the city's recent history as anything.

Originally, after speaking with the show's creator, Larry David, Buck didn't think he wanted to do it because of all the previous failed attempts by other media outlets to clear his name of losing the '86 World Series for the Red Sox. But Larry convinced Buck it would all be positive, which it was. So, despite being a little leery about doing it, he talked it over with his wife, and since the show was a comedy and he respected Larry's comedic talents, he decided to give it a shot. I know Buck was really glad he did it. He came out of it looking like the good sport that he is.

Buck and I were together for a whole day during taping. It made me feel so good watching Billy do the episode that it almost felt as if I were doing it myself. Everything on that show is ad-libbed and it looked like he was having a lot of fun with it. I also enjoyed watching the professional comedians at work. It was amazing to me how many people are involved behind the scenes in a show like that and all the different takes they do in order to get the scenes just right. I was so impressed with how they put everything together.

The closest thing to acting I did before *Curb* was back in '83, when Keith and I did a few skits for *Sesame Street*. We worked with The Count, Snuffleupagus, and Cookie Monster. But I think the only one that aired was the one with The Count. We didn't count anything with him, but the three of us sang this song called "Put Down the Ducky." I had the time of my life doing that!

It's remarkable to me how such a strong friendship with Buck has evolved over the years. Besides baseball-related topics, we talk about family, church, and how we can help each other. One example of the latter was when he was a batting coach in Toronto and he asked me if I would have any interest in working with him there. I would have, but I had a job at the time.

Another instance was when I had the coaching job with the Mets under Bobby V, who had come up with Buck in the Dodgers organization. We asked Billy if he would be interested in coming to the Mets as the hitting instructor. But he was under contract with the White Sox and his job gave him the opportunity to stay at home and watch his son play high school ball. But it probably wouldn't have worked because you just know someone would have said or written that Buck's already been "helping" the Mets win since '86 or something sarcastic like that.

More recently, when Bobby V had the manager's job in Boston, Buck interviewed for the hitting instructor's job. During the process, Billy said to me, "Wouldn't it be nice if we both went to Boston to work for Bobby?"

I said, "That would be nice. But the two of us with the Boston Red Sox? That's probably not going to work with the fans up there."

So Billy Buck and I must remain content with continuing our partnership at autograph signings and in our strong, if unlikely, friendship that continues to blossom after more than two decades.

3

My Great Escape

My brother Collis and I were joined by some friends at a local diner one night when we were teens. We waited for service. Waited a little longer. Still waiting, we came to realize that no one was going to take our order. Feeling humiliated, we left.

Of course, we knew why we weren't served. It was the same reason we sometimes had to enter local businesses through the back door. And it was the same reason doctors would put gloves on before touching us.

We were Negroes in Ehrhardt, South Carolina—a one-horse town with a population of around five hundred—during the social turbulence of the civil rights era and the dawn of desegregation.

I was just seven years old when President John F. Kennedy

was assassinated in 1963. When Kennedy was elected three years earlier, many Southern blacks were denied the right to vote, were barred from public facilities, and were subjected to terrible abuse, both physical and mental. Kennedy sought to change the landscape and his assassination was a tremendous blow to the black community, as he helped lead the civil rights movement forward by appointing a large number of blacks to high-level positions in his administration, spoke in favor of school desegregation, and put Vice President Lyndon B. Johnson in charge of his Equal Employment Opportunity committee.

Five years later, Dr. Martin Luther King Jr., the most important black leader during the civil rights era and the single biggest advocate of integration, was assassinated.

At the time of both killings, I was attending Lewis L. Butler Elementary School, an all-black school. I was too young to fully understand the importance of each event, but I remember how terribly sad the adults were when they found out the news.

There was a deep Southern culture in the sixties and early seventies in which white people were very open about their feelings toward people of color. To hear such derogatory terms as "nigger" or "boy" when they referred to blacks was common, and it happened much too frequently.

It was a period when many Southerners shared a common goal of manipulating the lives of blacks and some less-fortunate whites. They were proud of being able to display their superiority over the black race in social status and employment. It was a culture that rejected growth and embraced oppression. Education was stressed only to maintain an already decaying community supported mainly by farmers. New ideals were not welcomed, which limited the chance for any new opportunities. The powers that be were more than content with the status quo because they feared losing control.

For young blacks like me, it was a challenge growing up in this environment. I often wondered how strong black men would allow themselves and their families to be subjected to such unfair and degrading practices. I felt ashamed, angry, and helpless. But when I got a little older, I began to understand the way things were planned and implemented. I realized that blacks had few or no options.

While slavery was, of course, unlawful in twentieth-century America, "legalized slavery," as I call it, was rampant in the South.

One of the more popular tactics of the manipulation of blacks was used on the farms. A farmer would allow a black worker and his family to live in a house rent-free for as long as he worked on his farm. In most cases, the homes ranged from subpar to condemnable.

While this arrangement might seem passable, the farmer could show up at the black worker's front door at any hour with something he wanted done. So while the normal work hours were long—literally sunup to sundown—there was no such thing as overtime. They referred to this arrangement as "straight pay."

Black workers felt obliged to honor any request at any time for fear of losing their jobs, homes, and other necessary items provided by the farmers, like cars and household appliances. I believe in an honest day's pay for an honest day's work, but this was clearly a case of abuse.

Most of the workers I knew were content with this arrangement until they had a serious disagreement with the farmer and wanted to leave. That's when reality hit them. Many had a family to support and the idea of not having shelter or owning anything of their own made it complicated. They really had no alternative except to stay in a hopeless situation.

Many people have written and read about the struggles of the black man in the South, but I often wonder how many have actually experienced or understand the struggles as I do. I'm also realistic enough to understand that my challenges paled in comparison to blacks that lived generations before me. Besides the physical abuse they encountered, the mental anguish and humiliation is often too difficult to comprehend.

My father, James Wilson, was a sharecropper who supported our family of fourteen on a $25 a week salary. But he was astute at "living off the land," and most of our food was grown and stored during the summer, with the exception of meats, which were processed and stored during the winter. The only items we purchased were flour, sugar, rice, and seasonings.

There was no room for any mistakes because this food had to last through the winter and into spring when we would start eating directly from the garden.

The living conditions were hard.

Our four-bedroom home, built with twelve-inch cement blocks on a concrete slab, wasn't much different from that of the homes that housed the other black farmworkers. We initially had no running water, so all fourteen of us relied on an outhouse. A single fireplace provided the main source of heat for the entire house. Our wood-burning stove, which I learned to cook on, would also become an effective heating source while meals were being prepared. Still, it was a nightmare keeping warm in the winter because the cinder block walls didn't give us any insulation.

The summer presented the exact opposite problem. While the tin roofing kept the house dry, it also made it extremely difficult to cool down the interior. And I'm sure you could guess we didn't have air-conditioning.

We all helped my father with his heavy workload. I worked tirelessly in the heat, sometimes missing school because, as my parents would sometimes say, "There's work to do on the farm." While my parents valued education, school would, unfortunately, begin at the same time as harvest season and all hands were needed for gathering crops for sale and storage.

The best thing that came out of our harsh lifestyle was how close we became as a family. As I grew older, I missed that closeness, that sharing, that looking out for one another. The funny thing was we didn't consider ourselves poor. Our parents made sure that we always had plenty to eat and the clothes that we had were always clean and neatly pressed.

When we worked, we gave all the money that we earned to our parents to help with whatever had to be paid for. With a large family like ours, it made the burden easier on Dad, especially after we eventually moved off the farm and had to pay for more things. But moving off the farm was definitely a step up. While we didn't grow as much food as before, we were able to get jobs with normal hours (no more waking up at four a.m.!). Plus, it was the first time we had indoor plumbing.

We learned quite a bit from our parents. Dad taught us skills of survival: farming, carpentry, masonry, auto mechanics, and other things that helped us become resourceful and more independent. Mom taught us cooking, cleaning, and how to better take care of ourselves. And jointly, they taught us to do things together and share one another's clothes, food, and even Christmas presents.

It's funny how some simple pleasures of your childhood stay with you forever. I still remember and miss the melody of the raindrops that pelted our tin roof as I slept.

Alternatively, I guess the one thing that I don't miss from my youth is the getting up in the middle of the night to make my way across the backyard to the outhouse. That could be brutal, especially during the winter.

But all in all, there was plenty of value that I learned from my whole growing-up experience.

I am proud to say that my father had the greatest influence on my life and was a major reason why I eventually became a professional baseball player. I was always amazed by how much he knew and was able to do, despite the fact that he only had a seventh grade education. Besides being a very good catcher, he played both the piano and guitar; had the ability to diagnose, repair, and rebuild most automotive engines; was a wiz at mathematics; and had the general wisdom of a college professor.

Most kids think that their father is the greatest man in the world and they probably have plenty of good reasons to think that way. But there was something different about my father. He always seemed to know the right things to say or do at just the perfect time.

The game of baseball was our family's outlet on the weekends to forget about the hard work we did during the week. It might seem funny, but we worked just as hard at perfecting our play in baseball as we did at farming. Personally, I saw baseball as a life commitment and my "great escape" from the real world. At first, baseball was a relief from the long work hours—just pure enjoyment. Later, it was a way to a better life. I would end up going to college because of baseball.

Baseball came to be a family tradition and all of us, including my father, six brothers, five sisters, and a host of cousins nearby, were quite good at it. While most other families went to parks, beaches, and movies for recreation and amusement, my family played baseball. We played on sandlots on Saturdays with both family and friends and then put teams together primarily just from our large family on Sunday afternoons after church.

Today, most kids who love baseball play Little League, AAU, or on some club team and dream of one day playing in the major leagues. I didn't play organized ball until high school and the idea of playing big league ball never crossed my mind. My only thoughts were to hope it didn't rain on Saturday and that we got out of church early enough on Sunday to get a game in.

As a young boy, my entire approach to baseball came from my father. His philosophy was never to work on mechanics or technique, but rather to simply emphasize enjoyment of the game. It was meant to be fun. He didn't put as much stock in winning and losing as he did in doing your best. His favorite saying was, "All you can do is your best, but some days your best will not be good enough to win." I lived by that philosophy throughout my entire baseball life.

Despite all the work there was to do on the farm and how much Dad depended on his children to help out, he still encouraged me to try out for the baseball team at the then-recently integrated Bamberg-Ehrhardt High School. It was an interesting time there. Everyone seemed out of place and many white kids either stopped taking the bus to avoid being with black students or enrolled in private schools. Black parents expressed outrage, too. They were concerned that while the material their kids would learn would be the same as the whites, the white teachers would treat the black students differently. Many believed that it may have been better to receive the same funding and material as whites but have their children remain in all-black schools. It was not an easy transition for either blacks or whites.

Trying out for the high school baseball team made me nervous for a couple of reasons. First, blacks playing ball on the same field as whites in the South was not the norm. And second, I wasn't accustomed to competing for a place on any team that was not made up of family members.

I will never forget the feeling of intimidation on my first day entering the gym for tryouts. At just 140 pounds soaking wet, I was astonished at the size of the first two boys I saw—one was around six-foot-ten, the other about six-four and 250 pounds. Feeling like a boy among men, I turned around and went straight home. But my dad talked me into going back the next day and, thankfully, one of my older brothers, James Richard, whom I rarely saw because he worked all the time, and a cousin, Monique Singleton, were at the tryouts as well, which really put me at ease.

Once I made the team, overcoming the issue of my size thanks to the skills I developed from years of playing with my family, there was an assortment of new challenges I would need to overcome. Besides learning to play and socialize with other players who were not family, close friends, or of the same race, we lived fifteen miles away from school. Since we were a one-car family with twelve children, most days my brothers and I would rely on hitching a ride with people driving through on their way home from work. However, because our practice and game schedules didn't always match up with the working hours at the factories, either our father would have to come pick us up or we would go to a nearby bus station and wait for someone we knew to drive us home. The good thing about a small town is that everyone knows one another and, in Ehrhardt, they were always glad to give you a ride home.

Winning baseball became a Wilson family tradition at Bamberg-Ehrhardt High School. The varsity team won every 2A title in South Carolina from 1974 through 1981, a period in which no fewer than two Wilson brothers or cousins played on the team.

Thanks to my father, the game of baseball is more than just a sport to me. It continues to be a reminder of happier and simpler times when family and friends took precedence over everything else in my life.

One thing I've learned over the years is that success is rarely ever achieved alone. Often, it takes another person's assistance to help you accomplish your goals. I was certainly no different.

Because I was raised in a family with limited resources, I consider myself to have been blessed with parents who gave plenty of love and support, as well as money they did not have, to provide me with an opportunity to succeed in life. I will always be grateful for that and can never repay them for their sacrifices. However, there were some things that were beyond their capabilities to provide for me. This is where I was fortunate to have had a friend like Judge Julius B. Ness—known to many simply as Bubba—in my life.

Aside from my father, Judge Ness was the other early influence in my baseball development. Our relationship started in an unusual manner during my senior year in high school. That was when Mr. Ness, a prominent white judge in South Carolina and the father of our high school catcher, approached me one day outside my school and asked if I wanted to play baseball for the American Legion team in Orangeburg that he planned on coaching.

Although the high school season was over and I wanted to say yes, I told him that I had to work to help my parents out. The other issue was the long distance between Ehrhardt and Orangeburg. I couldn't possibly ask my father to drive me back and forth every day.

Judge Ness politely said he understood and walked away.

A week later, I arrived home from school to find this strange car parked in the yard. I assumed it belonged to a friend of my parents from church. However, when I walked into the house, I instead saw this short little man—Judge Ness—sitting in the living room.

My father calmly said, "Mr. Ness says that he wants you to play baseball this summer."

"Yes, sir," I quickly replied. "But I already told him that I couldn't because I need to work."

I was hoping my father understood that I did not invite Mr. Ness to make the request on my behalf. I looked nervously from my father to Mr. Ness and relief flooded over me as I realized from their body language that there was no tension or unease between them. I sensed that the judge had already made it clear that I had turned down his offer.

Recognizing the dilemma of my wanting to play baseball versus the need for me to bring some money home to the family, Mr. Ness said to my father, "I understand your situation and would not want to cause any more hardship. But what if I got Mookie a job working hours that would allow him to play ball *and* get a ride back and forth every day?"

Dad repeated the judge's words to confirm what we just heard.

"That's right," Mr. Ness said. "He can work and play baseball."

Relieved, my father looked at me and asked, "Well, do you want to play?"

Wanting to jump through the ceiling, yet trying to maintain my calm, I answered with a simple, "Yes, sir."

After Dad gave his consent, the judge explained more about American Legion baseball and how the other players would be coming from all the surrounding towns. When the conversation ended, my father and Mr. Ness stood up and shook hands.

As Mr. Ness drove off, I stood in the doorway in disbelief of what had just transpired. The end of the school baseball season had always been boring for me because there was nothing to look forward to after a day of classes. Now, thanks to the judge, that was about to change.

True to his word, he had arranged for me to be picked up either at school or at my house during the summer. Little did I realize it would be in a squad car driven by Deputy Sheriff Grimes. I had never been in a police car before so I was a little ill at ease. With a bunch of kids from school watching me drive off with Grimes, I knew I would have a lot of explaining to do the next day.

The Sheriff drove me to the courthouse and directed me to the courtroom where Judge Ness was presiding. Mr. Ness saw me standing at the courtroom doors and signaled for me to take a seat. Fifteen minutes later, he adjourned court and we went to his office so he could get out of his robe and into street clothes. From there, we got into his car and drove eighteen miles to the field for our practice.

During the drive, he told me that he was a Navy veteran who went to law school after completing his service. As he spoke, I noticed the absence of part of one of his fingers. I was curious about what had happened, but it would have been impolite to ask. I just assumed he sustained this injury while in the Navy.

Shortly after our first practice began, it became obvious to me that this was going to be a different level of baseball, far more challenging than I experienced in high school. All the players were All-Stars. It would be exactly the kind of environment I needed to improve my skills.

During the ride home, the judge informed me that a police officer would be picking me up every day for the remainder of the school year and driving me home after practice when I wasn't riding with him personally.

He also confirmed for me the promise of a job, something not easily found for a teenager in those days—especially in Ehrhardt. The options were typically limited to farm work, pumping gas, or bagging groceries, which made jobs particularly rare, since Ehrhardt had just two gas stations and one grocery store. As for farming, working a full day in the fields and then trying to find the energy to play ball at night was not going to work. Knowing full well that Mr. Ness was aware of the limited options, I couldn't imagine what kind of job he would be able to find for me.

A few days later, he instructed me to see a Madison Bishop, who owned a fertilizer spreading business about two miles from my house. I had no idea what I could possibly do there, but arrived bright and early the following Monday morning.

"Good morning, sir, my name is Mookie Wilson. Judge Ness told me to come see you about some work you may have for me."

"Yes, Bubba said that you would be coming by," Bishop said. "You're one of James Wilson's boys, aren't you?"

"Yes, sir," I replied.

Bishop, in a joking manner, said, "Bubba told me to give you a job and that you had to be off by noon. Imagine that Bubba, telling me to give you a job and how much work you could do."

At first, I was put off a little by his tone, but I quickly realized that Mr. Ness and Bishop were very close friends and that he was giving me a job as a favor to the judge.

The conversation became more comfortable from there.

"Bubba says that you're a pretty good ballplayer."

If I had had a lighter complexion, he might have seen me blush.

The next day I reported to Bishop's office.

"Ready to work, Mookie?"

I said I was, still not knowing what to expect.

We walked into a building filled with fertilizer that needed to be put into bags. But that wasn't going to be my job, because the last thing Bishop wanted to do was tire me out and make the judge mad at him.

"I want you to paint the outside of this shed."

I was no painter, but I knew this could be done in a matter of a few days. But somehow, and I still don't know how to this day, Bishop found a way for me to work on that same shed for the entire summer. I worked four hours a day painting it and repainting it.

At first, I was a little uncomfortable knowing that I was working a job that didn't need to be done and getting paid for it. However, my desire to play baseball overcame any lingering apprehensions I may have had.

It was then that I realized the degree of influence that Judge Julius B. Ness had in the state of South Carolina.

During the American Legion season that summer, Mr. Ness and I got into a conversation about college. I told him I had been given a baseball scholarship to play at South Carolina State but that, for financial reasons, the school had just recently discontinued their baseball program. They would still honor my scholarship, but I was extremely disappointed I would not be playing college ball.

A week or so later, the judge brought up college again and said when we played a game in Sumter, South Carolina, later that week, I was going to pitch. There was nothing odd about this, as I was one of the best pitchers on the team. But what did surprise me was that he also said that he had someone coming to see me play that game, but wouldn't say whom that was going to be.

We would win that night in Sumter, and it was a game in which I played particularly well.

The next day, while Mr. Ness drove me to practice, he revealed to me who came to watch me play. I was shocked to learn that it was Bobby Richardson, the former New York Yankee great and the head coach of the University of South Carolina baseball team—the best college baseball team in the state.

For a brief moment, I was both excited and nervous. I was thrilled just thinking about a baseball man of this magnitude coming to watch me play. Then I remembered the strong game I had both pitching and hitting. It didn't take long for my mind to register that I would be going to the University of South Carolina to play baseball.

The judge continued talking, but I had kind of tuned him out in my excitement until I thought I heard him say the words "he can't use you."

I asked Mr. Ness to repeat what he had just said.

"Richardson said he can't use you, Mookie."

As quickly as I had become elated, I now suddenly had a feeling of rejection. I don't know why I was so disappointed since the University of South Carolina was never in my plans anyway. But the wind had clearly been taken out of my sails.

As hurt as I was, I sensed that Mr. Ness was even more disappointed and a little upset over the snub. I wasn't sure if the judge was more upset because Richardson rejected a player that he endorsed or that Bobby did not respond the way Mr. Ness, a major financial supporter and booster to the school, had expected him to. In either case, the judge's usual strong influence didn't work in this instance.

As the summer was nearing its end, my dream of playing baseball at the next level was fading along with it. But then, without warning, Mr. Ness told me to meet him at his office the next day. He said we would be driving to Spartanburg Methodist College to enroll me there for school on a scholarship. The judge never asked me if I wanted to attend SMC, but it was a two-year college well-known for its baseball program at the junior college level. I realized I was being given another amazing opportunity by this caring man.

During the two-and-a-half-hour drive to Spartanburg, I couldn't help but wonder why this person was doing all he had for me.

In an environment where I was accustomed to eating on the back porch of white families' homes, he always invited me inside to join his family and dine at the same table. He had provided transportation for me and an opportunity to play baseball all summer long. He created a job for me, cashing in a favor from a close friend. He used his influence in trying to get me into the University of South Carolina. And now he was taking six hours out of his day to enroll me in a college where I could play baseball.

Why would this white man go out of his way for a black kid from the South? I really didn't understand, but I was certainly grateful. Judge Ness was validation of what my father had always told me about people: that every person should be judged by his or her own merits. It was also extremely important for me, as a young athlete, to know that some total stranger thought more highly of me than I did of myself.

Judge Ness gave me some wonderful gifts. Not only the opportunities to succeed, but also support, encouragement, and the belief that there are very good people in the world.

After two strong seasons at SMC, I was drafted by the Los Angeles Dodgers. But to most everyone's surprise, I turned them down. I certainly had second thoughts about that decision, but my reasons were simple. First, I didn't think I was ready for such a big move. And then there was the bigger reason of how deeply disappointed my parents would have been if I had left college. As much as my parents loved baseball and were proud of what I had accomplished, my finishing college was their ultimate dream for me.

Still, a lot of people I knew didn't understand how I could turn down a chance to play professional baseball for a franchise as great as the Dodgers. Those same people couldn't believe my next move. I would accept a baseball scholarship to attend the school that "couldn't use me" two years earlier—the University of South Carolina.

My friends and family had another reason for concern—I would be the first black player in the history of University of South Carolina baseball.

I would be lying if I said I wasn't at least a little worried about putting myself in that situation, but my desire to test my baseball abilities at a higher level and to prove to myself and others that I was ready to be a part of the best college program in the state outweighed any lingering concerns over how I would be treated.

As the only black player on the 1977 South Carolina Gamecocks, there were certainly instances on the playing field when I could truly understand how Jackie Robinson, who broke the color barrier in the major leagues thirty years before, must have felt. There were uncomfortable situations when I had to ignore an assortment of unflattering comments and jokes based on my race. And there were times when I was not just the only black on the field, but also the only black in the entire stadium.

But nothing could prepare me for what happened when we played a game at Georgia Southern University. The actions and language from the Georgia fans became so offensive that my head coach, June Raines, wanted to take me out of the game, but I refused. I would like to say the fans' resentment was directed toward the entire Gamecocks baseball team except for two things. They were not offering the rest of my team watermelon or waving the Confederate flag behind the other outfielders like they were with me.

Thankfully, the season reached the point where most people focused more on our winning ball games and less on my being the lone black player on the team. We were as good a college team as anyone had ever seen. We cruised through the Regionals, defeating all of our challengers in convincing fashion. And through all of the adversity I had to endure, my big season was rewarded in the June amateur draft held just before our trip to Omaha, Nebraska, to take part in the College World Series. I would go to the CWS knowing that I had been drafted by the New York Mets in the second round. But while that was certainly great news, my focus was still on winning the college championship.

We would make it all the way to the final game against Arizona State. But while it was one of the most thrilling games I had ever been a part of, we lost a heartbreaker, 2–1. With the college season now over, it was time to make one of the most difficult decisions of my life. Being drafted as high as the second round had a little more meaning than the previous year. Because of my strong season with the Gamecocks, I was now more confident, more prepared, and less afraid to take that next step into professional baseball.

The Mets made their offer and I discussed it with my parents. The money was almost a nonfactor, as any amount would have been more than we could have ever dreamed of. Nevertheless, my dad's words and body language implied how important finishing college was in comparison to going off and playing professional baseball.

Representing myself at the time, I called the Mets back and said that I needed more money. In some small way, I was hoping that they would make the decision for me and say they had made their final offer.

Well, the Mets increased it.

Having never negotiated anything before in my life, I was thrown off balance and, without giving it a second thought, accepted their higher offer on the spot. I would receive a signing bonus of $22,000 which I would turn over to my parents in appreciation for everything they had done for me.

When I told my parents what I had done, I saw confusion on their faces. For the first time in my life, I felt as if I had disappointed them. But at the same time, I think they realized, as did I, that I was taking the first step in accepting responsibility for my life and actions.

Before leaving for Wausau, Wisconsin, to begin my professional career with the Mets' A-Ball minor league team, I went to see my father, who was in the hospital recovering from a back injury he had suffered at work. He gave me a warm embrace, offering me his full support and telling me that he now fully blessed my decision.

I was shocked, but relieved. Now I could begin a new chapter in my life with a clear mind. I was ready to take my baseball career to the next level.

4

The "Say Hey Kid" and Me

Where's that Mookie kid?! Where's that Mookie kid?!"
The voice and the stature of the man who hollered those words out in the visiting locker at Candlestick Park in 1984 were unmistakable. Perhaps the greatest baseball player who ever lived, Willie Mays, was checking up on me.

It took me back to the first time I met the "Say Hey Kid" a few days into instructional league in St. Petersburg following my first minor league season for the Mets' A-Ball team in Wausau, Wisconsin, in 1977. Mays made such an effort to talk to me. At the time, the only theory I had for this was the sense that he saw in me some of himself when he was my age—the speed, the way my helmet often flew off like his did when rounding second base, and the fact we were both center fielders. That was pretty much it.

But maybe, just maybe, there was more to my Willie Mays connection that I had no way of knowing about back then.

Years later, after my playing days were over, I was kind of shocked to find out that my father's real last name was not Wilson. In fact, he was born with the name James Mays.

One of my sisters was motivated to find out more about this revelation through further research of our genealogy. But some of my family members weren't too happy she was doing it because Wilson was the only surname they had ever known. Plus, the discovery meant that the grandfather we all knew and loved wasn't our biological one. So after some pressure from family and a general desire to leave well enough alone, my sister stopped her digging and no longer pursued it.

But it is kind of a neat thought to think that I might have some relation to baseball royalty.

The instructional league capped off a somewhat disappointing introduction into everything I had previously dreamed professional baseball was going to be like. What a world of difference it was between playing Division One college ball at the University of South Carolina and A-Ball at Wausau. In fact, conditions in A-Ball were so horrible, I actually believed that I had made a mistake leaving college a year early to play minor league ball.

The dugouts were bad. The clubhouses were bad. The ballparks were bad. And the lighting was poor at best. Travel was just ridiculous, as they packed us in the team bus like sardines. It was normal for some of us to sleep on the luggage racks above the seats during long trips. But most disappointing of all were the showers in the clubhouses. While some didn't even have hot water, others had wood floors with no drain, which meant if you weren't the first guy in, the dirty water would rise almost up to your knees.

By contrast, at the University of South Carolina, everything was beautiful. We had manicured fields, beautiful clubhouses, and team officials that catered to your needs. It was awesome.

But while I had strongly considered staying at the University of South Carolina for my senior year, in the end I figured with this being the second time I got drafted that it was probably time to sign a pro contract. Besides, even my meager salary of $500 a month *before* taxes and $4 a day in meal money beat what I made at home doing farmwork. I was used to not having money, so I never missed what I didn't have. As long as I had food to eat, playing baseball was "it" for me. Never once did I consider giving up playing ball to go out and get a real job. As depressing as some aspects of A-Ball were, it was the love of the game that kept me going. I wasn't even thinking about moving up to the next level or one day playing in the major leagues. A-Ball, in spite of the conditions, was very competitive baseball, a step above what I saw at the college level. I got a joy out of that new challenge. The disappointments were just part of the process that all minor leaguers had to go through when starting out. It's not like I was the only one.

I ended up having a strong half-season at Wausau, hitting .290, stealing 23 bases, and scoring 50 runs in only 68 games. I enjoyed playing for manager Tom Egan, who, from the very first day when he told me to grab my uniform because I was starting that night in center field, always showed his confidence in me and my playing abilities.

The year was also significant on a personal level because I began dating my future wife, Rosa, who was separated from my brother Richard. They had a child named Preston together, who was a mere toddler at the time. It's important to note that Rosa and Richard's separation and ensuing divorce was mutual and very civilized. In fact, Richard had already moved on and was engaged to another woman.

After a few discreet dates outside of our hometown of Ehrhardt, we decided to let our folks know what was going on. My parents and I went over to see Rosa and her parents to discuss this dicey issue. Our parents had grown up together in the same church, were very good friends, and, of course, had been in-laws, so we all knew each other very well. But to say my dating my former sister-in-law in a small town like Ehrhardt brought about great friction from both Rosa's parents and mine would be an understatement.

My father was the first to speak and sought to relieve some of the tension in the room. Sitting up, he said, "You two are grown-ups and you're going to do what you're going to do. I appreciate the fact you thought enough of us to let us know."

Then he turned and looked directly at Rosa and said, "Now Rosa, I'm gonna tell ya. You know the type of person I am. I will always give you a chance. I am just going to take your relationship with Mookie one day at a time and we'll just see where it goes. But I just want you to know that I don't hold anything against you."

As he finished speaking, my mother was shaking her head side to side.

Seeing her reaction, Rosa said, "Well, Mom, I hear from Dad, but you're shaking your head no."

My mother told her, "You've already been with one son. I don't want you to be with another."

My father was a little more liberal than my mother and had a better understanding of the situation. He knew that Richard was an otherwise hardworking and generally courteous guy, but was only twenty-one, right out of high school, and Rosa just sixteen when they were kind of pushed into marriage by Rosa's mother. While that didn't excuse or justify them not working harder on their marriage, it was the major factor on why it didn't last. My father saw two kids that married too young and had set themselves up to fail.

My mother's different take on the situation wasn't a surprise to me. She really didn't know a lot about what went on between Richard and Rosa like my father did. Besides, it's normal for moms to feel the way she did about her son.

Rosa was hurt by my mother's reaction, but she didn't take it entirely personally. She felt my mom's biggest concern was how other people were going to perceive the news.

My father helped my mom come around at that first meeting and everything seemed to be a lot better. But then the parents were back at Rosa's parents' house for a second meeting two weeks later. My mother told Rosa's folks she didn't want me coming over to their house, that they needed to help break us up. Rosa's mom valued her friendship with my mother and agreed, which now created a new friction.

When Rosa found out, she told her mother, "That may be your friend, but I'm your child. How could you love Mookie's mother more than you love me?"

The negativity from our parents would ultimately only bring

Rosa and me closer together. It was me and Rosa against the world.

I was promoted to the Mets' AA team in Jackson, Mississippi, in 1978 and again put up strong numbers, hitting .292 with 38 stolen bases and 72 RBIs. Besides my continued productivity at a higher level, it was also a much better experience at Jackson than A-Ball was. Besides the parks and facilities being a lot better, for the first time I began thinking about the possibility of one day playing major league ball. AA-Ball is usually the stage in a player's career when team executives start looking at you a little more seriously in terms of getting promoted to AAA and beyond. Luckily for me, I had what I would classify as one of my "career games" the day Mets' general manager Joe McDonald made a rare trip to Jackson to see our team play.

It was a good time for me.

I also began playing with Hubie Brooks, the Mets' top draft pick that season. Despite my Gamecocks losing to his Arizona State Sun Devils team in the College World Series the year before, we became very close friends. The two of us were very much alike—very quiet. But I guess because we played against each other in college it gave a couple of reserved guys like us something in common to break the ice. We were also both just beginning AA-Ball, were roommates on the road, and were experiencing a new team and level of play together.

It was also during my season at Jackson that I proposed to Rosa. I had saved enough money to give her a ring with a little heart-shaped diamond you could barely see. I told her, "I know you need a magnifying glass to see it, but on our wedding day I will give you the biggest one you ever saw—a *baseball* diamond!"

The idea of getting married on the field before a Jackson home game started with our general manager. He got wind of the fact I was engaged and wanted to give us a full-blown wedding ceremony. At first, I was reluctant, preferring to get married in a small, private ceremony. But he was persistent, saying that Rosa would love it.

As it turned out, the team did a really nice job. They had the visiting team, the Arkansas Cardinals, and our Jackson Mets club line up facing each other from home plate toward the pitcher's mound, bats held high to form an arch so that Rosa and I could walk under them. Willie "Paco" Perez, a teammate and best friend whom I lived with at the time, was my best man. His wife was the maid of honor. Reverend Broom, recommended to us by the team, presided over the ceremony. I was a little embarrassed at first over the whole thing, but I was really glad we went through with the on-field wedding.

There was a little bit of a dark cloud over the wedding day as no family was present, not even little Preston. With my mother still upset, Rosa's mother talked Richard and her son Louis into coming to get Preston in Jackson and bringing him back to Ehrhardt—a 1,200-mile round trip—because our moms didn't think that he should be a part of the ceremony. I guess it was their way of trying to stop the wedding. I was a little hurt by it all, but not surprised, as I knew the predicament everyone was in. It wasn't like any of our parents had given us their blessing.

My dad and I discussed the circumstances several times prior to the wedding. The one thing that stuck out in my mind was when he told me, "Listen, I can't tell you what to do. You do what your heart says. Don't worry about your mamma—she'll come around. She's just hurt right now, but she'll come around."

I think his telling me that is really what led me to believe that everything was going to be okay. My father had a way of knowing things.

After the game, a reporter asked me why I decided to get married on the baseball field. I told him, "My wife wanted a big diamond." It was a throwaway line, but one that got a lot of play in the media and around the ball club. The team put us up in a hotel that night and Rosa and I watched clips of the wedding on the local news channel.

The very next morning, however, I had to leave Rosa and head off on a road trip with the club. It was her introduction to baseball as a player's wife—one night and then I had to go. Not exactly the "fairy-tale wedding" we dreamed of, but still very special.

Now married and the stepfather to a four-year-old boy, I had to struggle on a minor league salary with three mouths to feed instead of just one. The team gave me a fifty-dollar raise as a wedding gift, bringing my monthly salary to $750. To help us get by, we shared an apartment with another teammate and his wife. Also, when I went on the road, my roomie and I would pool our meal money together and buy stuff for sandwiches instead of eating out. In doing so, I was able to put away some of the seven bucks the team gave me each day. So, after a ten-game road trip, I would actually be able to bring home a few dollars.

I look back at it now and realize the whole thing could have turned out badly. I had *nothing*. But you find a way. We certainly couldn't save any money, but we got by.

As for Preston, despite the unique circumstances of once being his uncle and now being a father to him, it was surprisingly never an issue. We always had a good relationship. Aside from missing the wedding, he was generally always with Rosa and me. And when we did have him, he was always moving because *we* were always moving. Rosa's parents, not surprisingly, voiced their issues with young Preston's schedule. But I always sensed their greatest concern was with the whole situation of me, Richard, and Rosa, with Preston in the middle. Like the small Southern town of Ehrhardt they grew up in, our parents were generally unreceptive to anything different from what was considered normal. It wasn't so much about being right or wrong as it was just being different. And I don't think they knew how the whole thing was going to play out with Preston's psyche. That was their main concern, but when the boy was with us, there were never any issues.

In fact, I took Preston with me whenever I could. He basically grew up exposed to the baseball life. I took him in as my own, taught him to be honest, and whenever giving someone his word on something, to honor it—never flip-flopping. I gave him quality time and always stressed the importance of respecting women.

And it was no different later when it came to my daughters, Adesina and Ernestine, as well as Esthermae, a girl who was Rosa's brother Luis's child, whom she had assumed parental rights for when the mother contracted AIDS years after breaking up with Luis. Because of the way I was raised by my own parents,

I understood the importance of mentoring and raising children as best as I could.

———————

The off-season was a busy one. After some time in instructional league in Florida, I had my first opportunity to play winter ball in Puerto Rico. That was a terrific experience. The money was very good and the team I played for, the Arecibo Lobos, paid for our apartment and other living expenses. The cash I received at the end of each week really helped us make it through the winter.

I moved up to AAA Tidewater in the spring of 1979 and had a very good season. I made the All-Rookie team, finished second on the team in hitting, and swiped 49 bases as an everyday player. But in spite of the success I enjoyed in my first season at Tidewater, the thing I remember most was how difficult the jump from AA to AAA was. People don't realize how big a step that can be. Most notable was how the defenses were much better—balls you would get hits on in AA were, all of a sudden, outs in AAA. But like anything else, I had to adjust to the higher level of competition.

After the season ended, the Mets informed me that I was being put on the forty-man roster that following spring training. I was very excited about the prospect of making the Mets major league club. I was one step away from realizing my ultimate goal, but now had to face a winter of anticipation.

To stay sharp, I went down to Puerto Rico, playing once again for the Lobos. I loved Puerto Rico so much, I think the country designated me as a native! Rosa, Preston, and I had such a great time down there. I would bring Preston with me into the clubhouse and sometimes wouldn't see him again until after the game was over and it was time to go home. That was because other teammates would play with him or keep him busy. That's one thing I will say about ballplayers at all levels—they take care of kids. I don't care which ballplayer's child it is, they never have to worry about babysitters in baseball. Ballplayers, in spite of whatever faults they may have, are very family-oriented. They really know how to take care of kids, even when they don't have any of their own. They just love to see kids on the field or in the clubhouse. It does them a world of good.

Spring training finally arrived and I couldn't wait to get into a game. But to my disappointment, I waited and waited and waited some more, but I wasn't getting into any games. I didn't want to be one of those players who thought he was deserving of anything, but the fact was I wasn't getting anything out of spring training by riding the pine. I had been around the game enough to know it was only a matter of time before I was going down and I knew they were just waiting for the right opportunity to do it.

I wasn't happy about how I perceived what was going on because we had a poor team. I didn't feel like I was given the opportunity to make the club out of spring training. That was my disappointment. Still, I understood it was only my first year on the forty-man roster. I had already surpassed my expectations just by making the roster in spring training. It was a great accomplishment in my young pro career. But it just wasn't my time to go north with the club when spring training was over. They had made up their minds about that. They knew who was going to be in that outfield and I wasn't going to be one of them. This was especially true in center field, where Lee Mazzilli was "the guy," their drawing card.

Still, there was no question in my mind that I was as good or better than the outfielders they had with the big club. So while I sat and watched, I was really getting frustrated, which takes an awful lot for me. I didn't mind going back to AAA, but, if that was going to be the case, then I wanted to get sent down as soon as possible so I could get ready for the season.

As the days went by, a number of minor league teammates on the forty-man roster had pink slips put in their lockers, a maneuver done by management that meant you were getting sent back down to the minor leagues. But despite my not playing, my locker wasn't getting a pink slip. In a way, this was frustrating to me because I knew I was eventually going to get sent down, and I wanted to play.

After a few weeks on the bench, I made the highly unusual move by a minor league player of confronting my big league manager, Joe Torre, about it. My strategy was if they were going to send me down anyway, I was going to give them a reason to do so quickly. Or, better yet, maybe he would give me a chance to finally play some games on the big club. Looking for a reaction, any reaction, I went into his office and said, "Look, I know you're going to send me down. I want to go down and learn how to switch-hit."

Joe simply said, "Okay."

I was a little shocked by his answer. I never thought he would actually agree to it, because it had been just the year before at Jackson when, after messing around with switch-hitting during batting practice, I said to my manager, Bob Wellman, "Hey, Bob, I'd like to try this switch-hitting thing in some games."

After calling the team up in New York, Bob told me they said no. So I figured Torre would stick with the company line when I confronted him about it, but it backfired on me. Of course, actually learning to switch-hit would work out well for me in future years. It's interesting, but if I hadn't gotten so frustrated, I would never have learned to do it. But as I left Joe's office, it was the farthest thing from my mind. All I could think was, *Well, now what do I do?! What have I just done?! What I just said to Joe was completely out of frustration! I'm a good right-handed hitter who batted third at Jackson in AA and led the team in hitting and runs scored, and then jumped to AAA Tidewater last year and did the same thing as their leadoff hitter. I never really wanted to learn to switch-hit. Why would I want to mess with that now?*

I was very concerned. I didn't want to regress. I had already played a full year at AAA and wanted to make the jump into the big leagues sooner, not later. Learning to become a productive switch-hitter could add years to my time in the minors. I really regretted what I had just done in a big way.

Sure enough, in the next day's paper, there was a blurb about how I was going to be sent back down to Tidewater to learn how to switch-hit. But they didn't send me down right away.

Two days after my meeting with Torre, he actually started me in my first spring training game. I had to face Jim Bibby, a hard-throwing right-hander and one of the premier pitchers in the game. I had just started switch-hitting and in my first at-bat from the left side of the plate, Bibby jammed me with an inside fastball. I got an infield hit out of it, but my left hand hurt me for a week!

After the game, I finally got sent down, which was a relief. In just my second game back at Tidewater I hit a home run batting left-handed. I thought, *Wow, this switch-hitting thing is going to be easier than I thought.*

Of course, that wasn't going to be the case, but I was glad to be off to a good start. Learning to switch-hit correctly was all trial and error for me. I wasn't getting any help from my coaches. Nothing. I was completely on my own. Frank Verdi, my manager at Tidewater both years, never said anything about my switch-hitting one way or another.

I would go on to have a great season at Tidewater in 1980, stealing 50 bases and batting .295. I figured I had been around long enough that I would be a September call-up. Plus, if your team is losing like the Mets were, it was normal for them to call up guys from the minors to get a taste of the majors. If your team is in the pennant race, however, they don't call up as many guys because they don't want to disrupt anything.

My big moment, the one I had waited my entire life for, was nothing fancy or ceremonious. Verdi simply called me into his office after our last game of the season and said to me, "You're going up to the big club and you have to meet them in LA."

No hoopla. No parties. But at least I was going up with my buddy Hubie Brooks, who was going home to Southern California. I felt good about the fact I was major league–bound with a good friend and that we could experience what was to come together.

We caught a plane out to LA the next morning. My dream of playing major league baseball was about to come true!

5

Joe's Seafood

t was September 2, 1980. Earlier in the day, I had arrived in Los Angeles after a very long connecting flight from Norfolk, Virginia. I got to the hotel just in time to drop my baggage off in my room and catch the team bus to Dodger Stadium. The AAA season now over, I had been called up by the Mets to start my major league career.

I was scared.

Moments before getting dressed in my Mets uniform, I was called into manager Joe Torre's office. He said just two words to me: "You're playing."

I was a little shocked and unprepared mentally to play. I thought this would just be a token call-up, not a chance to break into the starting lineup! I got dressed, went out to take batting practice, and then game time came and Joe had me leading off!

As I strolled to the plate to face iconic Dodger players like Steve Garvey, Dusty Baker, and Ron Cey, I knew I wasn't at Tidewater anymore. This was Dodger Stadium, man! I mean, c'mon! To a kid growing up in South Carolina, this was the big time. *Everybody* knew about the Dodgers. It hardly mattered that I grew up hating them. Playing in beautiful Dodger Stadium was a surreal experience.

I was in a fog. As I stepped in to face Dodger pitcher Dave Goltz, it really hit me—I was actually starting in a major league game. In my first at-bat, I grounded out to short—Bill Russell to Garvey. I ended up going 0-for-4 with a strikeout in a 6–5 loss to the Dodgers.

It didn't get much better the next game, as I went 0-for-3 with another strikeout. But at least I drew a walk.

I finally got my first major league hit when we went down to San Diego. It was off John Curtis in my second at-bat of the evening, a clean single to left field to break an 0-for-8 slide.

The year 1980 was kind of a turnaround season for our franchise. The team was sold earlier in the year by Charles Payson to Nelson Doubleday and Fred Wilpon. The new ownership then hired a new general manager, Frank Cashen, to see if he could do for the Mets the great things he accomplished for the Orioles during their glory years of the late sixties and early seventies.

Their next move was to try to fill some of the seats at Shea Stadium, which had all the excitement of a mausoleum that year. Seriously, there were a few times when I thought, *Why are we even here?* You got a hit and you heard two people clapping. That's a tough way to play. Athletes play for the crowd, they play for the approval—the ones that don't, don't survive. But when you have a decent crowd out there, man, it's a thousand times easier. So the new ownership team hired a public relations firm named Della Femina, Travisano and Partners to come up with a new team slogan and increase attendance figures. "The Magic Is Back!" would be used in television commercials and on a banner outside of Shea Stadium.

But there honestly was no cause for optimism at all that year. We were real bad. I had naively thought I was going to make a big splash and, all of sudden, the Mets were going to start winning. When that didn't happen, and I saw the way the team continued to lose, it was a hard thing for me to comprehend. All my life I had played for winners, so this was a unique experience. To be honest, I was having more fun playing in the minor leagues. At least at Tidewater, we were winning and weren't getting booed all the time by the home fans. If given the option, at that time, I would have preferred to play in Tidewater instead of Flushing, Queens. Even with the big league lifestyle and the grand hotels we stayed in, I was first and foremost a baseball player. I didn't care about all the frills. The one thing that defined me was winning. I wanted to win ball games. I wanted to be a difference-maker. I didn't want to be on a losing team. So being on that dreadful Mets team and not being able to make an impact was a shock to me.

That first season, New York was a Yankees town. They drew over 2.6 million fans. We drew just over 1.1 million. They won 103 games. We won just 67. The face of their franchise was Reggie Jackson, a future Hall of Famer nicknamed Mr. October for his World Series heroics. The face of ours was Lee Mazzilli, a local boy from Brooklyn who was a good ballplayer marketed for his matinee idol looks. They had won back-to-back World Series just a couple of years before. The Mets' only championship was in 1969.

A friend of Ron Darling once described being a Mets fan back then as someone thinking the Monkees were better than the Rolling Stones. You couldn't even describe us as a distant second to the Yankees. People were like, "Oh, yeah, there's a team over in Queens, too." We were nothing more than a passing thought. Our spectators would come to see other teams' stars.

Mets fans were holding on to the '69 team. You went to the ballpark on a weeknight and there were sometimes as few as twenty-five hundred people. On a good day, like a promotional giveaway day against a popular team like the Reds or the Dodgers, we might draw twenty thousand if we were lucky. Shea was a huge place and it seemed like it was almost empty half the time. In a word, it was depressing.

But despite the atmosphere, I always busted my butt on the ball field because it was the way I was taught to play the game. My father did a great job. My baseball ethic was ingrained in me before I even thought about playing professionally. I was taught if you were going to play baseball, play it well. My dad also told me, "No matter what you do in life, do it the best you can every day, because you never know who's watching you. If you're going to be a ditchdigger, then be the best ditchdigger in the world."

Because of that advice, I never wanted to go home and say, "I should have done this," or "I could have done that." I knew if I gave maximum effort all the time, I would never have any regrets. Baseball was more than a game for me. It was who I was, because I hadn't done many other things at that point in my life. So it wasn't hard for me to give 100 percent effort to a really bad team. Anything less would have been a cop-out.

The next season, 1981, we traded Steve Henderson, a veteran who had helped me get adjusted to the dos and don'ts of clubhouse etiquette after I got called up to the Mets, for Dave Kingman. Kingman had been on the Mets before and was one of the most feared power hitters in the game. But there was a reason he kept getting moved from team to team throughout his career—he had a reputation for not being a good teammate. But I can honestly say that in the three years we played together, I never had a problem with him. I thought he was misunderstood and was a much nicer guy than people gave him credit for. I never heard him say a bad word about anybody. He was just one of those guys who kept to himself—a very private person. And since I was much like that, too, I guess I understood him a little more than other people.

"Kong" was a phenomenal talent who probably was not tailored to the likings of a lot of people. Some believed he could have been more than what he was, almost like the case with Straw. But he was happy with who he was and, unfortunately, sometimes that can work against people.

Some of my teammates didn't like him. The press hated him. The fans both loved *and* hated him at the same time. When he hit one five hundred feet, they loved him, but when he struck out three times they hated him. But that's the player he was—all or nothing.

It was great having Hubie Brooks on the team. Hubie and I were roommates in AAA and in our first year up with the Mets. It made the adjustment to the majors a lot easier to have a fellow-rookie like him on the club. He was also a terrific hitter and a solid third baseman for us.

As for Mazzilli, I know he wasn't thrilled with my taking his place in center field during the '81 season, which led to him getting moved to right field or first base. Initially when I came up the year before, I didn't know how to take Maz. It seemed like he was a little caught up with that whole Brooklyn/Italian/*Saturday Night Fever* era and being a real heartthrob with our female fans.

In fairness, I don't know how he really took to me, either. Because we didn't talk a whole lot, I got the impression he was a little upset to see me come up and become a challenge for his natural position. Center field was an iconic position in New York going back to the days of Willie, Mickey, and the Duke. I think it meant a lot to Maz to play out there.

Joe Torre, at times, could be very intimidating to me. I thought maybe that was because of his mannerisms or lack thereof. He wasn't loud and didn't say much, unlike most of the managers I was used to. When your manager is a little quiet like that, it makes you wonder what he's thinking. But I still thought he did as good a job managing and communicating with us as possible, but he just didn't have the player personnel to win with.

Barely two months into the '81 season, the players went on strike. At issue was the owners wanting compensation for players they would lose to free agency. Of course, the players felt that any compensation given would diminish their value when they entered the free agency market. While I saw my brethren's point, it was a tough sell for me. One of my goals was to get out of debt. At that time, Rosa, Preston, and I would go home during the off-season and either live with my parents or in-laws, because we were still living on borrowed money. The first couple of paychecks that season were really putting a dent in my debt, so I was optimistic about meeting my modest financial goal. Now with the strike, I had to find a way to survive and provide for my family.

Luckily, we frequented this inexpensive restaurant in Woodside, Queens, called Joe's Seafood. The owner, Joe Diecedue, and his father were huge baseball fans and would come over to talk to us each time we dined there. Knowing I was just in my first full season in the big leagues, Joe would always give us a break on dinner.

One evening, the owner brought up the strike and asked me what I was going to do for money until it ended. I told him I didn't have any idea and that I was just going to take things one day at a time and hope for the best.

With some hesitation in his voice and perhaps a little embarrassment, he said, "Well, I could use you here a couple of days a week."

I was slightly taken aback by the offer, but needed a job. I immediately thought to myself, *I never worked in a restaurant before. I don't cook. I wonder what he has in mind.*

I responded, "Well, what do you want me to do?"

"On the weekends, it gets pretty busy in here. You could be our maître d'," he offered.

I agreed and the owner's surprised look was quickly replaced with a smile.

I had never been a maître d', so I had no idea what I was getting into. But I knew I had to work somewhere and that it needed to be at a place where, if the strike ended, I could be ready to go back to playing ball immediately. So he scheduled me to work on Fridays, Saturdays, and Sundays and paid me cash. It was just enough money to pay the rent and feed my family for the duration of the strike. We didn't have much spending money, but we survived.

At the time, we were living in Queens on Ditmars Boulevard, across from LaGuardia Airport. There was an older man, Mr. Stevens, who had a house with a furnished basement that was converted into a small apartment that he rented to us. Two other Mets had stayed there before me—Duffy Dyer and Joel Youngblood. Joel was the one who told me about the place after he moved to Greenwich, Connecticut.

One of the most bizarre experiences I ever had occurred while working at Joe's Seafood. It was a Sunday afternoon and the place was packed. Word had gotten around that I was working there and it was definitely good for business. People were lined up outside along the sidewalk to get in. The restaurant had tables that seated groups of two, four, and six people. As the maître d', I took down people's names and seated them. One group on this particular day was a party of four nuns. After I took down one of their names and told them that I would call them when their table was ready, they went back outside to sit on a bench.

Right after the nuns went outside, a couple walked in and, after looking around the restaurant, I noticed a small square table for two being cleaned off. I took them to it, but when I returned to my podium at the front of the restaurant, one of the nuns approached me. She kind of went off on me and sternly said, "We were there before them! Why did you seat them before us?!"

Before I could explain to the nuns that the table only sat two people, she continued ranting and raving at me. I was shocked. Number one, she's a nun. Two, Sunday was a holy day. And three, that anyone, especially a nun, would come at me that way was really uncalled for. To me, I always thought a nun was supposed to be very proper and cordial. I had never seen that side of a nun before.

The people around the restaurant were looking at me to see how I would react, but I didn't know what to do. I thought, *I can't say what I want to say to her because she's a nun!*

I told a couple of the waiters to *please* help free up a table for these people. Someone must have heard me because a table became available pretty quickly after that.

I hope they had a good meal, because I never went back over to ask them.

I couldn't wait to get home that night. As soon as I arrived, I excitedly told Rosa, "I almost got into a fight with a nun!"

In general, though, the time I spent working at Joe's Seafood was fine. I had many good conversations with the patrons.

The strike ended on July 31 with the Players Association and owners finally reaching an agreement on the free agency issue.

Play resumed for us on August 10, a day after the All-Star Game was played. The season was split into two campaigns, one prior to the strike and the other after it. We didn't come close to winning a division title in either half of the season and went home. The Yankees, maintaining their stranglehold on the city's fan base, made it to the World Series.

But at least the Mets' brass kept on trying to turn things around in the off-season. Frank made a heralded trade with the Cincinnati Reds, getting slugger George Foster in exchange for light-hitting catcher Alex Trevino and pitchers Jim Kern and Greg Harris. George was then signed to a five-year, $10 million contract, the second highest annual salary in baseball at that time after the Yankees' Dave Winfield.

This was a major statement by the Mets' ownership and front office. George was a genuine star and a former MVP who hit 52 home runs in 1977.

Suddenly, there was a glimmer of hope. At our home opener in '82, more than 40,000 fans showed up to watch our new slugger in action. But it was Kingman, our other big bat, who supplied all the power we would need, hammering a three-run homer off Steve Carlton in a 5–2 win. Just as memorable was the reaction of our closer, Neil Allen, who went crazy on the mound after striking out George Vukovich for the final out. Shea was rocking and the scene looked as if we had just won a championship.

With Foster and Kingman, we had two power guys to go along with Hubie and myself to give us a formidable offensive attack.

The pitching, however, still wasn't where it needed to be. We had some older guys like Craig Swan, an outstanding pitcher, but one who struggled with arm problems. Pat Zachry was a serviceable pitcher, but not a star by any stretch of the imagination. There was Pete Falcone, a southpaw from Brooklyn who was a great talent, but lacked that fight needed to be successful. Mike Scott had a live arm, but was nowhere near the pitcher he would later become in Houston. And Randy Jones, a former Cy Young Award winner, was in the twilight of a fine career. In the bullpen, Allen was a solid closer and Jesse Orosco was very effective in the set-up role for us.

We now had, at the very least, a team that we could put on the field that people respected. We didn't get the number of wins that we wanted, but at least we were no longer embarrassing ourselves out there.

The addition of Foster to the middle of the lineup was huge for us. All we knew about him when we got him were the tremendous numbers he put up in Cincinnati that helped lead them to two World Series championships. What we didn't know about him, however, was that he was a self-conscious, private, no-nonsense kind of guy. Plus, he was always very suspicious of others.

Like George, I understood bigotry, but he seemed to believe that most every bad thing that ever happened to him was the result of some prejudiced act. He had a hard time believing that some things in life just happen. He was really outspoken about his suspicions. I'm all for people speaking their minds, but I think you pick your battles. A person shouldn't blurt out everything that's on their mind. I think the fact that he did hurt

George. It hurt him with the fans, with management, and with the players. Perhaps if he was still hitting fifty home runs in a season as a Met he could have gotten away with a lot of what he said, but he was no longer that kind of offensive threat.

Bigger than the Foster signing or that exciting home opener was a trade that would go down in Mets history as one of their best. On April 1, we got Ron Darling and Walt Terrell from the Texas Rangers in exchange for Mazzilli, who had expressed to management his displeasure over being moved from center field. Three seasons later, we would trade Terrell to the Tigers for Howard Johnson. Then, after the Pittsburgh Pirates released Maz in August of '86, we picked him up just in time for our stretch run that year. So, in a sense, we got Darling and Johnson, two of the brightest stars in club history, basically for nothing. Thanks again, Texas!

But despite all of the early optimism, we finished the 1982 season in last place, 27 games out in the NL East. George Foster, our superstar signing, homered just 13 times in over 600 at-bats and became the poster child of our continued woes.

The following spring training would be the strangest of my entire career. In an effort to take away some of my over-aggressiveness as a leadoff hitter and utilize my speed more, our manager George Bamberger came up with the *brilliant* ideas of not having me take batting practice and, during the games, only bunting until I got a two-strike count. This bold plan of his followed an off-season trip to Birmingham, Alabama, where he had Harry Walker work with me on slapping the ball and running in one motion. It was all pure junk.

I was always very comfortable with my approach to hitting. It may not have always looked that way, but I really was. Bamberger wanted to try everything he could to make me into a prototype leadoff hitter. It just didn't work.

Bamberger, a former pitching coach during the Orioles' glory days that Frank handpicked to be the manager the previous year, wouldn't last much longer. We were in LA early in the '83 season when, after batting practice, he called everyone into the clubhouse for a meeting to tell us he was "going fishing." He just basically quit on us, leaving Frank Howard to take over as interim manager. Bamberger later told reporters he had simply *"suffered enough!"*

During the off-season prior to that '83 season, we again made another big headline trade, this time bringing back the pitcher people once referred to at Shea as the Franchise. Tom Seaver was back with the Mets five years after they traded him to the Cincinnati Reds. But this was clearly a different "Tom Terrific" than the one that was dealt away in his prime. He was coming off a very un-Seaver-like 5-13 season with an ERA of 5.50.

Still, back in New York, he occasionally showed signs of his old self, like his outstanding 1983 opening day start at Shea against the Phillies when he pitched six scoreless innings. He would go on to have a decent year for us, but his presence on the club and his allowing us to pick his brain were worth a lot more, making it a good transaction for our mostly inexperienced team.

Rusty Staub was another veteran presence that helped the younger guys with how to approach the hitting aspects of the game. I'll never forget facing Nolan Ryan's 100-mile-an-hour fastball for the first time. The harder he was throwing, the quicker my swing, as I tried to get out in front of his blazing fastball. After returning to the bench one time after facing Ryan, Rusty said, "Listen, son. The harder a guy throws, the *slower* your swing has to be. Let *him* supply all the power."

The advice didn't make a lot of sense to me at the time, but I tried it and it worked. I went on to have relatively good success against Ryan for the rest of my career.

Perhaps the *greatest trade* in Mets history came on June 15 of that year when we picked up Keith Hernandez from St. Louis for Neil Allen and Rick Ownbey. Neil's numbers had dropped off over the last year and Rick hardly pitched for us, so picking up a former MVP and perennial Gold Glove first baseman for those guys seemed like a steal.

I knew Keith was having trouble dealing with Cardinals' manager Whitey Herzog, and my first thought was this was the classic case of one man's trash being another man's treasure. The Cardinals were as much concerned about their public relations as they were about their performance on the field and Mex, at that time, was a PR nightmare because of revelations of past cocaine use. So they were willing to move an All-Star first baseman to cut their losses and save face. Plus, the Cardinals were a very good team and felt they could recover from losing a talent like Keith.

I *knew* how good a player Keith was. I also knew about all of Keith's baggage. But at the time, we were only judging ballplayers by what they could do on the field and trying to become a legitimate contender in the NL East. There was no doubt Keith Hernandez could play a big part in accomplishing that goal.

I know Keith didn't originally want to play in New York. He didn't make any secret about that. The Mets and Cardinals hated each other and their cities, even when we knew so little about the latter. It's just the way it was. But Mex came to grips with the trade and we were happy to have him.

One thing I didn't envision was what kind of clubhouse presence he would bring. Even before we saw what he could do on the playing field every day, it was his mannerisms and professionalism that made him stand out. He didn't come in with the rah-rah stuff or any glitter. Instead, it was clear that he was a student of the game and learned a lot about leadership from guys like Lou Brock and some of the other great Cardinal veterans he played with.

Mex didn't instantly become the leader of the team. No one can just walk into a new clubhouse and proclaim themselves a leader. That's a bad idea. Instead, players will sit back and watch. When you don't think they're paying attention, they are. They'll watch you when you fail. They'll watch you when you succeed. And they'll watch you when it doesn't matter one way or another. But certainly by the end of the '83 season, Mex had made his imprint on the chemistry of the team. He became our go-to guy.

The acquisition of Keith was something we badly needed. We had young players coming up and we needed a veteran to show us how to win. No team wins by talent alone at the major league level, and Mex was the perfect player to come in and assume that role. Keith brought us his talent, his teaching ability, and some attitude all at the same time. We were changing the culture of the clubhouse and now, with Keith, a world champion with the Cardinals, we no longer came to the ballpark wondering how we were going to lose on a particular day.

With our young infield, Mex was like another manager out there. Instead of a Brian Giles, Wally Backman, Hubie Brooks, or Jose Oquendo having to guess if they were doing the right thing, Mex would make clear to them what needed to be done. You don't always want to look to your manager or a coach with questions. Instead, you want it to appear to them that you know what you're doing on the ball field. Keith was that sounding board for those guys and helped the infielders dramatically. You need to have that kind of experienced voice in the infield to keep everything together.

Keith also knew the trends of all the opposing hitters. It was that knowledge and the emotion he brought to each game that made being the captain of that infield a good role for him.

He was also inspiring to our young pitchers. During trips to the mound, he reminded them of what was going on in the game and gave them the confidence needed to get the job done. Instead of telling one of our pitchers something like, "Your fastball stinks today," he might say, "This guy can't touch your breaking ball." Coming from him, that was a huge confidence booster to them.

In the dugout, Mex was a motivator. He was always moving, always in the game.

Needless to say, if we were going to turn our club around, Keith was the one that would show us the way.

Suddenly, we had a strong top half of the lineup that one-through-five looked like this: Mookie Wilson, Hubie Brooks, Keith Hernandez, George Foster, and a twenty-one-year-old first round draft pick by the name of Darryl Strawberry.

The Mets brought up Darryl the month before we got Mex. Right away, I was impressed. I remember reading about him coming up, but when I actually got to see this six-foot-six, 190-pound physical specimen, I was awestruck. He *looked* like a ballplayer—strong and wiry, with a perfect home run swing. He was a very good player right from the beginning. I had no idea we had this type of player in the pipeline.

Straw just had limitless potential. He did everything with grace and nonchalance. When he first came up, right away I thought he was going to be a Hall of Famer. Darryl was, without question, the most naturally talented player I have ever been around. He was the total package.

He was also very cocky for a rookie which, surprisingly, didn't bother me at all. What did concern me was that his work habits may have come up a little short. That was the biggest knock most people had with Straw. Darryl was the guy who people always presumed had more than what he was willing to give. But in fairness to Straw, I don't think there was anything he could have done that people wouldn't have expected more of. If he hit 30 home runs, people thought he should have hit 35. If he hit 35, then he should have hit 40. Darryl would be the perfect example of someone with whom much was given, much was expected.

Ronnie Darling, another important part of our turnaround, made his major league debut for us in September, yielding just one run over six-plus innings against the Phillies. I didn't know much about Ronnie when he first came up. The book on him was that he had a powerful arm and good secondary pitches, but seemed to think too much on the mound. I could see, however, that if he threw strikes, he was going to be good.

Of course, in future years, we found out just how good.

Della Femina, Travisano and Partners came out with yet another slogan for us following the '83 season—"Catch the Rising Stars"—as Mets brass continued in their efforts to get people to take notice of the positive strides they were making with the ball club. But this slogan was different from all the others. It was the best and most appropriate because it was saying, "We're not there yet, but this is what you have to look forward to."

We were still losing games, but we weren't losing them like we were before. Progress is not always seen with wins and losses. It's how we win and how we lose. I was seeing effort that hadn't been there in previous seasons. I saw growth. It was a process moving in the right direction.

Despite another last place finish in '83, I couldn't wait for the 1984 season to begin.

6

Catching the Rising Stars

Davey Johnson was in awe. We all were. This tall, skinny nineteen-year-old kid, not even two years removed from high school, showed up at spring training in 1984 with a presence and confidence normally reserved for ten-year veterans. At first, we didn't know what to expect. Sure, we heard all about how he struck out 300 batters in less than 200 innings the previous year at Lynchburg. But that was just A-Ball and we had seen plenty of young power pitchers in the years before him come down to earth when having to face big league hitters. But there was something very different about this kid. Besides his unshakable demeanor, his ability to overpower hitters was nothing short of amazing.

The Mets had a phenomenon. And his name was Dwight "Doc" Gooden.

As the spring progressed, so did the rising expectations of what this young man could potentially achieve. We all tried to rein in our enthusiasm. After all, spring training is often a trap, a time of year when players and fans can get so pumped with optimism and excitement that they can lose sight of reality. Our experience had taught us that spring training success for young pitchers can be an illusion because of the adrenaline and lack of readiness of some opposing hitters.

But despite our attempts at caution, we believed this kid was the real deal. I was watching him pitch and couldn't believe his talent. In spring training, pitchers usually take more time before delivering and sometimes aren't sure what pitch they want to throw. Not Doc. He would just grab the ball and throw it. His control was slightly off, typically a little high, but when you can throw as hard as he did, you can pitch up there and get away with it. Oh, and he could mix his 98-mile-an-hour fastball with one of the *best curveballs* I've ever seen.

Davey saw what Dwight did to major league hitters in spring training and couldn't wait to bring him up north with the team, but Frank Cashen wanted to keep him in the minors for another year out of concern for the state of mind of a teenager pitching in the Big Apple. Davey countered that Doc had mound presence beyond his years and was always in control. The kid never got rattled.

Our new manager, whose relationship with Frank went back twenty years to their days with the Orioles, literally begged Cashen to promote Doc to the big leagues. Davey eventually sealed the deal by telling Cashen he would "protect" his young

CATCHING THE RISING STARS **95**

pitcher. Some people around the organization may have interpreted that to mean Davey would watch over Doc from a social
standpoint. But as it turned out, what Davey meant by "protecting" alluded more to watching his innings pitched, pitch counts,
and which teams he would allow him to throw against at that
early point in his career.

As it turned out, Davey didn't have to protect Doc at all—at
least not on the mound. Doc was something else, man! Davey
didn't have to worry about who he was facing, didn't have to
worry about favorable situations for him to pitch in. Dwight
would quickly evolve into the most dominating pitcher in
baseball.

Almost as impressive as Doc's pitching prowess on the
mound was his appetite at the buffet table. The food he could
put away in that skinny frame of his was staggering. Sometimes
I watched him in awe and would say, "Doc! Am I seeing this
right?"

Only Rusty could give Doc a run for his money in the eating
department, but even he could not best Doc. It was a good thing
he was a kid, man, because he could burn it off, too.

After losing on opening day, something we hardly ever did
even when we were terrible, we won our next six games behind
a suddenly stellar pitching staff that yielded only six earned runs
in those victories.

It was only April, but Shea Stadium had quickly transformed
into a completely different place. We suddenly had legitimate
drawing power. People wanted to see what Straw was going to
do. The Mets never had a position player like that before. And

when Doc pitched, it was nothing short of an *event*. And then you had Ronnie as our number two starter. There wasn't a big drop-off from Doc to Ronnie. Darling actually had more second-ary pitches than Doc had. So we had a one-two punch that was second to none in baseball. And they were so young.

Put those guys together with an assembly line of promising rookies coming up to join our veterans and there was a new and exciting brand of baseball in New York.

In those first couple of months of the season, I didn't know how well the kids were going to jell and come together with the rest of the club, but most of them surprised me by showing us just how good they could be. Despite some growing pains, we battled hard against a veteran Cubs team for the first three months of the season, never having more than a two-game divi-sion lead or being worse than 4½ games back. At the All-Star break, we were in first place by a half a game. Our 47-34 record made us the surprise team of the season to that point. While I had a sense in spring training of all the possibilities we had with our young talent on the farm and our much-improved attitude over previous years, for the average fan, our 1984 turnaround came out of nowhere.

As the summer wore on, and we would spend a total of 65 days in first place that season, I sensed a shift in power in our city. New York was becoming a Mets town. You could see it on the streets. Mets fans were wearing their orange and blue colors proudly. And as much as the media was rallying behind us, they were becoming increasingly critical of the Yankees and their way of running their team under the iron fist of owner George Steinbrenner.

We were like the little brother who finally grew up.

There was also a freshness and intrigue about us that I think New Yorkers were waiting for. The Yankees, by contrast, were static; they hadn't changed in 100 years. They had the same old uniforms with the pinstripes, no names on their backs, and prided themselves on their tradition. It was boring! We were giving people a new way to enjoy the game and it showed.

Before more than 51,000 fans at Shea on July 27, Doc pitched a 2–1 gem over the Cubs to move us a season-high 4½ games up in first place. It was our seventh straight win. By that point, I had been the starting center fielder for four years running and had never seen the electricity I witnessed at Shea that night. To be there through this sudden turnaround after the previous four dreadful seasons was the most fun I ever had in baseball.

But just as soon as we had put together that seven game winning streak, we lost our next seven, and moved back down into second place where we would remain for the rest of the season.

We just couldn't beat the Cubs. They won the last seven of eight games we played against them, including a four-game sweep at Wrigley in August. Chicago wasn't better than us, but they had more experience. They had guys that had been through a pennant race before, like Ron Cey, Larry Bowa, Keith Moreland, and Gary Matthews. Veterans in a pennant race mean *everything* to a ball club. They don't panic in most situations and seldom try to do more than the game allows them to. You can't force your will in a baseball game. You have to let the game come to you. Younger players like we had didn't have the discipline yet to do that.

Another reason we faded in August was due to fatigue. When you have a lot of guys in their first year in the big leagues, they're not used to playing a 162 game schedule. In the minors, they only play around 140 games. That extra month of baseball is grueling for the younger guys. They have to learn to play when they're dead tired in the heat of the summer. And if you are in a pennant race like we were in '84, it's even tougher because of the added mental stress.

Veteran teams like the '84 Cubs knew how to pace themselves. They likely did just enough to get ready for their games. They may not have done as many sprints or made as many throws to get loose before games. Vets understand the season is a marathon, not a sprint, and that makes a big difference. And no Cub veteran understood that or was more important to Chicago that year than Rick Sutcliffe. He was the biggest reason the Cubs won the division. He was 16-1 for Chicago following a June trade from the Cleveland Indians and earned the Cy Young Award over Doc. If not for him, I believe we would have won the NL East.

Sutcliffe's delivery was very unorthodox and it was tough to pick up the ball. He could throw your timing off and he threw hard. He was on a roll that year and his confidence level was sky-high. He had our number, plain and simple. On that Mount Rushmore of pitchers who could dominate us in the mid to late eighties, Sutcliffe was the first, later to be joined by John Tudor, Mike Scott, and Orel Hershiser.

But it was just so nice to play in meaningful games in August and September. When you're basically out of playoff contention in July, every day is a grind.

The connection we had with the fans that year was great.

Many, including current Mets announcer Gary Cohen, who grew up in Queens and has witnessed pretty much the entire history of the team, believe that our 1984 season may have meant more to "true" Mets fans than our world championship team of 1986. In '84, we ended a decade of bad baseball and shocked our fan base with our quick turnaround. By contrast, in '86, we joined a list of fewer than twenty teams in baseball history to win 108 or more regular season games. We saw winning the World Series as more of a coronation.

Personally, I probably enjoyed '84 more than '86 as well because I was an everyday player, my career was on an upward trajectory, and our team was young and exciting. I loved the fact that the front office at that time only went out and made trades for the pieces that we needed. For an organizational guy like myself, that's the best feeling you can have. The Mets produced this team from the ground up, shying away from bringing in a big free agent just for the sake of signing a big star.

Perhaps I would have enjoyed '86 more if I didn't have all the adversity with Davey and Frank and having to make all the concessions I did with Lenny entering the picture. There were no such concessions in '84. That may sound selfish, and maybe it is, but ultimately a person's value is what he feels he is contributing to a team or situation.

At the last home game of the season, all of us tossed our hats to the fans in the stands as a gesture to say *they* earned it. It was the first year we had done something like that. In previous years, we were hiding from the fans on the last day of the season, thinking they might throw something at *us*!

But seriously, it was the start of a love affair we had with our fans for the rest of the eighties. We had finally made good on our promise to the Shea faithful who came out to see us play no matter how bad we were. When you look at where we came from, a team whose annual goal was to not lose 100 games, to how we built that '84 team, it gave us all a tremendous sense of satisfaction. We finished with 90 wins, the most by the club since 1969, and gave Mets fans a pennant race that went down to the last week of the season. We had arrived and were there to stay.

We had fulfilled our "Catch the Rising Stars" slogan. We still may not have been quite *there* yet, but we were close.

The final piece of the puzzle to a championship, or so we hoped, was added in a December trade, when we acquired future Hall of Fame catcher Gary Carter from the Montreal Expos for Hubie Brooks, Mike Fitzgerald, Floyd Youmans, and Herm Winningham.

At the time, I didn't like the trade, but we *needed* to make it to get to the next level. I thought we were giving up too much—four quality players—not to mention seeing Hubie, my good buddy, headed north of the border. Plus, we were getting a catcher that *nobody* liked. Gary was nicknamed Camera Carter for a reason, as nearly everything he did was for the benefit of the cameras. The guys really resented that. Besides, we had an outstanding catching prospect in John Gibbons. Gibby was the whole package—a great hitter and defensive catcher. Think Jerry Grote with power. And a tough guy. Gibby wore his regular baseball hat backward, never wearing the hard cap designed to protect catchers' heads.

The problem was Gibby couldn't stay off the disabled list. Besides a banged up elbow, he broke his jaw near the end of the '84 season. I always wondered if he had stayed healthy and realized his full potential if Frank still would have made the trade for Gary. If Gibby had, I bet there probably wouldn't have been the need to make such a splash with the Carter deal.

Then again, Frank wanted to win right then and there. Cashen had a great stint as GM of the Orioles, but he knew that if he could turn our organization around in the same role, it would be the crowning achievement of his career.

Keith's initial reaction to the trade was elation. Not just because of Gary's offensive numbers, but also because of Carter's defensive skills and the influence he would have on our young pitching staff.

Ronnie took it a step further, saying Gary knew all the hitters in the league, knew how to get them out, made our pitchers throw inside, and was the computer readout and video that pitchers use today.

I agree there were certainly some advantages in obtaining Carter. As a catcher, he was as good as they came. But I still didn't like it with respect to how it would affect the chemistry of our team. My intuition, it turned out, would be vindicated.

When Carter first joined the club, his acceptance in the clubhouse was a slow process. Most of the guys were cordial to him, but it wasn't genuine. The guys never openly made derogatory remarks about Gary, but they still knew what Kid was—a "complicated" man to put it mildly. They didn't trust him, didn't know if he was one of us, at least not yet.

Gary had a reputation as a fraud, a great self-promoter who had a strong awareness of what the public deemed appropriate and inappropriate. That turned guys off to him because many thought what he was doing out there under the glare of the spotlight was not what he was showing them in the clubhouse. The guys just wanted him to be himself both in *and* out of the public eye. But Gary couldn't resist the spotlight.

The other knock in the clubhouse was that Gary was a selfish ballplayer, sometimes as concerned with his own statistics as with winning games. There were certainly examples of when Gary put himself in front of what the team actually accomplished. It didn't make him a bad person, but it did make him a selfish player. We're all a little selfish at times, but there are certain things you just don't say. Gary's problem was saying them at the most inappropriate times, which made your eyes roll.

As talented as he was, he was clearly insecure with himself and I've often wondered if he questioned his ability and whether he felt he should have contributed more. If that was the case it was a shame, because Carter was a great talent and the players were smart enough to realize that whether they liked him or not, he was now our teammate and could help us win some games.

Over his tenure with the Mets, Carter began to blend in. You began to see him eating dinner with some of the guys, joking with them, and interacting more than he had before. He would even occasionally make a trip to the back of the plane to hang with the Scum Bunch, our irreverent group of party animals that included, among others, Doug Sisk, Jesse Orosco, Danny Heep, and a host of honorary Scum Bunchers. Not surprisingly, Kid didn't stay long, but at least he made the effort to be one of the guys and, because of that, some of the players began to accept him a little more.

And the Camera Carter nickname bestowed on him was not entirely a bad thing. It was just a way of letting people know he was very photogenic and it depicted Gary's personality as well as anything else. Let's just say Kid never ran from an interview. He loved being up in front. It was important to him. But we had a bunch of guys who were not accustomed to that and didn't want what they were doing up in front—the so-called sanctity of the clubhouse.

But the one great thing about Gary right from the start was that you knew what you were going to get from him every single day. He put it out there on the field, even on days when he was playing hurt and maybe shouldn't have been playing. It was that toughness, in itself, that earned him a tremendous amount of respect from the guys. So despite our opinions of him, what he did on the field eventually overcame all of his off-field issues.

That Gary was a fellow Christian didn't really influence how I looked at him a whole lot, because I try to treat everyone the same regardless of their beliefs or nonbeliefs. I took Gary for who he was. While it may have been fortunate that we had religious beliefs that were compatible, if Carter had been, say, a Muslim, it wouldn't have made a difference to me. I would have treated him the same.

Take Kevin Mitchell. I *loved* Kevin Mitchell. But we couldn't have been two more different individuals in our playing days. Mitchell liked his hard liquor cocktails and I didn't drink. Mitchell was part of a gang growing up and I belonged to a church. Mitchell wasn't afraid to mix it up if he felt threatened; I avoided confrontation. But it didn't matter to me, because I took him for what he was—a terrific, if misunderstood, teammate. Today, Mitchell is more devoted to God, his church, and working with children. I spoke to him a year ago and the changes he's made in his life since we played together are unbelievable and he looks fantastic.

While guys like Mitchell and other Mets during the eighties liked to party hard, it never affected my strong relationships with them. I was still able to maintain my own values and didn't allow others to alter them. Some may not have liked me for that, but when you start trying to adjust your personality so that people will like you, you're going to fall down. And I'd like to think most of my teammates respected my personal beliefs, since I never interfered with what they wanted to do.

We had high expectations heading into '85. Unlike the previous season, when everyone had us pegged for last place, we now had everything in place and were primed to do what we fell short of doing in '84.

What was there *not* to be excited about? We had speed, power, pitching, and defense. There were no holes on that team. We had *everything*.

But there was actually one thing that was in the back of my mind that potentially could derail or cast a shadow over a season that showed such promise. The possibility of another baseball strike was looming sometime around the All-Star break. While I was better prepared to weather a strike financially than I was four years before, it was the last thing I wanted to see happen with the positive vibes we had entering the '85 campaign.

Opening day would be against the Cardinals. Every game we played against them felt like the last game of the season—in our minds, they were always the team to beat. Despite our other divisional rivals' various degrees of success, it was never about beating the Phillies, Pirates, Cubs, or Expos. It was always about the Cardinals.

As usual for opening day, it was freezing at Shea. As a South Carolina boy, I *hated* April in New York! I always dreaded it.

Gary introduced himself to the Flushing fans in the most theatrical and dramatic of ways—hitting a walk-off home run in the tenth inning to win the opener, 6–5. It was right out of Hollywood. That game and his home run meant everything to Gary. It was big for us as a team, as well, but for a newcomer like Carter, it was *really* big. The home run was Exhibit A on why we brought this guy over. It was perfect timing against the right team in the right situation. Good for the team, and even better for Gary.

Gary came out of the dugout for a fist-pumping curtain call in what was the first of many by our players that year. It really started a trend. Everybody started doing it. We did it, first and foremost, to please the fans, who loved it.

It's funny, but while we all did the same thing as Gary with respect to the curtain calls, when Carter did it, the perception of it by both his teammates and opponents alike was that he was doing it more for himself than anything else.

We won our first five games of the season. It was easy for us to think we were really on our way because everything in April gets magnified. But the reality was there were still another 157 games to go in the regular season. So despite that immediate rush, we didn't lose sight of how long the season is.

I had to take a couple of weeks off near the end of April to rest a sore shoulder. That was the very first time I met Lenny Dykstra, who was called up from Tidewater. I don't think any of us had ever seen him before because he wasn't even in spring training. Ronnie described him perfectly by saying he looked like he was from the Ty Cobb era. "Nails" was just a dirty-looking player, man, even in batting practice. He often was seen with tobacco juice dripping down on his uniform—just a horror show!

By June, it became obvious that the Cardinals, and not the defending division champion Cubs, would be our toughest competition in the NL East. At the start of the month, we had a five-game lead over the Cards, but they were still having a great season. St. Louis had the two leading base stealers and four of the top ten hitters in batting average in the National League. Then they had Jack Clark and Tommy Herr to drive them in.

I loved the Cardinals' style of play. They were so aggressive, always running on the bases until there was no place else to go. And it wasn't just one or two of their guys. *Everybody* ran on that team except for Clark. It was an exciting brand of baseball.

I always believed that I could have fit in well with that club because I liked running when there were no rules or boundaries. The Mets, by contrast, were more "opportunist runners." We were built differently than the Cards, so we didn't need to steal bases to get runs. We had guys who could hit the ball over the fence.

St. Louis also filled their lineup with switch-hitters—Willie McGee, Terry Pendleton, Ozzie Smith, and Herr—making it tough to set a pitching rotation against them. In the pitching department, we had the edge over the Cardinals in depth. St. Louis primarily depended on just two starting pitchers—John Tudor and Joaquin Andujar. But what they did have over us was a trio of southpaws—Ricky Horton, Ken Dayley, and Tudor—which the White Rat used to neutralize our predominantly left-handed power-hitting lineup in games whenever the opportunity came about.

On our side, we led with Doc and Ronnie, but could also throw quality starters out there, like Sid Fernandez, Rick Aguilera, and Ed Lynch.

But not even our strong pitching could keep us in first place for long once we lost Straw for better than a month, when he was put on the DL after an operation he needed to repair torn ligaments in his thumb suffered when making a diving catch. Danny Heep primarily filled in for Darryl while he was out and did well, but he wasn't the "enforcer" or "intimidator" that Straw was. Pitchers were more likely to pay a heftier price when making a mistake against a slugger like Darryl and, because of that, were much more comfortable facing Danny.

Darryl's absence also forced the rest of the lineup to press and try to do a little more than they were capable of. So important was Straw to our offense that the opposition viewed us differently and was less intimidated by us. As a result, by the time Straw returned to the lineup on June 28, we were in third place and 2½ games behind the red-hot first-place Montreal Expos.

Our bullpen, always so reliable, was reeling. McDowell went on the disabled list and Orosco and Sisk struggled, leaving us vulnerable in the late innings. I really felt the worst for Sisk because the fans could be unmerciful with him. It was a shame because he was a really good pitcher with movement on his pitches that was unnatural. I wouldn't play catch with him because his throws moved so much. Part of his problem throwing strikes was that he couldn't control his pitches. Nobody wanted to hit against him in batting practice at spring training for fear of getting their hitting stroke and timing all screwed up. He was *that* nasty! There's no question he had a wild streak on the mound, but he was a guy that was very aware of all the booing at Shea and it got to him.

Our mid-season slump was nothing compared to that of the Cubs. Suddenly, they were horrible. After they dominated us in '84, we would go 14-4 against them in '85—a complete reversal of fortune. Chicago was a one-dimensional team that relied on hitting and had no speed to speak of. Our young pitching staff was another year older, smarter, and better, and that was the difference.

They also got the injury bug, which peaked in August when their entire five-man starting rotation was on the DL.

The Cubs' descent was almost unprecedented. They went from winning a division crown to finishing '85 nine games under .500, in fourth place, and 23½ games out. At one point mid-season, they had a thirteen-game losing streak.

With Straw back, and my shoulder still in a great deal of pain on throws from the outfield, I had a window of opportunity to get surgery on it. I had taken all the cortisone shots I could take. I knew I couldn't go on the way I was going.

The surgery was a success, but I would be out for a couple of months resting at home in New Jersey and going to Shea every once in a while for treatment.

I watched from home as the club went on a roll. Mex was named National League Player of the Month in July, the first Met to achieve the honor since Dave Kingman exactly ten years before. Darryl seemed fresh after his long layoff and was also making a big impact on our offense. And Doc was putting together a season for the ages on the mound. We won 12 of 13 games heading into the All-Star break and were in second place, just 2½ games out.

Although it was still only July when the break was over, we had a sense of urgency to get back into first place. The Players Association had set a strike date of August 6. Our guys were divided on the whole strike issue. There was more at stake than all the political hoopla going on. We were playing for a pennant. There was concern that if we were out for a prolonged period of time, we would have fewer games and chances to come back and win the division.

As it turned out, we did have a strike—it lasted exactly two games. It was a good thing because we were in the midst of a nine-game winning streak that culminated with us being in first place on August 13 by one game over St. Louis. We believed we could win every game.

In the middle of the streak, Straw had the best game of his young career, hitting three home runs and a single at Wrigley Field. What was neat about it was how, with the Cubs basically out of contention, the opposing fans were pulling for Straw to hit a fourth home run in his final at-bat. Though still on the DL, I was at the game and really enjoyed the fan reaction.

I loved Wrigley Field. The closeness of their fans—some of the best in baseball—to the field made it an intimate place to play. I also liked the fact it wasn't commercial—just plain old baseball at the old ballpark.

Across town from us in the Bronx, the Yankees were in the midst of their own pennant race. Never in the twenty-three years since the Mets were born had both New York teams been so good in the same season. The city was buzzing and we were very much aware of the possibility of a Subway Series, something that had not occurred since 1956 when the Brooklyn Dodgers and the Yankees played one another.

On September 1, I was reactivated. But while my shoulder's condition had improved from prior to the surgery, I probably shouldn't have come back that soon. I misled myself into thinking I was completely better. It had nothing to do with the fear of losing playing time or where the team was in the pennant race. Primarily, I rushed back because I simply missed the excitement of playing ball.

Another reason, however, was the importance I placed on myself as one of the few experienced major leaguers on our very young team. I felt we needed all the veteran influence possible to mature and develop into a winner.

One example came into play with Ronnie, after a game against the Pirates that September. We were on the team bus on a getaway day and, as usual, I sat up front and Ronnie was in the back, a superstition of his. Some of the guys in the Scum Bunch began saying some really cruel and personal things about the Pirates' Dominican pitcher Cecilio Guante, who had a really awkward body and wasn't exactly the most handsome guy around. It was obvious that Cecilio had had a rough life.

Ronnie, just a kid back then, added something equally inappropriate about Cecilio's physical appearance. I got up from my seat and walked toward the back as if I was going to use the rest room, but instead stopped by Ronnie and said firmly, "Ron Darling. I expect that stuff from these guys. I *do not* expect it from you."

I then just turned around and returned to my seat.

I could tell it shook Ronnie up a little bit. Sure enough, when we got off the bus, he came up to me and apologized. I told him it wasn't necessary and that my little wake-up call was given because I thought so highly of him and didn't want him to fall in with that group. Ronnie was not your typical jock. He was a competitive player, but with intelligence, which was very rare on that team. Frankly, if I hadn't heard Ronnie's voice, I probably wouldn't have gone back there. I would have just thought to myself, *Those drunk, Scum Bunch idiots. That's just the way they talk.*

Besides Ronnie's competitiveness and intelligence, I also saw a budding talent. Ronnie could have been a number one starter on a lot of teams in the mid-eighties. While I got the sense he may have had some pitching-envy of Doc, I think he also realized that Dwight was a special pitcher in the same mold as a Bob Gibson or Sandy Koufax. Still, there's no question that Doc's greatness cast a huge shadow over Ronnie and, perhaps, made him feel underappreciated at times. He wanted to hear people say, "The Mets have Doc Gooden *and* Ron Darling," instead of just, "They've got Doc!"

And that's natural. You want to see that competitive side in your teammates.

I could see during that '85 season Ronnie sometimes trying to do more than he needed because of all the praise that was given to Doc. That was a mistake because Darling was his own pitcher and could do things Dwight couldn't do. As a player, you have to be comfortable in your own skin.

For me, I was envious and felt overshadowed by Straw and his seemingly limitless abilities. He was a specimen, man! When he walked onto the ball field, I sometimes thought, *Why couldn't I be like that?* What ballplayer alive wouldn't look at that kid and say "Wow!" But in the end, it would have been detrimental for me to try to do something other than what Mookie Wilson was able to do.

We won the first five games in the month of September, the fifth being one of the greatest pitching duels I have ever witnessed. Before an electric, sell-out Friday night crowd at Dodger Stadium, Doc pitched nine shutout innings, struck out ten, and didn't walk anybody, to lower his ERA to 1.74. Fernando Valenzuela countered by shutting us down for eleven innings to lower his ERA to 2.26.

The game went into the thirteenth inning, still scoreless, when Straw gave us the winning margin with a two-run ground-rule double. One of the guys who scored was Keith, who arrived during the game after giving testimony at the infamous Pittsburgh drug trial case against Curtis Strong.

I stood by Mex despite my own objections to drug use by simply accepting him in spite of his past mistakes. I didn't pretend to know all the circumstances behind why he ended up getting involved with cocaine and, at that point, it really wasn't any of my business. Stuff happens. Besides, none of the other Mets were that squeaky clean, either. By supporting Keith and welcoming him back into the clubhouse, I didn't do anything that I wouldn't want someone to do for me if I made a mistake. I was raised to believe that no one is ever as bad as they're portrayed, just as no one is ever as good as people may think.

What I saw in Mex, first and foremost, was a guy who genuinely loved the game of baseball, and that overrode anything that he may have done. And let's not forget, it's not like he committed mass murder. That would have been a different story.

In the final analysis, Keith only hurt himself and nobody else. He made a mistake and I think he underestimated what he had to lose. But did he cost St. Louis any games because of his recreational cocaine use from 1980 through 1982? I don't think so. They did pretty well with him, even winning the World Series in 1982.

It was great to have Keith back because we really needed him and his expertise on the field.

Two days after the Fernando-Doc duel, I started my first game since returning to the active roster. In another great pitching matchup, this time between Orel Hershiser and Sid Fernandez, the game went into the fourteenth inning before I homered off Dodger reliever Carlos Diaz to give us a 4–3 win and pull us to within a half game of St. Louis.

As a team, more important than building some winning momentum into the stretch run was the fact we were healthy and had our full arsenal in the lineup. The timing couldn't have been better, as we returned to Shea to host a crucial three-game series with the Cardinals locked in a first place tie.

Besides the obvious significance of playing for first place, there was also the anticipation surrounding how the crowd would react to Mex as he returned home for his first game since the well-publicized Pittsburgh drug trial. It was no surprise to me when the Shea crowd gave Keith a standing ovation before his first at-bat, because New York fans are very forgiving. Plus, they really appreciated what he meant to the club.

Mex responded with an RBI single to center to drive me home with our first run. A few batters later, HoJo hit a grand slam to give us all the runs we would need in a 5–4 win. We were back in first place by a full game.

With Doc going the next game, we had an excellent chance to really begin putting some distance between us and St. Louis. Dwight didn't disappoint, throwing nine innings of shutout ball. But John Tudor was up to the challenge, countering with ten shutout innings of his own. César Cedeño's tenth-inning home run off Orosco was the difference in a 1–0 loss to deadlock us with the Cards once again.

The final game of the three-game series was every bit as pressure-packed. After we took an early 6–0 lead and knocked Joaquin Andujar out in the second inning, the Cards battled back and would tie it in the top of the ninth on a Willie McGee solo home run off Jesse. But we willed ourselves to win the game in our half of the ninth when I beat out an infield single and later scored on a walk-off single by Keith.

With a little more than three weeks left in the season, we were again clinging to a one-game lead.

We continued playing good ball for the rest of the month,

with Gary even winning Player of the Month honors. But the Cards were nearly unstoppable, at one point winning an astounding 14 out of 15 games.

We went to St. Louis to begin a three-game set on October 1, down two games with six left in the season. We knew we had to sweep the series to have a legitimate chance of winning the division and were very confident we could pull it off. No one was on edge.

In the opening game, Darling and Tudor were sensational. Ronnie threw nine shutout innings and Tudor ten. It was like a heavyweight bout out there on the mound. But ultimately, with the game and, likely, our season in the balance, Straw came to the plate in the top of the eleventh inning with two outs to face Ken Dayley. Straw hit an absolute missile off the Cardinals' scoreboard and our bench went ballistic! He knew it was gone as soon as the ball left his bat. Darryl then may have made the slowest trot around the bases I ever saw. Jesse shut down the Cards in the bottom of the eleventh to secure the 1–0 victory. It felt like we had just won the World Series, but we still had two more games to win.

The second game was all about Doc and his ability to close a game out. Dwight was cruising along with a 5–1 lead until, with two outs in the ninth and nobody on base, St. Louis started a rally that would ultimately bring Tommy Herr to the plate as the winning run with the bases loaded. But Doc got him to line out to Wally to end the game, a 5–2 win. Dwight improved to a remarkable 24-4, striking out ten in the process. As an example of the kind of season he was having, his ERA actually *increased* to 1.53. I have never seen a more dominating season than the one Doc had for us that year. He had a fastball as good as Nolan Ryan's and a curveball like Bert Blyleven's. He was simply magnificent.

We were now just one game back with four games left in the season. The final game in the series against the Cards was as big as they come. We were right there!

In this, our biggest game of the season, we came out strong against Cards' pitcher Danny Cox. I began the game with the first of four singles in the first inning, scoring on an RBI single by Mex to give us a 1–0 lead. We would load the bases with just one out with Foster and HoJo coming up. We had the right guys hitting to drive in some runs and I remember thinking, *C'mon! One of you guys has to come up big.*

With the Cardinal infield up, George hit a hard grounder to third that Terry Pendleton fielded and threw home to Darrell Porter for a force out. That brought up HoJo, who had hit a grand slam against Cox just three weeks before at Shea. We still had a great chance to blow the game open early. But this time, Cox got him to hit into a force out at third to end the threat.

It was a moral victory for St. Louis. Usually when a club doesn't cash in on an early opportunity like that, it comes back to haunt them. We really needed to come out of that first inning with at least two or three runs.

We entered the ninth inning down 4–3 with the top of our order coming up. As the leadoff hitter against Cards' reliever Ricky Horton, I was just looking to do anything to get on base to give the big bats a chance to drive me in. With Busch Stadium being as big a ballpark as it was, the last thing on my mind was trying to tie it with one swing or anything like that.

Unfortunately, I ended up popping out to Tommy Herr at second for the first out.

Up next was pinch hitter John Christensen, who flew out to right for the second out.

Now it was all up to Mex to keep our dimming hopes alive. And like he usually did in the big spots, he came through with a single. Now we had the tying run on base and the go-ahead run at the plate in Gary, the hottest hitter in baseball. Herzog brought in right-hander Jeff Lahti to match up against Carter. I was thinking, *Make a mistake in. Make a mistake in.* But it wasn't to be, as the Kid went with a pitch away and flew out to right to end the game.

It ended a series that was the greatest I had ever been a part of. Considering the magnitude and importance of each game and how each of the three came down to the final at-bat, it was like two gladiators fighting with the ultimate will to win. Even though we had such a deep dislike for each other, the two teams had so much mutual respect. We *forced* each other to play to the best of our abilities.

Despite still having three games left, we knew our season was over. We needed the Cards to drop three straight to the suddenly lowly Cubs while we needed to sweep the Expos. Sure enough, we were officially eliminated two days later.

I was really disappointed. While I was proud of the way we played and the way we battled back after the injuries we had, I thought we played well enough to win the division. We certainly didn't give anything away, so there was some comfort in that. But four more lousy wins over a 162-game schedule and *we* would have been the ones going to the playoffs instead of St. Louis. While we certainly had to tip our hats to the Cardinals, if we would have stayed healthier, we would have made up the ground we lost when Straw and I were on the DL. St. Louis may have trumped us in a couple of areas—like with left-handed pitching and speed—but overall, we were the better team. It shocked me we didn't get it done. But sometimes the best teams don't finish first.

I have reflected often about how if there was a wild-card system in the 1980s like the one that began in 1995, we would have qualified for the playoffs in both 1984 and 1985. And with the pitching we could have sent out there for a short playoff series, we would have had a good chance to win a World Series, particularly in '85.

The fact that we won more games in 1984 and 1985 combined than any other team in the major leagues, but had nothing to show for it, made us a very hungry, and confident, ball club looking toward 1986. Our latest slogan, appropriately enough, would be "Baseball Like It Ought to Be." I was counting the days to opening day.

7

The Unforgettable Season

We're not just going to win this year, we're going to *dominate* the league," Davey Johnson told us the first day of spring training in 1986. "We're going to *win* the World Series."

Unlike some managers who make bold statements like that to get their team going, I think Davey meant every word.

In 1984, we all saw this club blossoming. The following season, with the acquisition of Gary, we felt we were the best team in baseball. By '86, with two pennant races under our belt and the emergence of all of our young talent, we came to camp believing our time had come. We all believed like Davey believed.

It was that bravado that would make us one of the most loved *and* hated ball clubs of all time. We were a team flush with talent and confidence. There was not one player on that team that I wouldn't want to play with again. Not one guy. But if you played in a uniform other than the orange-and-blue, you hated our brashness. You despised our cockiness. You resented the press for giving us all the headlines, for crowning us victors when we hadn't actually won anything. We were arrogant because in 1986 we knew we were good and weren't afraid to let people know. In short, we demanded that you treat us with the respect we felt we deserved as baseball's best team. We now had a swagger that we didn't have the year before.

The expression "growing into your pants" applied to us as we looked forward to the 1986 season. We had a tremendous cast of young players who'd needed to grow the last season or two and learn how to win. Winning is more than just physical ability. It's walking into a rival's ballpark and not being intimidated.

For us, that rival was the St. Louis Cardinals, the defending National League champions. We felt that we now matched up against them most favorably. Their strength in the first half of the eighties was their speed. For a long time, I was the only guy who was a threat to run for the Mets. Now all of a sudden, we also had Lenny, Wally, and Straw, so we matched up pretty well in that category.

We *knew* we had more power than the Cardinals and, for that matter, any other team in the league.

In the pitching department, we had a strong young staff the year before, but had added a critical piece to the puzzle with veteran Bobby Ojeda, which gave us stability.

The trade really didn't get a lot of publicity. Bobby's pitching numbers with the Red Sox over the first six years of his career were pretty average. Yet there were two reasons we traded four promising prospects—Calvin Schiraldi, Wes Gardner, John Christensen, and LaSchelle Tarver—for him.

The first was we didn't have a need for those players because of who they were competing against. Christensen was a versatile guy who could play third base and the outfield, but we already had Mitchell. Tarver, a left-handed hitting outfielder, was basically Lenny. Gardner was a good pitcher, but he was never going to break into either our rotation or bullpen. And we all knew Calvin's story. He was a pitcher who possessed a tremendous arm, but he tended to crack under pressure.

The other reason was we knew what we were getting in Bobby. Even though he played on another team in a different league, we had faced him plenty of times when he was with the AAA Pawtucket Red Sox, because our AAA team, the Tidewater Tides, played in the International League against them. With only eight teams in that league playing a 140-game schedule, you got to see the players on the other teams on a regular basis. So we were very familiar with Bobby and what he was capable of doing.

We also felt Bobby O would benefit greatly by pitching at the more spacious Shea Stadium, better than at that little ballpark in Boston. For a left-hander, leaving Fenway Park can make all the difference in the world. It did not go unnoticed that another average former Red Sox left-hander named John Tudor became a star after he went to play in St. Louis.

The Mets were looking for pitching depth and experience at the time and numbers can be very deceiving when evaluating pitchers. Bobby O was always a good pitcher. And left-handers are just crafty, man. This game is tailored for left-handed pitchers.

Bobby O understood the importance of never trying to overthrow and was very smart when it came to pitching.

A bonus that we came to realize immediately with Bobby at camp was how much he hated being with the Red Sox and how quickly he loved the guys we had on the Mets. He made no qualms about that. He would say how he felt like a square peg in a round hole there. He said a lot of guys' careers were winding down when he was coming up, comparing the clubhouse to an old golf club that was dying, and how some of the veterans were hoping he would fail so they wouldn't lose their jobs.

Bobby was as opinionated as anyone I ever played with. But that was fine because we had a club so culturally diverse that his brashness was just another part of that diversity. You ask Bobby a question, beware of the answer. He had no filter. But all of our guys respected him for that.

I think that Fenway was a bad park for him and, as far as his relationship with some of his teammates in Boston, sometimes players' personalities clash. Bobby was made for New York. His brashness made him feel more at ease with us than the clubhouse in Boston. He was now going to be playing with guys who were like him and sometimes that allows you to be yourself. He had found himself a bunch of other square pegs.

Bobby O would have a tremendous season for us, going 18-5 with a 2.57 ERA.

So the way we felt about it, the Cardinals weren't as much a threat to us as we now were to them.

This was also going to be a more vibrant team than Mets teams of the previous few years, one that would take on more of a "biker club" mentality. Elder statesman Rusty Staub had just retired. Before him, guys like Dave Kingman and Tom Seaver, also older players who had returned to the team after several years of being away, had moved on. George Foster was on his way out. All great players in their own right, but they weren't going to connect with this group at all.

The personality of this club was going to be invigorated by a new generation of young stars like Mitchell, Lenny, Backman, Roger McDowell, Darling, Doc, and Sid Fernandez, all of whom had spent time in our minor league system and knew they now belonged. As a result of their similar beginnings, those guys had a special bond after they were promoted to the big leagues. Davey knew what special talent he had with his younger players, having managed some of them at Tidewater in 1983.

We knew we were going to win big and have a lot of fun doing it. From the very beginning, there was a lot of razzing and practical joking going on. I never took part in any of that. I just didn't believe in it. I felt that something bad always came out of it. I think they respected me as one of the veteran leaders on the team and had a sense of what I tolerated and what I would go along with. But I still enjoyed watching it like everyone else.

I think all the fun the club had that season made us unique. What other team would allow a player to crawl under the bench and light a guy's heels like Roger McDowell was always doing? He even repeatedly gave hotfoots to poor Bill Robinson, once having one ignite *while* he was coaching first base. C'mon! You really had to keep an eye on McDowell. You're watching a ball game and then, all of a sudden, someone's jumping. No one was immune.

You couldn't always find Roger, but you knew he was behind it. You also knew his sidekick HoJo wasn't far away, that he had something to do with it, as well. It was awesome! That was Exhibit A on how there were no boundaries in that clubhouse. Everyone was the same, even the coaching staff. That is not typically the case on other ball clubs. But with our club, it really was like that.

I remember one time when Wally and Darryl's razzing got out of hand and grew into a real argument, with Straw calling Backman "a little redneck." But the next day, after an opposing pitcher threw at Wally, who do you think was the first person to go out there to defend him? Straw.

"No, no, no," Straw said. "I can mess with Wally, but nobody else can."

And that's the way that team was. It showed me so much.

Another time, Bobby O and Kevin Mitchell had a practical joke they played on each other that also went too far. They ended up cutting each other's pants off. It was crazy, but everybody laughed about it afterward. It was just another example of when things were said or practical jokes occurred, no one took it personally.

About the only needling I ever got was done in a good-natured way from Doc. From day one, he called me Old Man. He still calls me that today.

I think sometimes guys just want to fit in and all the joking and razzing was the way they tried to do it. I never really felt the need to do so with that club because I was there before any of them. But I really enjoyed watching them and their high jinks.

It was clear that as long as we played on the field like winners, Davey wasn't going to lay down any boundaries on us. I think when you look at the arrogance of that team, Davey was certainly no slouch. He did things his way no matter what. The general manager, Frank Cashen, didn't always like it. The players didn't always like it. And Davey and I certainly had our disagreements. However, I think we all really respected him for being his own man.

People called Davey a "player's manager." I don't know how that phrase is always defined, but I think he understood his players. He knew what buttons to push; he knew what buttons to leave alone. But he relied heavily on the veterans to control that clubhouse to make sure things didn't get too out of control.

Say what you want about the value of a good coaching staff, but it's the players who police each other. Coaches are great to have to bounce ideas off of, but ultimately it comes down to the players to ensure success. When players respect one another, you can be a coach or manager who does everything wrong and it won't matter. I'm convinced of that and it would take an extreme situation to prove otherwise. I've been on good teams and bad ones and on all the good ones, you've got one or two players who guys rally around.

For us, there was no veteran in that clubhouse who had more influence than Keith Hernandez.

Mex wasn't just the inspirational leader on that team, he was also the bridge between the players and Davey. It wasn't anything that he was appointed to do and there was no "C" on his chest, but our guys let him know that he was the leader of our team. Keith was our field general.

A leader has to be two things. First, it helps to be outspoken, which Mex certainly was. Then, they need to be forthcoming and practice what they preach. Keith was both.

We were like, *"Something's going on? Have a little talk with Mex."*

I know Davey listened to Mex, though I don't know if he always followed through on his suggestions. But at least Mex did have Davey's ear.

Gary always felt that because Mex had been a cocaine user while in St. Louis and was involved in the Pittsburgh drug trial, it was him, and not Keith, who truly deserved to be looked at as the Mets' team leader and the player who had earned Davey's ear. Our guys clearly didn't think that way at all. I think Gary may have been a little taken aback by the fact that it was so blatantly obvious who most of the players looked to for leadership. Gary may have been the final piece in making us a championship-caliber team, but Mex was our general.

When the Mets made it official and Keith was named captain the following season, Gary had a problem with it. He felt the captaincy should go to someone who was held to a higher moral standard than the average player. Guys like Gary didn't take that position lightly. I don't think Mex ever really said he wanted to be the captain, officially or unofficially. But Gary voiced his opinion anyway, letting it be known he felt that Keith was unfit to play the role of a captain. That sentiment kind of rubbed some people the wrong way.

Gary, at that point, hadn't really won over the whole clubhouse yet. Some of us were harboring some ill feelings toward him because he was still considered an outsider. Keith had been there for more than three seasons, so he was one of us. To me, there was no real reason not to like Gary. I simply didn't like him because, in my mind, he was still the enemy, a Montreal Expo.

Despite some of the negativity, Keith and Gary coexisted without any animosity between them. Both had tremendous respect for one another's talents and were smart enough to realize how they needed each other to win a championship. And in Keith's view, he was secure in the fact that the players were going to go to him whenever an issue arose. There was no competition in that regard.

As far as practicing what he preached, Mex gave his all every day. There were a number of times when he was injured but would play anyway.

I have always thought Keith would make a good manager, but a terrible coach. Mex is just so cerebral. He might say, *"This guy's going to throw me a slider because that's what he did in this situation three innings ago."* Then sure enough, *bang!*, he was driving the ball up the gap. You can't teach that.

He also wouldn't be able to teach a guy to play first base the way he played it because *nobody* could play first base like him. I am sure if he didn't see the results he wanted, he might become agitated.

On the flip side, Keith probably would make a good manager because he knows the game so well and he knows what he wants to do. He thinks about everything. He knows how everything should look. He's one of the smartest guys I know in baseball.

Despite all the optimism circulating around the team while training at Al Lang Stadium and our three practice sites in St. Petersburg, I had a calamitous start to the spring.

It was only March 5 when a routine rundown drill in which I was one of the base runners turned into a disaster.

On the last play of the drill, I got picked off first as planned. Trying not to get tagged out by using my patented move, I took two quick strides forward to entice Gary Carter, who was playing first, to throw the ball. Once he bit, I began to make a hard move back toward first base, but not before turning right into Rafael Santana's throw back to first. *Pow!* The ball smacked me right in my sunglasses, causing a lot of bleeding in and above my right eye from the shards of broken glass.

I went down, surprisingly not feeling any pain. But Gary was frantic. His voice was the only one I heard. Gary just kept repeating, "Mookie! Oh, Mookie! Oh, Mookie!"

I was thinking, *What is going on up there?*

I didn't realize it at the time, but my retina was hanging on by a thread. I later found out from the surgeon that if I had just sneezed, coughed, or anything, I might have lost sight in that eye.

They covered my eye with a bandage, but since I didn't have any pain, I didn't know how bad it was. The next thing I knew, I was at the hospital. I only began to get scared when it sank in how quickly they wanted to operate. After that, they must have given me a sedative or something, because I lost track of time.

Following the surgery, I was a little concerned I wouldn't be able to play or see well enough to hit again. The thought did cross my mind that my career might be over. I had already prepared myself mentally for that possibility. I was expecting the worst. Since my eye was closed and covered during much of the recovery, I couldn't see a thing. I didn't know if I was going to see again in that eye. After the bandage was removed, there was some blurriness initially. I could really tell the difference between my good eye and my bad one. And I worried how my lack of depth perception might affect my baseball career. That was the scary part. But it was a relief that the blurriness only lasted a few weeks.

Besides recovering from my eye injury, I was just coming off shoulder surgery. When I injured my eye, I had just started throwing and resuming baseball activities. So, in a way, the time off actually helped me get my arm strength back. Before returning to the club, I had an extended spring training working out in St. Petersburg with the Mets A-Ball players before moving up to play a few games with the AAA team in Tidewater.

To this day, I still have my eye checked each year for scar tissue, but it's really just a formality. Thankfully, I had a full and lasting recovery.

I would be out until May. Dykstra took over for me while I was on the disabled list. However, a platoon was already in the works whether I had begun the season healthy or not. Dykstra may have hit just .254 with only one home run in 236 at-bats in 1985 while I was a consistent .275 hitter with speed, but it appeared that the Mets were looking for a more traditional lead-off hitter than I was. Lenny fit that bill because he took more pitches than I did.

The Mets still needed me, though, because Lenny wasn't strong against left-handed pitching. The platoon caused a little friction. Not between me and Lenny, but between me and management because they wouldn't give me a reason why they were doing it. Frank Cashen would always say, "Davey's running the field down there and it's his call." Then when I went to Davey, he would send me back to Frank.

I was going back and forth for a big part of the season. They wouldn't give me any explanation at all. Nothing.

The problem with the platoon and having me only hit from my natural right-handed side was the fact I had become a better hitter from the left side. Over the years, I saw far more right-handed pitching, which helped make me a better left-handed hitter. Plus, I could use my speed from the left side to beat out infield hits. Now they were taking that part of the game away from me and I was going to see fewer pitchers. The move was kind of confusing to me. I had worked so hard to develop my left-handed hitting and then, for no given reason, was primarily being relegated to hitting right-handed. The other thing working for Lenny was the fact he played for Davey at Tidewater. I think Davey knew more of what he was getting than Lenny's statistics showed. Davey inherited me. That was a big difference for him.

It was the same thing with Wally. After Backman bounced back and forth between the minors and the majors, Davey told him at Tidewater that if he ever managed the Mets, he was coming back up with him for good. It was becoming obvious that Davey was going to show loyalty to *his guys*.

I've been around a lot of people, but Lenny was borderline psycho. He loved adventure. He loved the unknown. He loved pushing the envelope. He loved being on the edge. He loved a challenge. He was a small guy and maybe that was a part of his makeup. He always felt like he had to prove he could do the impossible.

Lenny bet on everything. I liked to joke that if there were two flies on the wall, he would bet to see which one would leave first.

Lenny had a handheld video golf game that had just come out. He actually bet people money he could beat them at this thing. Watching Lenny in action on bus trips was amazing. No matter how short the bus trip was, there was always some kind of video or card game he was gambling on. Then Lenny would go out and play real golf for a hundred dollars a hole. He just couldn't help himself.

I can honestly say I never really went out with Lenny anywhere. We went to dinner sometimes with a bunch of teammates, but I never got to see him in action doing anything else. Instead, I heard the stories the next day. Lenny was a great guy to play with. When I played on either side of him in left or center field, I never had to worry about where he was or covering more ground than usual. I was used to playing center field with George Foster on one side and Dave Kingman or Rusty Staub on the other. I would get dead tired from all the running I did with those slower guys in the outfield. But when Lenny played, I could concentrate on just me.

We did once have a terrible collision on a ball hit into the left center field gap. It was in that no-man's-land. I went for it, he went for it, and it was in one of those areas where nobody can call for the ball. We locked heads but I managed to catch and hold on to the ball. It was pretty ugly but we both stayed in the game. That's probably the biggest danger of having two center fielders manning the outfield.

I think the life Lenny lived after his baseball career ended was the same reckless one he had during it. He was daring. He took chances. In baseball, risks are calculated. If you take a shot at something and lose, okay, you lost. But life ain't like that. In the real world, you can't just take chances and hope that things work out without any planning and then deal with the consequences later.

I saw Lenny shortly after his retirement and did a double take. I remembered how he had this little speech impediment, like a lisp, but now he didn't sound or look anything like his old self. I said, "Lenny, is that you?"

His recklessness was affecting not only his health but also the fortune he had amassed in baseball. One minute Lenny was buying Wayne Gretzky's $17 million mansion in the hopes of flipping it for a profit, and the next he was completely broke. Why would he need to take such a risk?

The last time I spoke to him was at Gary Carter's funeral in 2012 and he looked and sounded a little better. He was under house arrest while awaiting his prison sentence the following month for three grand theft auto charges and one count of filing a false financial report.

Sadly, Lenny spent some time in jail because of the same recklessness that made him such a tremendous competitor on the field. He could play for me any day. He gave you everything he had between the lines.

Wally was cut from the same cloth as Lenny. He was another hard-nosed, gritty player, but Wally wasn't quite as daring when it came to areas off the field as Lenny was.

When Wally came to the ballpark, you knew what you were going to get. He was a fiery guy who would fight anyone. He just mixed right in with that group. I think we may end up seeing Wally manage a major league team someday. He's no more fiery than Billy Martin or Earl Weaver was. Plus, a lot of people love that passion and want to see it in their managers.

Wally's temper has gotten him in some trouble during his life, but I think he has mellowed a little bit in recent years. He doesn't manage with the same reckless abandon he had when he played. I've been around him when he's managed minor leaguers and I know that he demands and receives maximum effort from his players. He is managing AAA ball for the Mets right now, so he's only a step away. It's just a matter of when an opportunity comes up and whether a team is willing to roll the dice on Wally.

I don't know what was in the water, but that '86 team sure had a lot of spirit. The Mets roared out of the gates during my absence. At the end of April, they swept a four-game series in St. Louis to really set the tone for the season. Our 11-3 record was the best start to a season in franchise history. By the time I returned on May 9, the team was 18-4.

One of the reasons for the fast start was Kevin Mitchell, who had been promoted to the big league club while I was on the disabled list and made the most of the opportunity when he had the chance to play. Mitch was used as a utility player who would play at six different positions during the course of the season. The only guy I ever played with who was more versatile was Jose Oquendo. Jose came up with the Mets in 1983 and played two seasons for us before being traded to the Cardinals. He once played all nine positions for them in 1988, including four innings as a pitcher.

Mitchell had a reputation as a thug, but he was just a super nice guy. He did have a temper, but I think he came to the Mets with an undeserved bad reputation due to his gang involvement as a youth in San Diego. I think the Mets thought he was a time bomb just waiting to blow up, but he never did.

I do know one thing. Mitch immediately helped us defend our turf and could be just as brash and intimidating as the veterans. He had a mentality toward other teams that basically cautioned, *You can talk all you want, but unless you've got some credibility, you're just talk.*

———————

Once back with the club, I was nervous about my role with the Mets. I felt it was going to be short-lived. I honestly thought that since they were winning without me, they really had no need to put me back in. I knew that I would have to go out and prove that I could play the game at a high level all over again. That's just the way it is. You get hurt, somebody like Dykstra comes in and does a great job, and there are no guarantees you'll get your job back. I couldn't complain because I once replaced someone—Lee Mazzilli—as well.

The fans liked Dykstra's scrappy play. Some guys, like George Foster, thought there may have been a race issue on the club, that they wouldn't promote the black players as much as the white players. As someone who grew up having to deal with racism, I didn't get George's race thing at all. Maybe I was naive, but I just felt that the Mets believed they had found someone in Lenny who would eventually grow into a better player and that it would happen sooner rather than later. You can always look back and think, *Hmmm, I wonder if race had anything to do with it.* At the time I didn't think that way at all because Dykstra gave the team a dimension I didn't have even when I was healthy.

However, it's only natural that as a veteran player, there was some bitterness—but never toward Lenny. Outwardly, I never showed that bitterness, as I wanted to do what was best for the team. But as a professional athlete and fierce competitor, it bothered me. I think I was like most people who demand answers, even if they don't agree with them. I never got an answer and that bothered me more than anything else.

Not wanting to be a hood ornament as a fan favorite, I actually went to Frank and Davey and told them to give Lenny the full-time job. I didn't want to be sitting on the bench waiting for this kid to fall on his face and then all of a sudden hear Davey tell me, "Okay, Mookie, show us what you can do now."

But Davey would insist on keeping the platoon on, with Lenny and I alternating nights in center field depending on who was pitching for the other team.

I'd say to Davey, "This doesn't make any sense."

I just felt that if Lenny could play full-time, then they had no reason to keep me. There were teams that wanted me and I wanted more than anything to play every day.

I know Baltimore wanted me. Some of the coaches on the Orioles I was friendly with told me they thought they had a deal to get me but, for some reason, it didn't work out. I know Philly and San Francisco had strong interest in me as well.

I know everybody thought of me as Mr. Met, a happy camper with a positive attitude and a big smile, but I was ready to be traded. I would have invited it. I know people will be surprised to read that, but it was true. I understood the business of baseball and I was content to let the '86 season play out. But the next year, I either wanted to play full-time or be set loose. I wanted a resolution one way or another. I didn't want to be strung along.

To make matters worse for me, I started slowly after my return, going just 2 for 17 in limited action. But then, thankfully, I got hot, culminating in a 5-for-5 game on May 23 in my third straight start. My triple in that game scored two runs to tie it at 7–7 in San Diego. We ended up losing that game, but I got my center field job back, at least for the time being.

Lenny fumed on the bench. He didn't handle it well and didn't take the high road in sharing time with me. The only difference between the two of us was that I didn't show my displeasure outwardly like Lenny did.

After my 5-for-5 game, I felt like I was all the way back from my injuries. I thought, *Thank you, young man, for filling in, but I'm back now. I'll take it from here.* At the time, I didn't know playing regularly again was going to be short-lived. I think they had their minds made up in what direction they were *ultimately* going to go in. Eventually, it worked out best for the team when they had that Lenny-Wally combo at the top of the lineup. That one-two punch of scrappiness was so effective that other teams had to strategize on how to contain them. I couldn't argue with the results as the season went on.

Roughly a quarter of the way through the season, we were already twenty games over the .500 mark. HoJo had introduced the "rally cap" to baseball, McDowell the aforementioned "hotfoot." Opponents were really starting to despise our swagger and there was a general feeling that we weren't taking the game seriously. They may have been thinking, *They're killing us and they're over there joking around.*

I think teams didn't understand why Davey would allow this type of stuff to go on. But Davey understood our collective personality as well as anybody. He understood what it took to make us click. Throwing in a whole bunch of rules and regulations would have destroyed that team.

Most clubs didn't share in our enthusiasm. The Dodgers were one of them and, on the night of May 27, they showed their disapproval when Tom Niedenfuer plunked Knight with a pitch right after giving up a grand slam to Foster. It never took a lot to get Knight's blood boiling and he charged the mound and clocked Niedenfuer with a right hook just under his left eye. Ray may be a Christian, but he had some quick hands. He was a member of the Golden Gloves boxing association. It still shocked me because I had never seen that violent side of Ray. I had missed a lot of time with the team to that point, so I really didn't get to see everything during the spring. So man, when I saw that, I thought, *Oh boy! Here we go! This is a very different team from last year. Ray and Mitch are like enforcers!*

We would certainly need those guys as the season went on because the brawl with the Dodgers would be just the first of four fights we would get into with other teams that year. We were never going to go down without a fight—that you could count on.

Halfway through the season, Ed Lynch got traded to the Cubs for two prospects. He was with me at the University of South Carolina, then at Tidewater, and through all those down years with the Mets. Now with the division title practically a certainty with our 9½-game lead, Ed was going to miss the party. I am sure it was devastating to him.

I didn't say a whole lot to Ed after the trade. He knew there was no longer a place for him in the Mets' rotation. If he still wanted to pitch in the major leagues, he was going to have to go someplace else. Ed couldn't compete with the guys we now had. Sid Fernandez and Rick Aguilera had the last two rotation spots and had much better arms. Ed had to be realistic about the whole thing. He would have loved to have stayed, but he is a bright guy and I'm sure he understood the cold reality of the baseball business.

We ended June with a four-game winning streak and then won another four to start July. We were really cooking now, extending our lead to 12½ games.

In the July 3 game, down 5–3 to the Astros in the tenth inning, Straw tied it with a dramatic home run off Frank DiPino. Then Ray, who had struck out four times that game, redeemed himself and took DiPino deep with a game-winning blast.

At this point in the season, the curtain calls were happening after pretty much every home run we hit and that big win over Houston was no different. Yes, it was cocky and emotional, but it was what the fans wanted. If they didn't love it, we wouldn't have done it. Still, the other teams really resented us for doing that and the more they did, the more we wanted to do it because we knew it got under their skin. Our guys were begging to do the curtain call. The curtain calls' "irritation effect" created an edge over our opponents because when teams want to beat you so badly they tend to go outside of their comfort zone to do it. The problem was there was no game plan that you could go by to beat us because we had everything—power, speed, starting pitching,

At the Payson Complex in St. Petersburg during my
first spring training as a major leaguer in 1981.

Courtesy NY Mets

Rounding third and heading home! My running technique was enhanced after lessons with Olympic sprinter Steve Williams during the 1980 U.S. Olympic boycott. *Courtesy NY Mets*

Phillies shortstop Luis Aguayo and I watching a pop-up to first base during a game in 1985. The Phillies were more like a "little brother" than a rival to the Mets in the mid-eighties. Our only true rival during that period was the St. Louis Cardinals.

Courtesy NY Mets

Ripping one deep into the right field corner in a game against the Braves. The catcher's glove is positioned for a pitch down and middle in—just where I liked it!

Courtesy NY Mets

We were the "toast of New York" in 1986. But I always wondered why Doc and Straw weren't included in this picture. From left to right: Lenny Dykstra, Howard Johnson, Ray Knight, Gary Carter, Keith Hernandez, Mookie Wilson, and Wally Backman.   *Courtesy of Mookie Wilson*

This is the iconic photo of when my slow roller up the first base line went through Bill Buckner's legs to win Game Six of the 1986 World Series. Buckner's error was just one of numerous mental and physical lapses the Red Sox made that cost them that game, and Bill has received far too much blame for his miscue. Had he fielded the ball cleanly, would I have beaten it out anyway? You decide!

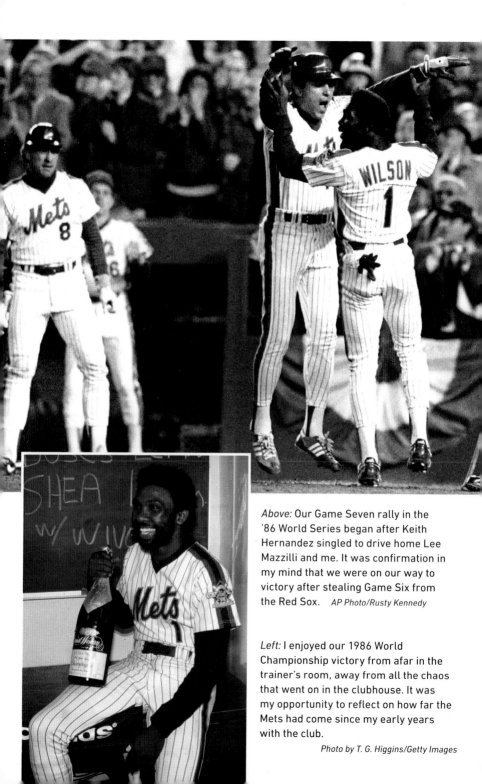

Above: Our Game Seven rally in the '86 World Series began after Keith Hernandez singled to drive home Lee Mazzilli and me. It was confirmation in my mind that we were on our way to victory after stealing Game Six from the Red Sox.   *AP Photo/Rusty Kennedy*

Left: I enjoyed our 1986 World Championship victory from afar in the trainer's room, away from all the chaos that went on in the clubhouse. It was my opportunity to reflect on how far the Mets had come since my early years with the club.

Photo by T. G. Higgins/Getty Images

With Rosa, my love and partner for life, after thirty-five years of marriage. *Courtesy of Mookie Wilson*

My wife, Rosa (far right), and I promoting a Gospel CD we wrote together at Shea Stadium with daughters, Adesina and Ernestine, and son, Preston. Our words came to life on the CD when performed by family and members of the Zion Mill Creek Baptist Church in Columbia, South Carolina. As my father often told me, "Make a joyful noise."

Courtesy of Mookie Wilson

Fulfilling the dreams of my father and Judge Ness, I graduated with a degree in behavioral science at Mercy College following my playing days. *Courtesy of Mookie Wilson*

Managing the Brooklyn Cyclones in 2005. Brooklyn is the greatest venue in minor league ball. A packed house every night and beautiful views of the Atlantic Ocean and Coney Island. *Courtesy Brooklyn Cyclones*

Me with the World Series trophy during the weekend celebration of the twentieth anniversary of our '86 World Series Championship.

Courtesy NY Mets

and a solid bullpen. Not many teams can say that they have it all, but we truly did.

That '86 club wasn't satisfied with just winning two out of three or three out of four. No, no, no, no, no! We weren't having any of that. We wanted to crush our opponents in every game. Like Bobby O once said, "We didn't just want to win, we wanted to step on the opponent's neck."

Ronnie called us "Must-See Baseball." No one could predict what would happen during one of our games, but it was usually something pretty entertaining. We might win 10–1, Gooden might throw a two-hitter and strike out fifteen, or someone might get hit by a pitch and a fight would break out. It was like a circus atmosphere every night.

The country has a genuine dislike for anything New York to begin with, but when you threw in our team's bravado and talent, it just made that contempt for us that much stronger. We would go into parks like Atlanta, San Diego, or San Francisco, where they typically drew between 8,000 and 10,000 fans, and have 35,000 show up to boo us. We were the villain. People came to watch the Mets—whether they loved us or hated us. Mostly, they hated us. We were the toast of New York, and we were the benchmark for every other club in baseball.

People would come up to us and say stuff like, "You guys suck! You guys are overrated!" I would simply respond, "Oh yeah? Just check the standings." As a Met, you didn't have to say much else. You either bought into that arrogance or you just didn't fit in with the team. I think trying to change that culture in later years really hurt us.

Having had two stints as the Mets' first base coach, I can tell you we had much more fun in the 1980s than the teams do now. Today, everyone's in their own little world. They have their cell phones, iPads, and video games, and they're checking their stock portfolios and everything else they're invested in. It's not a bad thing, but they forget about baseball.

Our players would sit and talk for thirty to forty minutes after games. Wives would sit outside the park asking, *What's taking them so long?!* Sure, the guys had a couple of beers in the process, but they were talking baseball. That doesn't happen now. When the last out is made, some guys have one foot in their pants and the other in their car. That doesn't make them bad players, it just means they have other interests outside the game. We did, too, but nothing got in the way of baseball.

We also made good money in the eighties by comparison to the average worker, but today's ballplayers make astronomical figures. And that plays into it. We didn't make so much money that we could afford to throw it away. Every dollar was accounted for and there wasn't a whole bunch left over for splurging.

The money really took off in the nineties when my son, Preston, played. It became a different environment. There are now more and more corporations owning teams. Back when I played, clubs were mostly family-owned and they were a little more cautious about where their money went.

The biggest problem with the huge money nowadays is that ballplayers don't have to worry as much about winning as they do about themselves. Whether they win or lose is irrelevant. It's just their numbers that really matter. In the old days, teams would say things like, "We'd be in last place with or without you." That's not the case now. Money plays a big part.

Today's ballplayers are much better athletes as a whole than in my day. They're bigger, stronger, and some of them are even faster. They work out year-round and many take supplements. But I don't think they respect the game as much as we did.

We had some real party animals on that '86 team. That's well documented. But when those guys got to the ballpark, it was *all* baseball.

———————

As was typical of the summer, Mets fans would plan their vacations around where we were playing on the road. In '86, though, there were more New Yorkers traveling to see us than I had ever seen before. We were like rock stars.

Even though I was then and still am today a devout and married Christian man, I would be lying if I didn't say there were temptations. It's tough to ignore what's in front of you every day. But what I quickly found is that it's not the temptation that gets you into trouble, it's the putting yourself in the position to be tempted that is dangerous.

You've got to go to the ballpark. You've got to go to work. That's a nonnegotiable. You've got to go to the hotel. You've got to walk the lobby. Okay, that's another nonnegotiable. The best thing to do to avoid temptation is to put yourself in a position where you are not sending the wrong messages to groupies. Some guys love the attention. I really never have. I've always told myself, *Let me do my job, then let me go back home and enjoy myself.*

Every once in a while, though, temptation does find you. The one thing I did as early in my career as I could was have my wife travel with me. I would buy her a ticket at my own expense and even bring our son along whenever possible.

We've all had issues as ballplayers with ladies calling our rooms. Sometimes you get yourself into a situation that you can't explain and nothing sounds like the truth. That's why it helped to have my wife *with* me when things like that occurred. One time, a lady called my room and I put her on the speaker phone. The lady said that I met her in such and such city when George Foster introduced us the previous month. There was just one problem with the lady's story. George was no longer on our team at the time. It made it easier for my wife to understand how some ladies will make up anything just to meet you.

I've had some other situations that were sometimes difficult to explain, but I have never put myself in a compromising position. One thing is certain. If you constantly go out, eventually something is going to happen because everybody knows who you are. It's a tough life for a family man.

A perfect example of how trouble can find you is what happened to a bunch of our guys on the night of July 19 after a game in Houston. Tim Teufel's wife gave birth to their first child and Bobby O, Ronnie, Aguilera, and Straw took him out to a place called Cooter's to celebrate. Straw left early, but the rest of the guys stuck around and drank until closing time. The guys ended up getting pretty hammered and they ran into some trouble with a couple of off-duty policemen hired by the club for security detail. My four teammates ended up spending the night in the Houston City Jail.

I remember them coming to the ballpark the next day and there were already T-shirts being sold around the ballpark with Mets jailbirds on them.

I was surprised when I saw Teufel, a man of faith who hardly ever drank. I shouted to him, "Teuf, what in the world were you doing in that club with *that* group?!"

I was a little surprised at Ronnie, too, but only a little bit. I knew Ronnie was a closet partier, the kind of person who was highly intelligent but never let that get in the way of his having a good time, because he liked to sit in the back of the bus with Straw and some of the rowdier guys. Still, I was taken aback that the young man from Yale ended up in jail. But Teufel? That *really* shocked me. It also goes to show that all it takes is one time out for trouble to find you.

We all had a nice little laugh about the Cooter's incident, though. No one with the club really took it too seriously. Any time you get negative publicity, club management isn't too happy with it, but it was just another one of those things with the Mets. The press, in part because we were a New York team, really blew what happened out of proportion.

Of course, had the trouble with the off-duty cops led to one of the guys getting injured or charged with a more serious crime, that would have been a different story. But this was just a case of a little harmless trouble after a few too many drinks.

Doc got the nod to start the All-Star Game, but his 10-4 record and 2.77 ERA, while still good, were not close to being as dominating as the stats he put up in '85. Not only was he not the top pitcher in the National League, he was no longer even the best on the Mets' staff.

At that point, there was no talk at all about Doc in terms of what was wrong with him. There were no whispers about whether or not he was using drugs. Not yet. After all, he was still 10-4, and other teams were now throwing their best pitchers and lineups against him while adjusting to his pitches. It was easy for us to justify his not being the dominating pitcher he was the year before. Nobody, after all, could pitch like that forever.

People may think it's easy to look back now and see the signs. People will point to how much he sweated on the mound. But Doc always sweated a lot. He was a horrendous sweater. He would get drenched out there even on relatively cool days. Plus, he was the same fun-loving Doc, not acting any differently.

So we all just went about our business. If team management knew anything, they kept the secret pretty well from us.

I believe the Mets mishandled Doc and, for that matter, Darryl, too. They were both very young and had tremendous talent. I think the team did not protect them as well as they probably could have. When you're winning, teams sometimes turn a blind eye to what's going on.

I am not up to speed on what the Mets knew or didn't know or what they did or didn't do for Doc by the All-Star break. But if they knew or suspected something was going on with Doc, then they shouldn't have waited and pretended it was all a big surprise.

When I found out about Doc testing positive for cocaine the

next spring, I was floored. I didn't see any signs that Doc was doing drugs. I didn't know anything about it.

I've said many times that maybe some of us veteran players should have figured it out and done something. It's still upsetting to me when I think about it. Here was Doc, a promising young star, and we probably could have saved him. In my eyes, despite his gracing the cover of *Time* magazine and becoming the youngest millionaire in the game's history that year, he was still just a kid. C'mon, you can't give a kid the proverbial "key to the city." But that's exactly what the Mets did.

To this day, on occasion, I still talk with some of the guys on that team about how we may have been able to help Gooden. Keith once said to me, "Doc was a man. You couldn't watch him 24/7."

Ronnie, in hindsight, thought one idea might have been to hire an unmarried bullpen catcher that could hang out with Doc and keep an eye on him. No expense would have been too much.

As for Straw, he wasn't performing close to the tremendous potential he possessed. Worse yet, he wasn't always hustling in right field and on the base paths. As one of the vets on the club, I thought about talking with Straw about it, but Bill Robinson beat me to it. I thought Bill was enough, so I didn't step in. There's a fine line between mentoring and being a nag. Plus, it's fine to talk, but talk is only good if people listen.

I didn't know what the reason was for Straw's prolonged slumps. Guys go through them all the time. I've had my own. But hustling is a different story. He did some things in the field that were unacceptable. And when he wasn't hitting, it got even worse.

I think the reason I may have missed some of the warning

signs with Doc, and then later with Straw, was because I was having my own issues with how I was feeling about the club, management, and my diminished playing time. That probably had a lot to do with what I didn't see or just chose to ignore. I did think the team's partying ways often went overboard. While management can't be expected to keep an eye on their players 24/7, I think more could have been done to rein in some of our guys, especially if there was even a hint of suspected drug use going on. It almost seemed like the Mets were willing to put up with some collateral damage as long as the team was winning.

On the morning of July 22, we were 13 games in front of the division and cruising. I was beginning to get the sense that we could run away with the race by historic proportions and that the rest of the season might lack the excitement that we had in the first half of the season. I couldn't have been more wrong.

That night we played a game in Cincinnati that was the strangest, weirdest one I ever played in. Of all the games we played during that regular season, this one probably should have gotten more ink than any of them.

Down 3–1 in the top of the ninth with two outs and nobody on base, Lenny walked and Teuf followed with a double to give us second and third.

The Reds brought in future Met left-handed reliever John Franco to match up against Mex. Keith hit what appeared to be the final out of the game to Dave Parker in right field, but "The Cobra" dropped the ball to allow Lenny and Teuf to come around to score and tie the game at 3–3. The game would go into extra innings and that's when things really got interesting.

The Reds' player-manager, Pete Rose, lined a one-out, pinch-hit single to center in the bottom of the tenth inning. He sent Eric Davis into the game to pinch-run for him and Davis wasted little time stealing second base. Davis then took off again and stole third, beating Gary's throw. But this time, as Davis popped up from his slide, he found himself face-to-face with Ray. The two of them started shoving each other before Ray punched Davis in the head.

A big brawl ensued.

Reds pitcher John Denny and two other teammates went right after Mitchell and attacked him, which, based on Kevin's reputation as one of our enforcers, was surely planned.

Even I was involved in the fracas, slugging Reds pitcher Bill Gullickson. There was no reason for doing it, but when you get into a brawl like that, you just go after the first person you can find.

All of us, except for George Foster, got caught up in the moment. George stayed on the bench during the brawl while the rest of us were out on the field. His reasoning was that all of our fighting was not sending a good message to kids. That excuse didn't score many points with us.

George wasn't a violent person. For that matter, neither was I. But there are some things that take precedence over everything else. I was taught in high school that when you're a part of a team, you defend that team even when they're in the wrong sometimes. That's just the nature of it. You straighten everything else out later. Your team gets into an altercation, everyone goes out. It's not the time for you to sit there and try to figure out should I or shouldn't I?

If that wasn't the beginning of the end for George with the Mets then the end was certainly coming soon. Actually, I believe the end was going to come for George no matter what he did or didn't do that night. George clearly was not in the Mets' plans for the future. He was an inherited player from manager George Bamberger's regime. He was a Band-Aid at the time they acquired him; he was brought in to get some people in the stands. The Mets' PR guys had this big thing about the power of Kingman and Foster in our lineup, but we were still a really bad team anyway. But the trade to bring Foster to the Mets was a good trade at the time. He led the team in home runs and RBIs in 1983, his second year with us.

I knew George was on his way out. I talked with him quite a few times in '86 and he was convinced that there was a conspiracy to get him out of New York. I didn't disagree. George always had a way of being overly honest and, in baseball, it is sometimes best to tap-dance around the truth. Unfortunately for him, George wasn't much for "dancing."

George probably felt the credibility he had built up after two world championships with the Reds and winning an MVP award would stand up on its own, but no one is bigger than the game, even when the game is not fair. And not going onto the field during the brawl just gave the Mets more ammunition to move him out. A week later, the Mets signed Mazzilli, the once-bright young star of the team whom I replaced as the center fielder, to a minor league contract with designs on quickly promoting him to the big club. The writing was on the wall. Foster, one of the most celebrated acquisitions in team history just four years earlier, would be released on August 7.

The brawl really put us in a hole in that game. Straw had already been ejected after arguing a called third strike in the sixth inning. Now, with Ray and Mitch both thrown out of the game for fighting, we were out of position players. Gary had to move to third with Ed Hearn taking over the catching duties, while Orosco and McDowell flip-flopped between pitching and playing outfield depending on whether a left-handed or right-handed hitter was coming to the plate. I stayed in left field until the thirteenth inning when the left-handed hitting Parker came up and I swapped positions for that one at-bat with McDowell and played right field. It was so bizarre.

Thankfully, we held it all together and HoJo won it for us in the fourteenth inning with a three-run homer.

I thought it was very innovative for Davey to move guys around like he did. We were also fortunate to have had two great athletes in Roger and Jesse. They shagged fly balls every day during batting practice so I wasn't worried about either of them playing outfield. I was more concerned about them pitching to one batter, then running to play the outfield before again coming back in to pitch. It was an odd set of circumstances, to say the least.

That game, more than any other we played all season, showed everybody that our team was serious about winning and how every guy on our roster would do what it took to win and be happy about doing it.

With George gone, the Mets promoted Maz to take his place on the big league roster. Unlike our first go-around, we ended up becoming very good friends. He said he had matured since he left the Mets and he was right. He had accepted his role as a part-time outfielder and first baseman and was a good pinch hitter for us down the stretch. It was also around this time that Gary missed eleven games due to a partial ligament tear to his left thumb that he injured while playing first base one night. But even with Gary on the disabled list, we still won eight of the games he missed. I think it helped our psyche to see that we could still play dominating ball without our future Hall of Fame catcher in the lineup. Carter's absence proved to us there was nothing that could upend the confidence we had going for us at that point. We didn't rely on any one guy, even one of Gary's stature.

We finished the season strong. Over the final two months of the season, we won roughly two-thirds of our games. We had pretty much wrapped up the division by the start of August, so all that winning wasn't necessary. It was our killer instinct that kept us going. We didn't know how to coast. We were never satisfied with just beating the opponent. Our collective thinking was, *"Until you bow down and say 'You're the best,' we're going to keep beating you down."*

I guess we didn't have to act like that, but we did.

On the evening of August 30, we had a twenty-game lead in the division. Best of all was the fun we continued to have. One of the symbols of that frivolity was put on display that night with the release of our team music video, "Let's Go Mets." The guys really embraced the whole idea and I thought it came out great. The song ended up going triple platinum. It was a team thing and was just *so New York*.

We were different. No other baseball team had done anything like a music video celebrating its greatness. I didn't know how it was going to be perceived. I thought it was going a bit overboard initially, but once we started doing it, I was thinking, *This team is made for this.*

A couple of weeks later, we traveled to Philadelphia looking to officially clinch the division. We were a season-high 22 games in first place entering the series. Lots of Mets fans were there. The Phillies were playing like it was do-or-die. They were determined not to let us win the division on their turf. In Philly, just like in Cincinnati, St. Louis, and other cities in the National League, their team and their fans couldn't stand the Mets. They thought we were the worst group of guys and were getting way too much publicity.

We needed two out of three to clinch the East in Philly. Instead, the Phillies swept us. In all honesty, I don't think we put all we had into that series. We were at the point where we felt if we didn't clinch on a particular day, there was always tomorrow.

We then went to St. Louis for a two-game series and dropped the first one, which actually gave us the opportunity to clinch at home after winning the following night. But clinching at home wasn't in the thought process at the time. I just think we may have been too relaxed and had too little urgency to close it out. Maybe if the schedule had us playing our archrival Cardinals at the time of the Philadelphia series, we would have played with more intensity. Winning in St. Louis would have been even better than clinching at home. But the idea of doing it at Shea was a nice way to finish the division off.

We finally got it done on September 17 against the Cubs, winning 4–2. Doc threw a complete game six-hitter. It was a pretty one-sided game. There was nothing satisfying about beating the Cubs, who weren't very good. It would have been much better if it had been the Cardinals or even the Dodgers.

Although the Dodgers weren't a division rival, I felt as much disdain for them as some other teams had for us. They got a ton of publicity. They could do no wrong in the eyes of the media. They seemingly were always featured on the NBC Saturday *Game of the Week*. Worst of all, their manager Tommy Lasorda was always on the top step of their dugout hugging guys and talking about bleeding Dodger Blue. For all of his own bravado, Lasorda could never have been our manager. He was too much of a self-promoter. When we played, the focus was *never* on Davey. Instead, the attention was *always* placed on the players. With the Dodgers, the cameras were glued to every move Tommy made.

In the clincher, the surprise hero of the game was yet another one of our kids, Dave Magadan, who had three hits and drove in two runs in his first career start. Dave was filling in for Mex, who had the flu that night. Still, Keith dragged himself out to first base for the final two innings because it meant so much to him, the team, and the fans to be on the field for the celebration. Like me, Mex had been there throughout the whole transformation of the team from losers to winners.

Magadan's day was coming. He would be the heir apparent to take over first base after Keith left the club as a free agent following the 1989 season to finish his career in Cleveland. It was good for Dave, just *ten days* after his major league debut, to experience what he did that night.

After the last out was made, the fans stormed onto the field. I remember thinking just before that happened how I was not going to join the celebratory pile on the mound, but instead head straight for the clubhouse to avoid injury. It was a chore getting off the field, but I made it back to the dugout unscathed. Some of our guys weren't so lucky, but thankfully none of them was seriously hurt.

Nothing good happens when fans rush the field. I don't like taking it away from the fans, but some of them bring shovels and other gardening tools to dig out big clumps of grass to keep as souvenirs. It doesn't make it easy for the groundskeepers to fix the field in time for the next game, which, in our case, was the following night. So my only two concerns are making sure nobody gets hurt and keeping the field playable for the next game. Other than that, the fans should join in the celebration. Many of them stayed loyal to us despite suffering through a lot of bad seasons since the Mets' last division title in 1973. They earned the right to go a little crazy.

We drew over 2.7 million fans in '86, a New York sports attendance record. I always enjoyed a great rapport with Mets fans. The big crowds made me a better and more intense player. I always played for the fans, played for their approval.

I recall what it was like at Shea Stadium during the days when it seemed there were as few as 200 people in the stands some nights, making it almost feel like a spring training game. But the more fans that came as we kept getting better, the more energy it gave us. I always hustled between the lines, but the difference with playing before a sell-out crowd as opposed to performing in a morgue-like atmosphere is that you don't have to motivate yourself or remind yourself to do this or do that.

The crowds at Shea in '86 gave us a tremendous home field advantage. We were very good in that ballpark. The fans really embraced that team. I don't know how other fans were with their teams, but at Shea we could really feel it. In their eyes, our team could do no wrong.

We would finish the regular season with 108 wins, the most by any team in the eighties, and 21½ games ahead of the second place Phillies. Most gratifying was the 28½ games we finished over St. Louis.

After going down to the wire in '85 with the Cardinals, battling down to the last week in '84 against the Cubs, and losing to both of them, no one could have predicted the extent of our domination over the division in 1986. Not even Davey. We knew back in spring training we were going to be good, but we ended up being *even better* than we imagined.

With our bravado, I would have never thought that possible.

8

The Dread Scott Series

After having so dominated the highly competitive National League East, much of the media and our fans envisioned us using the Houston Astros as a mere stepping stone on our way to the World Series. While we were seen as a team without any weaknesses, the Astros came into the NLCS with a .255 batting average, only one legitimate home run threat, and not even close to the pitching and bullpen depth that we had.

But I knew better. And so did a lot of my Mets teammates.

We expected a very good series. They may have had twelve fewer wins than us, but they equaled our team with their thirty-nine come-from-behind victories during the regular season. More than anything, that showed us they could be as gritty as we were.

I knew their pitching was very good, particularly in a short series, and matched up well against us. They relied on their pitchers like we did to keep them in games. And while Houston didn't have the power we did, they had very good speed on the base paths and played solid defense in the field. The Astros were a fundamentally sound ball club that didn't beat itself.

Despite how great we thought we were, I think we all would have preferred an easier team to play. It wasn't that we feared the Astros, but we knew that it was probably going to be a much tougher job to waltz through the championship series than if we faced a different opponent. We knew they were going to win at least one ball game; a four-game sweep was not going to happen.

Houston was as red hot as we were entering the championship series. Both of our clubs finished the season winning ten of their twelve games. But whereas we used our bats to beat teams into oblivion during that stretch, the Astros' starting pitching staff, which consisted of Mike Scott, Nolan Ryan, Bob Knepper, and Jim Deshaies, and their bullpen, anchored by Charlie Kerfeld and Dave Smith, were on an incredible roll. Over the final twelve games of the season, Houston pitching registered a minuscule ERA of just 1.34. Included in that run were an astounding five shutouts in six games, with a division-clinching no-hitter by Scott in the middle of it.

But despite the Astros' impressive pitching numbers, statistics didn't really play a big part in our planning back then. We believed in the proverbial "eye test." We believed in what we saw and what we had faced. We took seven of our twelve meetings against them during the regular season, so our plan was fairly simple: they had two pitchers—Scott and Ryan—that we had to beat in a short series or we would be in trouble.

Truth be told, as great as the Hall of Famer Ryan was, when it came to the biggest of obstacles standing between us and the World Series, Mike Scott stood alone. The amazing thing about Scott was that he was an average pitcher at best when he was with the Mets earlier in his career. I got to see him firsthand both in AAA and then for four seasons with the big club. He was very good at Tidewater and we thought he was going to be a solid major leaguer as well. Scott was a power pitcher, but one of his problems was that he kept his fastballs up in the zone too much. His other issue was that he didn't have a secondary pitch. In the big leagues, that's a recipe for disaster.

After leaving the Mets, Scott finally did develop that second pitch he needed—the split-fingered fastball he learned from former major league pitcher Roger Craig—and it changed his life. While the split-fingered fastball became a popular pitch in the eighties, you needed to throw it over 90 miles an hour for it to be any good. And Scott had that ability.

But that wasn't the only reason Scott's pitching improved dramatically. We thought that there was something else about the way he threw that pitch that just *really* put him over the top—namely, that he was scuffing the baseball.

Scott's pitches came in looking like a regular fastball—no unusual rotation—and would sometimes dart to the right and other times went straight down. The pitch was pretty much unpredictable and did what it wanted to do. That's why that pitch is so very difficult to hit. As a batter, you have less than a second to decide whether you are going to swing or not swing the bat. You're basically up there swinging where you *think* the pitch

is going to go. So with Scott's split-fingered fastball, if you antic-
ipate it going one way and it goes another, it kind of puts you in
a funk.

Was it cheating or gamesmanship? If you think it was cheating, then you would probably have to go back and accuse a whole
lot of other pitchers of doing the same thing. There's an old saying that goes, "You're only cheating if you get caught." I think
technically what Scott did was cheating, but so is putting pine
tar or Vaseline on your fingers or glove, so how can you distin-
guish between them what is cheating and what isn't?

Gaylord Perry is in the Hall of Fame and not only admitted
to throwing an illegal pitch, the spitball, but wrote a book about
doing it! I love Gaylord. We did a charity function together once
at the Mohegan Sun in Connecticut and he even joked about
having thrown that pitch. And there's nothing wrong with that.

People say to Gaylord, "Oh, you cheated." That may be true,
but not everyone could throw a spitball as effectively as he did.
Because Gaylord could, it gave him the edge that every pitcher
looks for when they're competing.

I put Scott in the same category as Gaylord. If Scott came out
now and admitted what he did, I would look at both pitchers
the same way. It was one of those little things Scott got away
with and that others may have tried, but didn't do half as well as
he did.

As a Christian man, I define cheating differently in baseball
from how I do in the real world. There is what is acceptable gamesmanship, which, while not always legal, can be somewhat rational-
ized. That's because baseball's only a game. While cheating is still

cheating, in baseball there has always been what is referred to as "honor among thieves." Players have been cheating in baseball since the game was invented. Guys are always looking for ways to get an edge, whether it's by doing steroids, doctoring a baseball, corking bats, watering down the infield unnecessarily, or lowering and raising the mound. There have always been ways to give players an edge, so you have to look at cheating in baseball as part of the game.

If Houston had another advantage over us besides Scott, it was their home crowd at the Astrodome. Under normal circumstances, it was a tough place to play because of how loud it could get in an enclosed stadium. But because we were the arrogant team from New York, it only added fuel to the fire. We were despised by the Astros fans well before the Cooter's incident earlier that season—that just confirmed what they already thought about the Mets. Also, the fans resented the fact we were on the back pages of every paper whether we were home or away.

But as players, we loved their venomous reaction to us. Just as we loved rubbing their noses in the fact that we were a great team. If the Astros thought they were better than us, we dared them to come out and prove it.

Their crowd was certainly amped up for Game One of the NLCS, a pitchers' duel between Doc and Scott. Gooden was really on that night, only giving up a second-inning home run to Glenn Davis. But when facing a guy like Mike Scott, you didn't ever want to get behind, even by just one run, because he really knew how to hold on to even the slightest of leads. We needed to try to force the issue somehow, but I knew it was going to be extremely difficult.

I just didn't like our attitude that night at all. We were talking on the bench with a very defeated attitude and that bothered me. Guys were distracted by the perception that Scott was doctoring the baseball. If you're thinking about something other than your job, you're probably going to lose. Scott was in our heads, no question about it.

We didn't ask to examine the balls, because we knew that nothing was going to come out of it. We figured if the umpires, who had been tipped off about Scott all season long, hadn't done anything by then, why would they do something now? We just had to go on and play the game.

Scott ended up with 14 strikeouts en route to a 1–0 Astros victory in Game One. The prospects were very real that we would see him twice more in the series if it went the full seven games. Despite this, I still felt we were going to win the series, but it would be important to make sure we didn't see Scott three times. That couldn't happen. We had to try to win it in six games at a maximum.

After the game, Mex summoned some of our key guys to a bar to offer reassurance. I think it served its purpose. His message to them was, "Hey, we've done it all year. You can't allow one game or one pitcher to get in the way of all we've accomplished."

I'm certain the pep talk helped. Keith had a way of talking to guys and really making them understand that we were in this thing together. He wasn't always politically correct with a lot of things he said, but the guys gravitated toward his honesty and that's what made him such a great leader.

Game Two was as much of a must-win game for us as you can have, but we felt good going into it because we always had pretty good success against their starting pitcher, Nolan Ryan. While he certainly had overpowering stuff, he had a tendency to walk a few guys a game. That was important because the opportunity for a few of us to steal second and third if we reached base was almost a given due to his big windup. We had a much different feel and confidence level facing Ryan as opposed to Scott. Plus, we had Ojeda going for us, who was as solid a pitcher in '86 as we had, and that included Doc.

We put up our first runs of the series in the fourth inning when Carter torched an RBI double off the right field wall and Straw followed with a sacrifice fly to left to give us a 2–0 lead. Getting out in front got the monkey off our backs. Psychologically, particularly in a situation when it's the playoffs and games are a precious few, it's critical to score first and let the other team play catch-up. Sometimes it even disrupts the way the team that is behind usually plays its game.

We got our swagger back in the fifth inning when Ryan knocked Lenny down with what was clearly a purpose pitch. But Nails got right back up and ripped a single to help ignite a three-run rally that gave us a 5–0 lead.

Nolan's purpose pitch didn't surprise anyone because he was not afraid to put you on notice, so to speak. He was very tactful with the way he did it, but you understood. He would throw a fastball high and tight and then walk around the mound, rubbing the baseball while staring you down. The fact that he chose to knock down Lenny definitely didn't surprise us because Ryan understood that Dykstra, along with Backman, were really the guys that made us go. If either reached base against him, he knew he would be in trouble.

Bobby O went the distance in a gutsy performance, winning 5–1. Now it was back to Shea to try to go up a game in the series before having to see Scott again the following day.

We faced Knepper in Game Three and, like Davey had done all season long, we loaded our lineup with righty hitters versus a southpaw. Davey moved me over from left field to center, and had me lead off. Mitchell was brought off the bench to play left field and hit second, while Teufel played second base and batted seventh. Mex and Straw were our only left-handed bats in the starting lineup that game. Davey was always big on playing the lefty-righty matchups, even if it meant sitting our two spark-plugs, Lenny and Wally.

Darling started for us and was wild early, walking a guy, hitting another, and throwing a wild pitch before yielding a two-run homer to Bill Doran to dig himself into a 4–0 hole after just two innings. Davey and Ronnie, both really cerebral guys, often went head-to-head over pitching strategies and this game was no exception. Davey and most of us thought that Ronnie was trying to be too fine with his pitches. He had a very good fastball and sometimes we felt he went to his off-speed stuff too soon. I know that was a point of contention between him and Davey. But Ronnie was very smart. He did things that were calculating. But we were like, *"You've got a good fastball, throw it!"*

It's not always that easy. Ronnie achieved a level of success doing things his way and he was certainly not the first player to disagree with Davey.

In the bottom of the sixth, still down 4–0, I was thinking we were in a hole, but we had come back so many times before and, based on the pitcher we were facing, we were still confident. It would have been a different story if Ryan or Scott were out there pitching with a four-run lead. Then we would have had some issues. But with Knepper out there, there was no panic and we felt there was an opportunity to get back in the game.

Sure enough, after cutting the lead to 4–1, we tied it up when Straw lined an absolute laser over the auxiliary scoreboard in right for a three-run homer. Now we not only had tied the game but felt like we were in control of it. We had the better bullpen, the psychological edge of coming back to tie the game, and the Shea crowd in a frenzy. We were feeling pretty good about our chances to win the game.

But I give that Houston team a ton of credit, as they bounced right back and manufactured an unearned run in the top of the seventh thanks, in part, to an error by Knight on a sacrifice bunt.

The Astros held on to their slim 5–4 lead going into the bottom of the ninth with Dave Smith, their closer, now in the game. Still, because of our lineup, I liked our chances to pull it out.

Sure enough, Backman, inserted at second base in the top half of the inning for Teufel, led off the inning with a drag bunt up the first base line. In avoiding the tag by first baseman Glenn Davis, it appeared that Wally may have gone out of the baseline, but was still called safe. Astros' manager Hal Lanier argued vehemently with first base umpire Dutch Rennert, but to no avail. It was a judgment call and if Rennert had called him out, it would have been Davey going ballistic instead of Lanier. Either way the play was called, you were going to get an argument from one of the managers.

With one out and Wally now at second, Lenny, having entered the game two innings earlier, strolled to the plate. Nails, the classic overachiever who played like he had a chip on his shoulder, got out in front of a pitch and lofted one high down the right field line. At first, it looked like a routine fly ball. I wasn't even thinking it had a chance to clear the fence, especially at Shea, a pitcher's park. But there must have been a breeze up there or something, because it surprisingly landed in our bullpen for a game-winning home run!

There was no question that was the pivotal game of the series. If we had lost that game, we would have been down 2-1 with Scott pitching next and in a Game Seven if necessary.

So here he was again: our nemesis Mike Scott back on the hill for Houston in Game Four. Or, as Bobby O would call him, our very own Freddy Krueger. There was no strategy to beat this guy. Before the game, I was thinking, *Guys, just keep your heads. Don't worry.*

But I knew how much Scott was bothering some of them. I took a different approach because I never cared who was pitching. I was always like, *C'mon, you're throwing it, I'm swinging at it.*

Nobody was more psyched out by Scott than Carter. Gary was obsessed with Scott scuffing the ball. It was all he could focus on. I was thinking, *C'mon, kid. We need you. Don't leave me now, man!* It was the only time I had ever seen Gary behave this way. Maybe it was also the pressure of the moment, the meaning of the series. After all, this was the farthest he had ever gone in the playoffs his entire career.

Keith was upset, too, but it didn't surprise anyone because he was outspoken by nature. We all had seen Keith lose it before, even yelling at opposing managers, but never Gary. Carter was one of those guys you always thought was in control of everything. And here he was just *losing* it, man!

The other guys didn't seem as concerned about Scott's "witchcraft" on the mound. But the risk was there that when you have your two leaders react like they did, it could filter down to the other players.

Because the game was at Shea, our batboy Mike Rufino was able to collect some of the foul balls that Scott had pitched. Mike must have collected between fifteen and twenty of them. I had no interest in looking at the baseballs in question, but most of our guys on the bench did, noticing the same size scuff mark in the identical spot on every ball. All I was thinking was, *Oh, that's all we need now, for us to see the evidence. We are beating ourselves just by worrying about what Scott is doing on the mound.*

There are a lot of theories about how Scott was able to scuff the ball without anyone noticing. Some of our guys thought it was their third baseman, Phil Garner, who was doctoring the ball. Others thought it was their catcher, Alan Ashby. I have no idea, but I talked with some of our pitchers and they said the easiest way for Scott to do it would be to have something taped to his glove. But no one, other than Scott, really knows for sure. And to this day, he's not telling, and I don't blame him one bit. Until one of his old teammates comes forward with something definitive about his doctoring the baseball, it's still *officially* all just speculation.

I don't believe we will ever know the truth from Scott. Why would he come out now?

Houston scored all the runs they would need in the top of the second inning in a manner that broke our hearts. With two outs and Glenn Davis on first, Ashby hit a pop-up in foul territory that appeared to be the third out. Santana called off Knight, but failed to make the catch as the ball dropped in the first row of the seats by third base. On the very next pitch, Ashby took Sid deep for a two-run homer. The 2–0 lead seemed like 10–0. A sequence like that hurts no matter who's pitching, but when you're facing Scott in the NLCS, it magnifies the whole situation. You had an out and you end up two runs down.

Houston won the game, 3–1, to even the series at two games apiece.

After the game, the balls that Rufino collected were sent by the Mets to NL President Chub Feeney's office, but he chose to disregard all the evidence that had been gathered against Scott. Personally, I wasn't disappointed or surprised by Feeney's decision. I was thinking, *Why would he say anything now?*

Besides, it really wouldn't have served baseball any good to penalize the Astros after the fact. We just had to live with it. That's why I was so upset with the guys being worried about it in the first place. It was what it was. Scott won two ball games against us. There was no way Feeney was going to take those wins away from Houston at that point.

After the game, Knight gave a clubhouse speech to simply tell the guys to stop complaining about Scott and to just go out and play ball. I was glad he stood up because he said what I was thinking since Game One. Scott was so into the heads of some of our key guys that we were beaten before the games he pitched even started. It was pathetic.

The one big deal about losing to Scott in Game Four was that it guaranteed that the series would end in Houston, not New York. While we were a pretty good road team, you always want to have that edge you get by playing at home. Houston was also a tougher place to play because of the artificial turf, the ceiling (which made it tough to see fly balls), the size of the ballpark, and, of course, their raucous crowd. If you weren't used to all that, it put you at a disadvantage. We were a power-hitting team and the spacious Astrodome played more into their brand of baseball than it did into ours.

There was a perception that the baseball gods dealt us another bad break after Game Four. The following game was postponed by rain, allowing the great Nolan Ryan, and not Jim Deshaies, to start Game Five. But I saw it differently. Deshaies was a southpaw, which typically was a slight advantage for a team when facing all of our lefty hitters. And, personally, I had as much trouble hitting against Deshaies as any other pitcher in the National League for some reason.

Also, even though Ryan was a power pitcher, we had hitters who didn't worry about fastballs because, aside from our sluggers, we also had slap hitters, guys who could bunt, and others who could do all kinds of disruptive things on the bases to break

Ryan's rhythm. So Nolan's 100-mile-an-hour fastball didn't concern us as much as it did other clubs.

Ultimately, from both a personal and team standpoint, I thought that seeing Ryan pitch in Game Five instead of Deshaies was going to be to our advantage because we would have our best lineup out there.

The one truly bad break that did come out of the rainout was that it assured that Mike Scott would be fully rested and ready to pitch in a potential Game Seven. Despite Knight's impassioned speech in the clubhouse after Game Four, this reality made winning the next two games critical for us. If the series reached another game against Scott, we knew we would be fighting an uphill battle in that decisive game. It made winning both Games Five and Six almost imperative to us advancing to the World Series.

Game Five would turn out to be a classic and largely underrated game. It was a rematch between Gooden and Ryan. Doc was impressive for the second time in the series, giving up just one run despite yielding nine hits over ten innings. On the other side, Nolan was even better, retiring our first thirteen hitters to start the game, and allowing just two hits through nine innings while striking out twelve.

The only runs scored through eleven innings were registered in the fifth inning. The Astros took a 1–0 lead on a Doran fielder's choice and we tied it when Straw hit a solo home run down the right field line.

For the next six innings, both offenses were comatose. But with the score still tied at one a piece, we would finally break through and win it in the bottom of the twelfth when, of all people, a slumping Carter came to bat with Backman on second and Mex on first with one out. For someone of Gary's stature, even though he had gone just 1 for 21 in the series to that point, the move by Lanier to intentionally walk Keith with first base open to get to Carter was an insult. And the Kid made him pay by grounding a single up the middle off of Kerfeld to score Backman with the winning run.

For Gary, it was extra sweet that he hit the game-winner off of Kerfeld, a big goofball who showed Carter up earlier in the series when, after fielding a comebacker, he held the ball up for a moment before throwing it to first. Kerfeld wore these big glasses like the ones the Hanson brothers do in the movie *Slap Shot* and acted like he was a better pitcher than he really was. He provided plenty of motivation for us to beat him.

We realized that even though we won that game and took a 3-2 lead in the series, it was far from over. But it did move us one step closer to avoiding a Game Seven showdown against Scott. And for Gary to get that hit that won it for us was big because he had really been pressing. We needed Gary to be Gary and to stop being intimidated by the mind games Scott's scuffed baseballs were playing on him.

When that epic Game Five was over, it was the longest ever in NLCS history. But that distinction would last only one day. And for as dramatic as it was, its intensity would pale in comparison to what lay ahead in Game Six.

9

The Greatest Game Ever Played

My chest was hurting so bad, I'm surprised I didn't have a heart attack! I had been nervous before, but never had I seen my heart pounding against my jersey. It felt like I had just run a marathon and, in a sense, while standing in left field in the bottom of the sixteenth inning of Game Six of the NLCS, after nearly five hours of baseball, I had.

It was the best game I was ever a part of and probably the greatest baseball game ever played. For eight gut-wrenching innings, from the ninth until that sixteenth frame, the Astros had the last at-bat and could beat us at any time. The pressure became so great that, at one point, I was hoping if we couldn't end it quickly, the Astros would. I honestly didn't care if we lost. I thought, *Lord, please! Let's just end this one and start fresh tomorrow.* I simply couldn't take it anymore.

Coming into Game Six, none of us had an inkling of how brutal that game would be. We were confident we would close it out and return home with the pennant. We figured that as long as Scott wasn't on the mound, we could play our typical fast and loose style of baseball. Plus, we knew we had a job to finish. This was one of those rare games when we were actually thinking ahead to the next game, the one where Mike Scott would be looming if we lost. Losing was not an option because there was a legitimate fear of Scott on our ball club. We *had* to win this one. It was the *only* game of my career that I felt that way about.

As I strolled to the plate as the game's first hitter, the decibel level in the dome from the 45,000-plus screaming Houston fans was off the charts. They knew in their hearts that if their Astros could just extend this series one more game to get to their ace, they would be on their way to the first World Series in club history.

After I swung at and missed a third strike from Knepper and slowly walked back to the dugout, the noise in the Astrodome grew deafening. Then the place nearly broke the sound barrier two batters later when Knepper struck out Mex looking to end the top of the first inning. It was definitely not the way we wanted this game to start.

To make matters worse, in the bottom half of the first, the Astros were taking it to Bobby O, spraying a flurry of hits to all corners of the outfield—a leadoff single by Doran to center, a double by Garner to left, a single by Davis to center, and a single to right by Jose Cruz. When it was over, Houston had plated three runs and, if not for a missed bunt by Ashby on a suicide squeeze attempt that resulted in Carter picking off Bass at third, it could have been even worse. Even the outs were hit hard. It was clear that Bobby O was not on his game.

While there was still a lot of baseball to be played, falling behind 3–0 after one with Ojeda not looking sharp was not what we had in mind. Still, I wasn't overly concerned because we had come back from games like this so many times before.

The next seven innings were like a heavyweight title fight. After the Astros' initial blow, Bobby O settled down and retired the next ten batters he faced and didn't allow another run through five. Then, in a prelude to how big a role our bullpen was going to play in this game, Aguilera followed with three shutout innings of critical middle relief.

On the other side, Knepper was nothing short of spectacular. As he left the Astros' dugout to take the mound to start the ninth, he was working on a two-hit shutout, having given up a mere pair of singles. I had never seen superior pitching like what we saw from the Astros in that NLCS. You see a pitcher here or there that stands out, but not an *entire* starting rotation.

Houston was now three outs away from forcing a Game Seven and the nightmare scenario of us having to face Mike Scott. We were worried. We really hadn't been challenged like this all year, and now our character was about to be tested for the first time. While we entered the NLCS with a healthy respect for the Astros, they proved to be a lot better of a team than we had given them credit for. They had a three-run lead and a crafty lefty I knew they wanted to keep in there because he neutralized a lot of our best hitters. While I still thought we had a chance to break through against Knepper, since he wasn't overpowering, I was already preparing mentally for the next game.

Davey had Dykstra pinch-hit for Aggie to start the ninth against the southpaw. It was an unorthodox move by Davey because he had a small fleet of right-handed hitters on the bench, most notably HoJo, a switch-hitter. But I agreed with the strategy if Davey was thinking about saving HoJo for a long-ball opportunity. One run via a home run at that moment wasn't going to help us any more than Lenny doing what he did best— getting on base with a single or a walk.

Dykstra would hit a long fly ball to center that Hatcher may have lost sight of in the ceiling—a common hazard of life in the Astrodome for outfielders if they merely blinked—and the ball sailed past him to the wall. Lenny raced around the bases and arrived safely at third with a leadoff triple.

I came to bat next with no other strategy except to get on base any way I could, knowing that if I succeeded it would bring the tying run to the plate with the heart of the order coming up. The steady roar from the Houston crowd was now taken up a notch and echoed throughout the Astrodome. I hated playing in domes—it just seemed so unnatural. Doing my best to block out the frenzied surroundings and concentrate on the task at hand, I managed to bloop a single into right field to drive Lenny home with our first run, making it a 3–1 game. But of most importance was getting on base and bringing the tying run to the plate.

With Mitchell up, I ran on the pitch. Some may question the risk of possibly getting thrown out at second, but it was a good thing I went because it kept us out of a certain double play when Kevin grounded out to third. I really wasn't too concerned about a potential caught stealing there because Knepper didn't have a good move to first. I wouldn't have run if I wasn't 100 percent sure I could make it to second. After all, Mitchell represented the tying run and if I had gotten thrown out, it would have been devastating. But staying out of the double play was also critical, so I was running unless I got the "stop" sign from our third base coach, Bud Harrelson, which I didn't get.

That brought up Mex, who had struggled against Knepper all day. But like he did all year for us in crucial situations, he came through. Keith doubled into the right center field gap to score me from second to cut the lead to 3–2. Now I was thinking we were in a manageable situation to tie the game.

Playing the matchups, Lanier pulled Knepper in favor of his closer, Dave Smith, to face the right-handed-hitting Carter. After working the count full, Gary walked to put runners on first and second base. That brought up Straw with a chance to blow things open with one swing.

You could now sense that the crowd, which just moments before was euphoric with the anticipation of a Game Seven, was feeling it all slip away. The tension built with every pitch to Straw and the count, keeping up with the drama of the game, appropriately went full. But Smith didn't give in to Darryl and walked him to load the bases.

Now things were getting very interesting. With still only one out, not only could we tie the game without the benefit of a hit, but we could take the lead with a single.

Tensions were running very high and started boiling over after Knight took a very close pitch with two strikes that home plate umpire Fred Brocklander called a ball. In fact, a fight almost broke out between Astros shortstop Dickie Thon and Knight after Ray started hollering at Ashby behind the plate to stop complaining about the umpire's calls. Knight was a keg of dynamite under normal circumstances, but now he was on fire.

After peace was restored, Ray came through with a sacrifice fly to right field that scored Mex from third to tie the game at 3–3, with Straw and Gary advancing to second and third, respectively.

Now I was thinking we were going to win. You don't come all the way back from three runs down in the ninth and lose. Especially us. It just wasn't something we did. In fact, even with two outs, I thought we were going to pull ahead right there. Everything was in place.

Lanier decided to walk Wally intentionally to load the bases to bring up Santana. The move shocked and thrilled me at the same time. Hal had to know that Danny Heep was sitting on the bench ready to pinch-hit for Raffy. Now we had one of the best left-handed pinch hitters in the game facing the right-handed Smith with the bases drunk. It was Lanier's second highly questionable move of the inning, the first being when he brought in Smith, who didn't put any fear in anybody, to replace Knepper.

Danny worked the count full. We were just *one* pitch out of the strike zone away from taking the lead. But maybe Hal knew what he was doing by walking Backman, because Heep struck out swinging to end the inning. But we had come back from the dead and I was happy to be in the position we were in. I liked our chances with our bullpen, our bench, and our explosive offense in an extra-inning game. But first we had to get through the bottom of the ninth.

At this point, Mets Nation was captivated. When we tied the game, it was rush hour back home in New York. Millions of fans realized that one run by either team could potentially end the game.

I didn't have many friends in Manhattan because I lived ninety minutes away by the Jersey shore. But Ronnie likes to tell a great story that his friends from the city told him. Outside a Crazy Eddie electronics store, there were fifteen rows of people watching the game from in front of its window. After each play, those in the first row would shout out what was going on to the back row. The crowd was so deep, it went into the first two lanes of traffic and cars were forced to drive around them. No one wanted to leave the city and miss the end of the game. Between innings, bartenders were bringing them beer in plastic cups while they watched the game. Even Yankee fans were into it because it was their city, too. Ronnie's friends said they never saw anything like that in their lives. It was one of those real New York moments.

It just amazed me how much the entire city was behind our club.

McDowell entered the game in the bottom of the ninth. Roger was unmatched as a versatile reliever. He could go long as well as close out games. He had 14 wins for us that year and actually ended up seventeenth in the National League MVP voting—unheard of for a long reliever. But everybody saw how he excelled in his role for us. Still, for as great a season as he had, there was concern. He really struggled against Houston for some reason, losing to them three times.

But on this day, Roger would come through in a big way. Not only did he breeze through the heart of the Astros' lineup in the ninth, but Roger would go on to blank Houston through the next four innings as well. By giving up only one hit and no walks, McDowell's performance may have been the best relief pitching under extreme pressure I ever witnessed.

Houston's relievers were just as tough, not even allowing a hit over four frames, as the trio of Smith, Larry Andersen, and Aurelio Lopez held us scoreless through the thirteenth inning. By this point, I was beginning to wonder if this game would *ever* end! I was just done! I was thinking, *Enough already! We're wasting all this energy and we may have to play tomorrow!*

My biggest concern was the fact that we had burned Aguilera and McDowell and would be in big trouble in a potential Game Seven if we needed our bullpen. As this game went on, *we* were the ones becoming a weakened team. If we had to lose, I wanted us to lose quickly. Houston didn't have that concern, as they likely would have used Scott in a decisive game until his arm fell off. I'll bet Scott was lounging on a couch somewhere hoping the game would go twenty-five innings.

But in the fourteenth inning, we finally broke through. Wally's one-out single scored Straw with the go-ahead run to make it 4–3. Relief! Now we just had to hold the Astros scoreless in the bottom half of the inning and this marathon of a game would be over with.

Davey brought in Jesse to try to finish off Houston. McDowell had been magnificent, but five innings is a lot of work for a reliever no matter how well he pitched. Maybe Roger could have squeezed one more inning out of his arm, but Jesse was "the guy." I had no issue with Davey's move.

The decision to bring in Jesse looked good at the outset, as he struck out Doran to start the bottom of the fourteenth. One out. Two more to go.

Next up was Hatcher, certainly not a home run threat, as he had hit just eight in almost 600 at-bats during the regular season. No one could have predicted what was about to happen next. But as Game Six proved again and again, whatever could happen did happen.

With the count full, Hatcher hooked a liner down the left field line. I gave chase, but it would hit the screen of the foul pole for a game-tying home run. I was stunned. Now, for the first time since we tied the game in the ninth, some doubt about our chances of winning the game entered my mind. After all, we had the right guy on the mound to close it out facing three guys in their lineup who didn't have a lot of power. I figured as long as no one got on base and Glenn Davis didn't come up to bat, under normal circumstances, we should have been good to go. But I realized by this point that this game was anything but normal. I was thinking that maybe it just wasn't meant to be for us.

Another concern I had was with Orosco. I was wondering if, by the way Hatcher crushed his fastball, he had it that day or if we would have to replace him and go even deeper into our bullpen. But then I wasn't sure if I trusted the other guys more than our closer in that kind of pressure-packed situation. I was also wondering if Davey should leave Jesse in the game if he got through the inning without giving up any more runs. The problem with leaving him in was that any more work and Orosco probably wouldn't be available the next day.

Things just didn't feel good to me. Maybe that's why my chest was starting to hurt.

Jesse would get through the inning, retiring Denny Walling and Davis, no small feat when considering the two represented most of the power in the Astros' lineup.

After we went down in the top of the fifteenth, Davey had clearly made his decision to put it all on the line in this game, electing to have Jesse pitch a second inning of relief. A closer was typically used for protecting a lead and usually not for more than one inning. But Davey, like the rest of us, realized the critical nature of winning that game. And, at least for that bottom of the fifteenth inning, the strategy worked. Jesse was phenomenal, striking out Bass and Cruz swinging before getting Ashby to hit an inning-ending groundout to Backman.

We realized we were on borrowed time by this point with a near-depleted bullpen. There was a great urgency to put a run up on the scoreboard in our half of the sixteenth inning.

Straw started things off by hitting a high fly ball to center off Lopez that Hatcher misplayed into a double. I can't overemphasize how tough it was to catch fly balls in the Astrodome, even if it was your home park, like it was Hatcher's.

That brought up Knight in an obvious sacrifice bunt situation. But Davey hated giving up outs and, with Ray not being a very good bunter, elected to have him swing away instead. The strategy worked as Knight singled to right field. Bass's throw home to get Straw was late and Ray advanced to second base. Now we not only had a 5–4 lead, but also an insurance run in scoring position with nobody out.

Lanier replaced Lopez with Jeff Calhoun to face Backman. Perhaps feeling the pressure from the enormity of the moment, Calhoun somewhat unraveled. He promptly threw a wild pitch to advance Knight to third base. Then, after walking Wally, he threw another wild pitch to score Ray and move Backman to second. We now led 6–4.

We scored yet again when, after Jesse sacrificed Wally to third, Lenny ripped an RBI single to right to give us a three-run cushion at 7–4. I ended the inning by grounding into a double play, but it hardly seemed to matter. We had, at least temporarily, sucked the life out of the Astrodome and ripped the heart out of the Astros.

Now I was thinking it was finally over. My chest was telling me the same thing. It might still have been aching, but at least it wasn't pounding like it was earlier.

With a lot of breathing room, we took the field for the bottom of the sixteenth inning. With Jesse out there for his third inning of relief, it was obvious that Davey was going to stick with his guy until the end no matter what the outcome.

Jesse started off the inning by striking out Craig Reynolds. One out. Two to go. But then things started to get interesting yet again. Pinch hitter Davey Lopes walked and the Astros had the top of their order coming up. Doran singled to center on Jesse's first pitch to put runners on first and second with Hatcher coming up. Like Doran, Hatcher swung at Orosco's first offering and singled to center to score Lopes to cut our lead to 7–5.

Now Houston had the tying runs on base and the winning run at the plate in Denny Walling. Denny didn't concern me too much as a guy who could put one over the fence but, then again, neither had Hatcher. At worst, Denny was the kind of guy who could drive one into the gap, so I wanted to be sure to play deep enough so Hatcher, who represented the tying run, wouldn't be able to score from first on a hit.

To no one's surprise, the crowd was back into the game in a big way. Still, I liked our chances. Orosco could be tough on lefties and this matchup somewhat neutralized Walling. Jesse went right after him and, after getting two quick strikes, induced a ground ball to Mex, who threw down to second to get the force on Hatcher. We didn't get the double play that would have ended the game on that ground ball, but the good news for us was that we now needed just one out to win the game. The bad news was that Glenn Davis, Houston's only legitimate home run threat, was coming to the plate with runners on the corners and a chance to win the game with one swing. This was also not a good matchup for us, considering that Davis hit from the right side.

After falling behind in the count 0-1, Davis ripped yet another Astros' single to center to score Doran, move Walling into scoring position, and cut our lead to 7–6. Now the Astros were really in business, but I remember thinking, *Well, at least Davis only hit a single.* Prior to his at-bat, I would have happily taken a single in exchange for the dangerous prospect of his going deep, so in that respect there was relief that he kept the ball in the ballpark.

At this point, all bets were off. Jesse was overextended and I didn't have a strong sense he could shut down the Astros' rally. I am sure he was tired and fatigued at that point and I wondered if Davey was giving even slight consideration to bringing in either Doug Sisk or Randy Niemann to get the last out. But Davey wasn't moving in the Mets dugout and it was apparent he was putting all of his chips on Jesse. While Orosco didn't show any of the typical signs of nervousness on the mound, I certainly did while standing out there in left field. I was never more nervous on a ball field.

With Bass at the plate, and runners on first and second, our outfielders were now positioned even deeper than before so Davis, now representing the winning run, would not score on a hit. We would concede the tying run with a Bass single, but we wanted to make sure it would take two hits instead of just one to beat us.

While I wished I could have seen Gary's signs to Jesse from left field to better position myself in the outfield, I knew Orosco was either going to throw fastballs away or sliders down and in. The slider was Jesse's signature pitch, and he would use it frequently in this matchup.

Bass, a solid hitter who could spray the ball to all sections of the park, worked the count full in a prolific at-bat. The tension in the Astrodome was overwhelming. With everybody on their feet, the roar of the crowd grew louder and louder as Jesse delivered from the stretch. Going with his best, Orosco threw a hard slider that Bass could only wave at. Strike three!

As I watched Carter raise both of his arms in triumph and Jesse throw his glove as high as he could above his head, I shouted at the top of my lungs, "Thank God!" and raced in from left field to join my teammates at the mound to celebrate. It was a release of pure jubilation and a tremendous sense of relief. After sixteen innings of gut-wrenching baseball, Game Six was in the history books. No Game Seven. No Mike Scott. Now we could celebrate and wait to see if we would be playing the California Angels or Boston Red Sox in the World Series.

In retrospect, no game should ever be that tough. But to this day, I have an amazing appreciation for having been a part of it. It truly was baseball perfection—the game of games. Would I ever want to go through it again? Surprisingly, I think I would. As crazy as that may seem, playing in a game like that really defined what our club was all about. Of course, I would only want to go through it again if the outcome was the same.

To no one's surprise, we had a victory party on the plane ride home that was legendary. Because it was the playoffs, the team allowed wives and girlfriends on the flight and they were engaged in the celebration just as much as the players. It was the one time all season where everybody was a member of the Scum Bunch. After all, we had just climbed the highest mountain we possibly could together and, for one night, we were all the same. While I drank my usual 7UP and ginger ale, I was laughing just like the rest of them as they drank heavily and clowned around with one another.

After a while I returned to my seat to be with Rosa. Leaving the celebration and not having a beer didn't keep me from being considered one of the guys. My identity and religious convictions—what I would do, what I wouldn't do, what I would tolerate, and what I wouldn't—were already established from my length of time with the club. I was kind of an untouchable from being mocked thanks to my veteran status. On my side, I didn't shun the guys because I didn't drink. I made a conscious effort not to separate myself from my teammates. That was because they weren't just my teammates, they were *good* teammates. They respected me and never questioned anything I did or didn't do. They never tried to force me to drink anything. They didn't mind if I just ordered a ginger ale. I really loved them for that because it could have been a very different situation. They could have viewed me as thinking I was better than they were. The reality was that, for me, drinking was something I had just decided not to do. I never drank my whole life.

As the flight wore on, Rosa noticed how some of the wives were just as drunk as their husbands and I told her, "Well, how often do they get to celebrate together?"

But then things started getting a little wild and out of hand. I began to hear *snap, snap, snap!* Some of the guys were breaking seats so they could lay them flat and play cards on them—a complete disregard for the airline's property. I thought that as happy as we were, there were certain things that under any circumstance you shouldn't do—destroying property that doesn't belong to you being one of them. That was going overboard. I didn't realize the extent of the damage our chartered United Airlines plane sustained until later.

I have often wondered that if Game Six, and the whole

NLCS for that matter, wasn't as intense and long as it was, if the players would have reacted in the same raucous way on the flight home. My guess is that it wouldn't have been nearly as crazy.

Winning that series felt every bit as much like surviving as it did being victorious. It was hard-fought from the start. We had our 1–0 loss in Game One. Then we came back from four runs down in Game Three. Scott got into our heads in Game Four. And then there was the extra-inning classic in Game Five. So while it may have been inexcusable to destroy property, after playing sixteen innings in Game Six, maybe it's somewaht understandable if some of those guys wanted to let off a little steam. Perhaps I could have used a lesson in letting out more of my emotions instead of keeping them bottled up inside. Maybe then my chest wouldn't have hurt so bad.

The infamous flight would eventually land safely in New York and the team had a couple of days to recover from all the partying and nurse their hangovers. Despite popular theory, all the drinking would have absolutely no effect on how the club would be prepared for the upcoming World Series. Our guys were used to coming right out of bars and going to the ball field without any sleep. The only risk we faced was spending too much time admiring our epic victory over Houston and not enough preparing ourselves properly to play the Boston Red Sox, who finished off the Angels hours after our game ended.

Back in our clubhouse prior to the start of the World Series three days later, Davey gave a pre-game speech. Holding up a bill sent by United Airlines in the amount of $7,500 for the damage done to the plane on the trip back from Houston, he began item-

THE GREATEST GAME EVER PLAYED   187

izing, in a very serious tone, everything the team had broken on the plane. At this point, I thought to myself, *I ain't paying for no broken seat.* Of course, it would have been within Davey's rights to say, "You guys tore up the plane, now you pay for it."

But he didn't.

Instead, he surprised us all by saying if we took care of the Red Sox, all would be forgiven, then turned to his right, tore up the bill and tossed it in the trash. Everyone in the clubhouse cheered with approval. I'm sure Frank Cashen was incensed by this maneuver, but by doing what he did, if Davey hadn't earned every player's trust before, he definitely did at that very moment. It showed us that Davey was in our corner and not management's. I think that's what players always liked about him the most.

Davey Johnson had made it abundantly clear to us all that we could do no wrong as long as we kept on winning. It was great motivation for us with the World Series just hours away.

10

A Tale of Two Cities

t was the World Series matchup the networks dreamed about. The big, bad, arrogant New Yorkers from the largest media market in the country going up against one of baseball's oldest and storied franchises.

From our standpoint, the Red Sox were a passing thought, a mere formality. After winning 108 regular season games and then beating Mike Scott's Astros in a grueling NLCS, we really had no game plan at all for Boston. While the pressure to win was more on us because of all we had achieved to that point, we entered the World Series thinking there was no way we could lose.

Meanwhile, the Red Sox were coming off their own riveting league championship series—a seven-game ALCS that included two extra-inning affairs—against the Angels. In fact, Boston was just one strike away from elimination in Game Five, the Donnie Moore Game, when Dave Henderson hit a two-run home run off Moore to give the Red Sox a 6–5 lead. After the Angels tied it in the bottom of the inning, Boston put the game away in the eleventh inning on a Henderson sacrifice fly and won it, 7–6. The Red Sox won the next two games in Boston to take the series. Sadly, Moore was never fully able to get past the devastation of that defeat and would take his own life less than three years later.

Despite the feeling of fate seemingly working in the Red Sox' favor, they had their own history and demons to overcome, hurdles the media in both cities brought up incessantly. Boston had gone sixty-eight years without a World Series championship, losing their last three appearances all in 7 games. And then there was the Bucky Dent Game against the Yankees that ended their 1978 season after they led New York by 14 games at one point. The Boston media, which could be vicious at times, blamed the way losing always seemed to find the Red Sox in the most heartbreaking ways on the "Curse of the Bambino," a term created to remind their fans how the team foolishly sold Babe Ruth to the Yankees for $100,000 in 1919. Still, as I would soon find out, even with all the losing over the years, their fans were just as passionate and crazy as ours.

While I *knew* we were the best team in baseball, I still couldn't believe we were actually *in* the World Series. After all the early down years with the Mets, the sudden turnaround in really just two seasons was dizzying. We went from being so bad to so good at warp speed.

As you might expect, I was a little nervous and anxious about being in a World Series. I had watched many of them on television and heard people talk about them, but to actually experience one as a participant was incredible. The thing that stood out over everything else was the intense media surge. It was almost unbearable. Everywhere you went, there was a microphone in your face. It was a challenge making sure you didn't say the wrong thing. You really had to think things through before opening your mouth.

The only way to avoid the media was to play the actual games and, on a cool October 18 evening at Shea, Game One was played before a sell-out crowd of over 55,000. Davey inserted me in the leadoff spot against Red Sox starter Bruce Hurst. The southpaw had three good pitches—a fastball that ran away from you, a good change-up, and a breaking ball that went down. His fastball was a little better than most of the left-handers we faced, though I wouldn't consider him a power pitcher. But it was just decent enough to keep you honest. We were aware of Hurst's talent but, with our success against lefties that year, we weren't concerned about it.

Maybe we should have been.

Hurst would limit us to just four hits and no runs over eight innings in Game One en route to a 1–0 Red Sox victory. Bruce did an outstanding job of neutralizing some of the major left-handed cogs in our offensive machine—Lenny, Straw, and Mex—not giving up a hit to any of them. All four of our hits came from our right-handed hitters—me, Carter, and two from Teufel.

For at least one game, the Red Sox strategy against us—to

keep a lefty out on the mound as much as possible—worked. Only Carter, Knight, and, when in the lineup, Mitchell, gave us any power to match up against a good left-hander like Hurst. John McNamara planned to have Hurst go one more game in the series and then pray for a rainout so he could pitch him a third time.

Our defeat wasted an equally brilliant effort by Darling. Ronnie was on that night, displaying great command over the location of his pitches and showing good movement on his fastball. He was simply overpowering, striking out eight and only giving up three hits over seven innings. When he had his control, Ronnie was as tough a pitcher as there was in the game.

The lone run of the game came in the top of the seventh when Jim Rice led the inning off with a walk and then advanced to second on a wild pitch. Then, with one out, Rich Gedman bounced a routine grounder toward Teuf that went right through his legs to score Rice.

Tim was my buddy, but I didn't say anything special to him after his miscue during or after the game. Teuf was no different from any of the other guys. He felt awful about making the error but didn't need every other guy coming up to him, offering him encouragement, saying stuff like "Hang in there," or "You'll get 'em next time." He knew we felt badly for him. Besides, we had to get ready for the next game and didn't have the time to worry about it anyway.

Still, as much as Tim wanted to forget about the error, it came up the next day in, of all places, our team chapel service. Typically, the same Mets attended every Sunday—Gary, Teuf, Raffy, Knight, Aguilera, myself, and, on occasion, Mitchell. You never saw Lenny, Wally, or any of the Scum Bunch. Father Dan Murphy was our team chaplain and, in trying to help give some perspective on the task at hand, said, "You have to take the good with the bad. Some days you're Bruce Hurst and other days you're like Timmy!"

While it may have seemed somewhat inappropriate for Father Dan to say that with Teuf sitting right there, I think in his own way he was trying to make light of something that had just happened. Even at the time, it didn't seem like anything out of place. He wasn't throwing hidden remarks at Timmy or anything like that. Instead, he was just referencing the error to make a point, since it was the glaring play in Game One. Father Dan knew how a loss could put a player in a really bad place. His point was that losing isn't the worst thing in the world. You just try to do your best and sometimes you're going to fail—something I learned from my father early on.

If a New York–Boston World Series was what the media wanted, then the Game Two matchup of Doc versus Roger Clemens was the ultimate pitchers' duel they craved. The hype for this game was like none other in recent memory. Gooden and Clemens had been the starting pitchers for their respective leagues in the All-Star Game earlier in July. Doc was the NL Cy Young Award winner in '85 and had always mastered Shea, making it an event whenever he took the mound there. Roger was the bright young star for the Red Sox and the winner of the AL Cy Young Award and MVP that year. These were the two elite young hurlers in baseball—two power pitchers going at it. Everyone, including myself, figured it to be the game of games, man!

But not too long into it, I was disappointed. Everybody was. With all the buildup, both guys probably went out there emotionally spent and had nothing left for the game. Roger threw a little better than Doc, but nothing like what we expected. He was surprisingly very hittable and didn't seem to be at all like the unhittable pitcher we had all heard about.

Doc was shockingly bad, giving up three runs in the third to put us in a 3–0 hole. It didn't get any better from there. After we battled back to cut the lead to 3–2, Gooden surrendered a solo home run to Henderson in the fourth and a two-run blast to Dwight Evans in the fifth to fall behind 6–2. Davey took him out after just five innings.

Doc just wasn't himself. After having been so good against Houston the week before, it was like he wasn't even the same pitcher that night. He seemed uneasy, sweated more than usual, and couldn't seem to get into any kind of rhythm on the mound. I can't say it was nerves, because that kid pitched all year in big situations, when most young players his age were still in the minor leagues trying to find their way. He just physically did not have anything that night and I think he knew it. If it was fatigue, that would have been odd because he had an extra day's rest to get ready for the game. Perhaps the expectations, even for Doc, may have been set too high. The Red Sox, after all, were a good-hitting club. Or Doc, as we know now from his recent admissions in his own memoirs, may have been battling the effects of his drug use throughout that '86 season. But who knows? It could have just been one of those things.

Whatever it was, it was the only time in his young career where it seemed like he was very unsure of himself.

I didn't start Game Two—Heep started in my place in left— but entered the game in the sixth as part of a double switch after Doc was taken out of the game. Since it was the World Series and I didn't want to cause a distraction, I didn't talk to Davey about my benching, but I was pretty disappointed. I would have loved to have started in that game. But then again, since I wasn't playing against all the righties we faced anyway, I guess Davey thought that keeping me out against Clemens, one of the best in the game, was the right move. Plus, Heep gave us a little more pop in the lineup. But I also kept quiet because, since Johnson and I had already had our issues throughout the season with my playing time, I didn't want to beat a dead horse. Besides, I correctly antic- ipated there would be a time when he would use me in the game.

In another move, HoJo started in place of Ray at third. Ray was upset but, unlike me, he decided to make it known to anyone who would listen. Ray's argument was that he had the experience factor over HoJo, which was critical in a World Series. While Ray would probably be the first to acknowledge that HoJo had lightning in his bat, he felt he displayed what he could do in a tough series like the one we just had against Houston. Ray started every one of those six games against the Astros and Game One of the World Series. So not starting in Game Two with us down 1–0 against Clemens didn't make much sense to him. I understood his way of thinking, but when you're getting near the end of your career like he was, every move against you feels like a threat. He had to deal with that throughout the regular season, too. There were times when he would tell Davey if it continued that he wanted out. And to add fuel to the fire, I don't believe Davey consulted Ray before making this latest move. I know Johnson didn't consult with me. But Ray being disappointed was as far as it went. I think management felt the third base position was going to be HoJo's job soon enough anyway.

The only chance we had to get back into Game Two before things got out of hand was in the bottom of the fourth, down 4–2. With runners on first and second and Doc due up to hit—and laboring on the mound—I fully expected to grab a bat and pinch-hit for Gooden. But Davey inexplicably allowed Doc to hit instead. Doc would ground out slowly to Buckner at first to end our threat. I was very surprised Davey stuck with Doc in that situation. When you talk about games that managers can affect with their decisions, this was one of those times. You have to try to make something happen, even if you ultimately don't succeed. We had already lost the first game, taking away our home field advantage along with it. But if we could split the first two at Shea with a win in Game Two, we would still be in good shape. As it turned out, Doc only pitched one more inning anyway.

The Red Sox also hit our bullpen very hard that night. When it was all said and done, Boston had pummeled us for 18 hits on their way to a 9–3 rout. By not taking advantage and beating Clemens at his worst, we were now down 2-0 in the World Series. I was stunned. I did not think any team, much less the Red Sox, would come into Shea and beat us twice. Granted, the first game was a close one, but they really beat us badly in Game Two. And worse yet, they beat our best pitcher.

We had put ourselves in a situation where we had to go up to Boston and try to win at least two. There was a lot of second-guessing in our clubhouse. I thought we had an opportunity to win that second game but didn't try hard enough.

As for the bullpen's rare failure in Game Two, although we only used McDowell in Game One, I think those guys were still a little emotionally spent from the Houston series and the Red Sox caught them by surprise. Our bullpen just couldn't regroup quickly enough mentally.

But I think, as a team, our failings were due to much more than being mentally fatigued from the NLCS. We were also just too arrogant to accept that there was another team playing, too. We didn't take the Red Sox seriously enough and now we were paying the price. So you compound those two factors and you can see how we ended up in a 2-0 hole. Our shield of invincibility was gone.

The media, of course, was quick to let us know that only one team in the history of the World Series, dating back to 1903, had lost the first two games at home and went on to win the series. The press was just stating a fact, but I took it kind of personally. I thought they were making a point like, *"Hey, you guys think you're going to come back and win now? Maybe you're not as good as you thought you were."*

Surprisingly, our team's morale was better after a day off before Game Three. Davey had canceled our workout at Fenway Park the day we arrived in Boston, which really showed that he had confidence in us. It was like Davey was saying we didn't need the extra work, that we would be fine. Initially, I felt we needed to get to

Fenway to get used to the ballpark. But I soon realized it was a great move not going because it's easy to start overanalyzing things. In some cases, like this one, it's best to simply stay away. Davey wanted us to just sit back—no working on our swings, no working on pitches—and come to the ballpark the next day, take some BP, and play.

Davey, however, did go to Fenway on our day off and took the heat for us by dealing with all the negative questions from the media. If the rest of the team had been in the ballpark, there would have been a zillion reporters there just drilling into us that we were down 2-0 and asking questions like, *"Are you worried?"* or *"Are you concerned?"* But Davey kept us away from all of that.

I had my family with me, so it was easy to relax. We walked around town, went to Copley Place and did some shopping. It was nice to get away from baseball for a day.

Before Game Three, the Mets' advance scout and, ironically enough, the last manager to take the Red Sox to the World Series in 1975, Darrell Johnson, hit fungoes to me in left field so I could better judge the bounces coming off the Green Monster and practice the short throws in to second base. It was the type of drill you did whenever you went to an unfamiliar ballpark on the road.

I found left field at Fenway very easy to play. I don't know why people say it's such a challenge. You only really have to stand in one spot. If the ball is hit behind you and hits halfway up the wall, you just turn right around and it comes straight back to you. And if the ball is hit high off the wall, it's going to come straight down. That's all there is to it. Carl Yastrzemski was given way too much credit for the way he manned left field at Fenway all those years because it definitely wasn't difficult. It's just a matter of having a sense of the bounces the ball takes off the wall and an understanding where you are on the field in relation to them.

And that was my thing in the drill I did with Darrell. I wanted to know where and how deep I should position myself. I ended up giving the Red Sox hitters a lot of line in that ballpark because there was barely any foul territory. Anything hit in the corner was going to bounce right back onto the field. I would put what I learned to good use, getting a key assist the next night.

Game Three was a return to Boston for Bobby O. With the exceptions of Hurst and Rich Gedman, he basically hated much of the Red Sox organization from the top down. But despite how much Bobby wanted that game, he didn't seem any more intense than usual. That surprised me a little bit, because it's normal for a guy to want to sometimes do too much to prove to the team that traded him that they made a mistake. But he was really focused on what he wanted to do and the results were outstanding, as he held Boston to just one run on five hits over seven innings.

Outspoken Red Sox pitcher Oil Can Boyd, on the other hand, had a lot to say to the press about us before the game. But with him, half the stuff he said you just passed on as nonsense. He didn't give us any bulletin board material from his comments about how he could master us. There are certain people that say things and you just kind of shrug and say, "Okay, whatever." And then there are other people who say stuff and you pay attention.

Oil Can was one of those guys you didn't pay *any* attention to. He was a little nuts and that's being mild.

Knowing that Oil Can could be a loose cannon, some of our guys weren't bashful about shouting out anything they could to rattle Boyd while he was on the mound. The one that may have actually worked was when they started replacing "Oil Can" with "Shit Can." The goal was to get inside of Oil Can's head and make him angry enough to do more than what he was capable of doing.

We had some of the best bench jockeys in baseball. They could come up with some great lines. I often wondered how they came up with half the stuff they did. While Keith was a master at manipulation, HoJo was the biggest antagonizer we had on the bench. HoJo would come out with stuff that I couldn't believe. He was great. You might not think so because of his mild manner and how he looked, but he was.

We made a major statement by getting four straight hits to start the game. Dykstra led things off with a home run. Then after Wally and Mex singled, Gary doubled in Backman to make it 2–0. Heep singled home Mex and Carter later in the inning to increase the lead to 4–0 before Bobby O ever took the mound. We never looked back and won easily, 7–1.

Bobby would tell me years later when we coached together at Single-A Port St. Lucie that it was his greatest triumph on the baseball diamond.

Despite still holding a 2-1 series lead, Johnny Mac had to endure criticism from some in the Boston media for not bringing Hurst back on short rest to pitch Game Four. Instead, he opted to go with Al Nipper, who was just 10-12 during the regular season. But unlike some people, it didn't surprise me that McNamara didn't go for the jugular. The Red Sox were still up a game and it wasn't a time of desperation for them. It wouldn't have been a very strategic move to bring Hurst back then. If you do, you're basically telling your team, *"You have to win this game. Because if you don't, you're done."*

Davey, however, sensing the urgency of taking at least one of the last two in Boston, did bring back Ronnie on short rest instead of pitching Sid Fernandez. It surprised me a little bit that Davey didn't go with El Sid in that game, or for that matter, *any* other game in the Series. But I understood the thinking that, especially in the postseason, you try to go with your top three starting pitchers. Besides, Ronnie had pitched so well in Game One and was the kind of guy who didn't always need the full four or five days' rest anyway. And having Sid in the bullpen was a luxury because, aside from Orosco, our closer, we didn't have a big left-handed contingency. Niemann, our only other lefty, was more of a short reliever—two batters maximum. But Fernandez could give us multiple innings and we all knew that could prove valuable if one of our starters faltered. It was the same from the right side with Aguilera. Because he was used primarily as a starter during the regular season, he was capable of giving us innings from the bullpen as well.

Despite battling bouts of wildness, Ronnie overcame giving up six bases on balls and came through for us again, tossing seven shutout innings as we rolled to another easy victory, 6–2.

Gary had two home runs to start and finish our scoring, with

Lenny hitting a memorable home run in between that popped out of Evans's glove and into the right field bullpen.

Now we were really rolling! The Sox had come into our stadium and took two and then we returned the favor in their park, smacking them in the face real hard. With Boston thinking they *had* to win one at Fenway, the pressure was squarely back on them now. Plus, how could their history of blowing leads *not* be on their minds at this point? With the Boston media to help remind them, I'm quite sure it was.

I felt really good about our prospects in Game Five. Even though Hurst was going for the Sox, I felt he probably pitched as well as he could in Game One and would have a hard time duplicating that effort. Plus, we were emotionally back where we wanted to be. Our guys were being aggressive again. The momentum of the series had clearly shifted back into our favor.

As for Doc, I felt he would bounce back from the poor outing he had in his last start and pitch really well despite the short rest. Plus, the short left field at Fenway typically favored right-handers and could wreak havoc on southpaws. I liked the matchup and thought we were sitting pretty.

As it turned out, even though Hurst would not pitch as well as he did in his first game against us, this time giving up ten hits, he scattered them well over nine innings and went the distance in a 4–2 Red Sox win.

Doc, once again, was pretty bad, giving up nine hits and four runs in just the four innings he pitched for us that night. He didn't seem to have any confidence in his fastball and tried to get by with his secondary pitch, the curveball, which didn't work out well, either. Whenever a pitcher isn't comfortable with his fastball, and that's their number one pitch, they're in trouble. That's because the alternative, a breaking ball, is very easy to adjust to when you know it's coming. As a result, the Red Sox were sitting on that pitch and hitting it hard.

Like in Game Two, Dwight didn't appear to be himself. In fact, it clearly wasn't the same Doc we had watched over the previous couple of years or even during the '86 regular season and NLCS. He had gone away from what made him great—a good, hard, elevating fastball complemented by Lord Charles, the nickname given to his outstanding curveball by his teammates.

Looking back at it now, I don't see how his pitching on short rest in Game Five would have adversely affected him as much as some thought it might have. Short rest may make you go a few less innings or even take a little off your fastball, but to be totally out of it like Doc was, to not even be close to the pitcher he had been just a couple of weeks before, made you think that maybe there was something else going on. If not knowing the information out there now about Dwight's downward spiral into drug use, you could chalk it up to having a bad run. But Doc was a shell of himself in those two games and looked as bad as he pitched. I still wonder if Doc's off-the-field drug use impacted his performance when he pitched those games.

Losing Game Five was very disappointing. When we arrived in Boston, winning two out of three was the goal. But once we took the first two up there, we then wanted all three. Still, since we had accomplished our overall goal in Boston, I was pleased with our effort and confident we would go back to Shea and wouldn't play as poorly as we had earlier in the Series. We would be better prepared than we were for the first two games.

It was now time to play Game Six, a classic that would forever impact the lives of two ballplayers in a profound way.

And force a Game Seven.

11

Top of the World

The Red Sox were finished. All we had to do was look in their eyes during batting practice prior to Game Seven. So devastating a defeat was Game Six for them that Boston was done before the game even began.

It hardly mattered that they had received a big break the day before, when McNamara's prayers were answered and a rainout allowed them to start Hurst in place of Oil Can in the decisive game. But as far as we were concerned, Hurst pitching didn't worry us in the least. We pounded ten hits off Bruce the last time we saw him, but simply didn't get the key hits off him at the right time. It's not like he was an overpowering lefty like Sandy Koufax. While he was a good pitcher, he didn't have that one dominant pitch with which he could say, *"Here it is. Try to hit it."*

In any event, all that truly mattered was the battered psyche of the Red Sox after we rallied back from a two-run deficit with no outs and nobody on in the fateful tenth inning of Game Six. In my mind, that was truly the deciding game of the series.

To their credit, the Red Sox came out swinging in Game Seven and actually took a 3–0 lead in the second inning, thanks to back-to-back home runs from Dwight Evans and Rich Gedman to start the inning and an RBI single by Wade Boggs. Gedman's home run had me and Straw racing toward the wall in right center field. Straw leaped high for the ball and, for a brief moment, I thought he caught it, but the ball popped out of his glove and went over the fence. Straw did everything perfectly on that play, timing his leap just right, but his glove kind of went limp as it went back to catch the ball and it trickled out. I was thinking, *Ahhhh, man, that would have been a really big play.*

Straw was no longer feeling the sting from being pulled from Game Six in that double switch Davey had made. Maybe the extra day helped him forget about it, because with Darryl, if it still bothered him, everybody would know. To put it mildly, Straw was never good at hiding his feelings.

Even though we were down 3–0 after two innings, we were still riding high off of Game Six. It was going to take more than three runs early in the game to bring us down. It was nothing. I was thinking, *We survived Game Six! Three runs? You've got to do better than that to beat us!*

I know that may seem a little arrogant, but when I looked at the Sox faces in their dugout, they still seemed out of it. I could see it in their body language. They didn't look or act like a team that was winning a ball game. I've seen teams celebrate and go crazy when they score just one run. But they had *three*! Boston just had a look that screamed, *"We've been here before. What's going to happen to us now?"*

From that point on, it seemed like the Red Sox were playing "not to lose," like a football team at the end of a game playing prevent defense. That's a real bad feeling, waiting for the other shoe to drop. I don't think I've ever seen a team play like Boston did in that Game Seven—winning on the scoreboard, yet losing in their minds.

On our side, Ronnie was starting his third game of the series. But unlike his first two starts, he wasn't nearly as effective in Game Seven. Still, Darling was the best pitcher we had to go in that game. Even though he gave up those three early runs, I was confident we would get them back. I knew Hurst was not going to shut us down because, if given a chance to face the same pitcher, even a tough lefty like Bruce, three times in nine days, we were going to adjust and score some runs.

Sid came in to relieve Ronnie with two outs in the fourth and was nothing short of sensational, holding the Red Sox hitless through the sixth, while striking out four. This was on the heels of Sid's four shutout innings of relief in Game Five. Sid had 200 strikeouts in '86 and won 16 games for us. While you want to go with your three best pitchers in the World Series, no one would have complained if Sid had started Game Seven. I don't know what the decision-making process was and why they didn't insert Sid into *any* of the seven games, but I would speculate it was because Davey wanted to make sure he had long relievers from both the left-handed and right-handed side for whenever a double switch came into play. It certainly kept the Red Sox at bay with Sid and Aggie out there in the pen.

While nobody can argue with Davey's thinking on that, I can't help but wonder if Sid had started one of those earlier games if it would have made a difference. For example, if Sid started Game Four, then Ronnie could have started Game Five on full rest in place of Doc, who looked worn out in his previous start. While it was a luxury to have Sid in long relief, perhaps we made a move we didn't need to in bringing Ronnie back on short rest. Maybe we would have won all three games in Boston. But any way you look at it, Fernandez was used very well out of the bullpen and was simply outstanding in that role.

As we entered the bottom of the sixth, I honestly had a feeling that with our lineup about to see Hurst for the third time of the night, we would finally break through against him. With one out, Maz pinch-hit for Sid and started a rally with a single. That brought me up to the plate in a pivotal spot in the game. If I make an out, Hurst probably gets through another inning without giving up a run and stays in to pitch the seventh. But if I reached base, he was going to be in a real jam.

I had now faced Hurst so many times over the last week that he wasn't going to surprise me with anything. I had a little better feel for what his pitches did and was much more comfortable facing the lefty because of that familiarity.

I kept the rally going by ripping a line drive toward the left field line for a single, which put runners on first and second to bring the tying run to the plate. Standing on first base, I thought,

Here we go. This is our time to have a big inning and get back into the ball game.

Teufel, who hit better than any of us against Hurst in the series, was next up and walked to load the bases. Hurst would now have to deal with the heart of our lineup—Mex, Carter, and Straw.

Although Mex had struggled against Hurst, having gone just 1 for 7 against him in the series at that point, numbers didn't apply to Keith in these situations. I didn't care if he was 0 for 20 against Bruce, because he was the guy we wanted up there with men in scoring position.

Sure enough, Mex drove a fastball up in the zone, a mistake pitch by Hurst, and singled to left center to score Maz and me to cut the Sox lead to just one run, 3–2.

Carter was next and, although he hadn't had a great postseason, one pitch, man, and I knew he could blow the game wide open. He wasn't as clutch as Keith was, but if Hurst left one over the plate, it could be a beautiful story.

Carter swung at the first pitch and blooped one softly into right field. Evans came charging in and dove for it, but it wasn't clear from our vantage point if he had caught the ball or trapped it underneath his body. The right field umpire, Dale Ford, initially unsure if the ball was caught as well, was slow to make the call, causing Mex to hesitate between first and second. Once Ford ruled a non-catch, pinch runner Backman scored the tying run, but Mex was forced out at second base. Mex had done the only thing he could do. The Sox were going to get an out there whether Evans caught the ball or not. But if Mex was too close to second and Evans had caught the ball, it would have been an easy inning-ending double play with us still trailing by a run.

Umpires usually make a call right away and figure it out later. But when Ford hesitated on that play, it left Mex in a no-man's-land where he couldn't wander too far off first. It was a tough call for Ford and an even tougher one for Mex because he didn't know what to do. It was just one of those things— unless Keith was at an angle where he could have really seen the ball hit the ground, he was in an impossible situation. But he did the right thing, because the Sox only got one out on the play and it kept the inning alive with Straw coming up.

I remember Gary later saying that if Mex had shown better instincts on the bases on that play, Kid would have been credited with a single instead of a "ground out," which would have given him an average of over .300 for the World Series. Even for Gary, the comment was over the top and was *exactly* the type of thing that got him in trouble with the other guys. The only thing that should have mattered to him was that his fielder's choice tied the game.

Straw flied out to left to end the inning, but it was another great Mets comeback. Hurst was done for the night after that frame and, as far as I saw it, so were the Red Sox. Bruce was the best they had and, other than Joe Sambito, they only had right-handers in that bullpen. I thought, *Who are they going to bring in who is even close to as good as Hurst?* Well, Johnny Mac brought in Schiraldi.

Still tied in the bottom of the seventh, the very first batter to face Calvin was Ray Knight. Ahead 2-1 in the count, I truly knew what was going to happen next. It was written on the wall.

Boom! Ray launched a home run deep over the left center field fence to give us a 4–3 lead!

It reached the point where I *almost* felt sorry for the Red Sox. Playing in the World Series should have been the happiest time in their lives—win or lose. Instead, they had expressions on their faces that said, *Why are we even here? If we were going to lose like this, then we should have lost last week to avoid all of this pain.* Oh man, for them to come that far and then let the World Series slip away like they were doing was tough. I really believed they were still sulking from Game Six and didn't have anything left in the tank after that game.

After Knight's home run, we started to pile on against Calvin and then, later in the inning, Sambito, to extend the lead to 6–3. With the great bullpen we had, I felt that the three-run lead might as well have been a ten-run lead. We were not going to lose that game.

I do give the Sox credit for attempting a comeback in the top of the eighth, though. With McDowell in his second inning of relief, Buckner and Rice singled and Evans doubled them home to cut the lead to 6–5. With Evans standing on second and nobody out, Davey brought in Jesse to stop the Sox rally. Despite the Boston threat, I had no doubt we were going to hold on and win the game. Our bullpen was just too deep. Roger didn't have it that night, but we were able to bring in a guy like Orosco. The Sox couldn't do anything like that. Their best reliever, Schiraldi, gets taken out, and their answer was Sambito. There was just no comparison with respect to the depths of the two bullpens. I didn't think they could keep up with us at that point.

It was the exact opposite feeling I'd had in Game Six against Houston. Just like this game, we overcame a 3–0 deficit to tie it and then would take the lead. But the difference was that Houston *believed* they could beat us because of their bullpen. The Red Sox, while having more than capable hitting to get the job done, didn't have the pitching.

With Evans on second, I expected Gedman to move the runner to third by any means possible. Instead, we got a break when he lined out to Backman at second for the first out.

That brought to the plate Boston's most clutch hitter of the postseason, Dave Henderson, in the key at-bat of the game to that point. A single likely ties the game and a home run puts the Sox back in front. Henderson was a thorn in our side from day one, just as he had been to the Angels in the ALCS. After his home run in Game Six, I thought to myself, *Who is this guy?!* But Jesse was able to slay the dragon, striking him out swinging on a 1-2 pitch and was now just one out away from completing a phenomenal job of stopping the Red Sox eighth-inning rally.

Don Baylor, truly one of the game's great clutch hitters and a guy who hit 31 home runs for the Sox that season, pinch-hit for Spike Owen. It was another big challenge for Jesse, but he was up to it, inducing Baylor to ground out to Raffy to end the inning. Evans, the potential tying run, never moved off of second base. It put a dagger in their hearts and there was a sense of relief on our side that we were able to keep them from tying the game. Though I felt sure we still would have won if they had tied it, you never want to put yourself in a position where one swing can beat you—especially with that clutch hitter, Dave Henderson, on the opposing team.

In the bottom of the eighth, Straw led off against Al Nipper and launched one deep into the night sky to make it 7–5. You knew at some point in the series he was going to connect and, when he finally did, it was a beautiful thing. Darryl had one of the classic power swings in baseball—a long, looping stroke with a great finish.

The majestic home run felt like the final exclamation mark on what would be a World Series championship for us. Straw sort of Cadillac'ed his home run trot while circling around the bases, taking his time to soak it all in. Nipper didn't care for it, but it was Darryl making a statement to Davey more than anything else for pulling him out of Game Six. Of all the home runs I ever saw Darryl hit, he never showed up a pitcher.

Later in the inning, we added another run when Orosco singled home a run against Nipper. But that's not necessarily a slight against Nipper, because Jesse was a good athlete who, along with other pitchers we had like McDowell, Aguilera, Doc, Sisk, and Sid, could have been a position player.

Jesse's single made it 8–5 and brought me to the plate with first and third and a chance to really blow open the game. Steve Crawford was brought in to replace Nipper and promptly hit me with a pitch. I don't believe he did it on purpose, but I was disappointed because I was swinging the bat well and *really* wanted that at-bat. With the game in hand, I knew it was going to be my last at-bat of the year.

With the bases now loaded, Crawford settled down to get Backman and Mex on groundouts and the score remained 8–5 heading into the bottom of the ninth. The three-run lead gave Jesse some breathing room. He deserved it after getting us out of that jam in the previous inning.

Jesse actually looked fresher in the ninth, no doubt from the adrenaline rush that must have been going through his body. Three outs away from a world championship has a knack of doing that to a pitcher. I could tell he really wanted to get it over with. He knew it was there and he had to contain himself to get those last three outs. It wasn't a matter of if he would get them, but rather a matter of how many pitches he would need.

Jesse and I went way back to before the Mets' renaissance, even playing together at AAA Tidewater in '79. He had a similar appreciation of our team's ascent as I did, which made this moment so extra special for us both. Ironically, Jesse came to the Mets organization from the Minnesota Twins to complete an earlier deal when the Mets traded away Jerry Koosman, the first pitcher in team history to get the final out of a World Series. Now Orosco was getting the chance to be the second one to do it.

Jesse worked quickly and got Ed Romero to pop out to Mex for out number one. Now he would face the top of the Red Sox order—Wade Boggs and Marty Barrett. I was thinking unless they both get on base, we would be fine. For a legitimate threat to develop, both of them would need to get on.

After getting ahead quickly 1-and-2, Jesse got Boggs to ground out to Wally for the second out. We were now just one out away from winning the World Series. I would love to say I was romanticizing the moment, but the reality was I was plan-ning my escape route. I was thinking, *All the king's horses ain't gonna keep these fans off the field!* And that thought seemed all the more likely to become a reality when a smoke bomb, thrown from the second deck, hit about twenty feet in front of me in left field. But because I was used to things getting thrown onto the field at Shea, the smoke bomb didn't faze me in the least. I just waited for the smoke to clear, my thoughts again completely focused on us getting that final out and getting off the field as quickly as possible.

Barrett, who enjoyed an outstanding series against us, was the final hitter. With the count at 2-and-2, Jesse got him to chase a pitch high and away for strike three!

Standing in left field, I shouted, "Yes! *Finally!*"

I watched as Orosco hurled his glove into the air, dropped to his knees, pounded the dirt on the mound with both fists, and raised both arms straight for the heavens. It was a *great* reaction by Jesse that really said it all. A great climax to our season.

Sprinting toward the pitcher's mound, where our guys had piled onto Jesse and Gary, I noticed an army of mounted police officers trotting in from right field to keep the fans in the stands. I was surprised it worked because I thought it was going to be like the scene when we clinched the division title at Shea earlier that month. Those fans had been waiting a long time, a *verrry* long time, for another championship, and I wouldn't have blamed them if they wanted to share in the glory by celebrating with us on the field.

The clubhouse was what you would expect it to be—a

madhouse. The bright lights from TV cameras lit up the room, with the guys screaming, yelling, and pouring champagne over each other's heads. I stayed away from much of the craziness and retreated to the trainer's room with a huge bottle of champagne, watching my teammates from a distance, reminiscing about how very different that locker room was when I had first come up to the Mets six years earlier. I didn't drink or spray any of the champagne, but I was enjoying the moment every bit as much as they were by just watching them. To experience a World Series Championship after playing for a perennial loser those first four years with the club was good enough for me.

Still reflecting, I thought about how we won that World Series in typical 1986 Mets fashion. Like our season, there was never a dull moment. It was one of the most exciting World Series I had ever seen. I can't think of another one that had more twists and turns and drama. Not a single one. The series had everything, man, with highs and lows throughout the seven games. We were down two games, then went into Boston and took two right back. Our ace pitcher threw like crap, but then we had Sid, who didn't get a start, end up being the star pitcher. You had that crazy Game Six when Davey made some really bold, questionable, and stupid moves, but we were able to snatch victory from the jaws of defeat with our tenth-inning comeback. It was like riding on a seesaw.

If someone goes back and reads the whole story of the 1986 World Series, before they get to the end they would come to the conclusion that there was no way the Mets could possibly have won it. You can't make up half the stuff that happened. And here we are, almost thirty years later, and you still have players and managers arguing about what they did and didn't do, what they said and didn't say, in that World Series. It's crazy.

As for the season as a whole, the little things that happened between management and the players, the heavy partying, the four guys who got arrested, our veteran superstars—Gary and Keith—having an ego thing going on, all would have totally destroyed some teams. Yet we found the strength to overcome it all and achieve all that we did. It was almost as if we won not in spite of our conflicts, but because of them. I guess we were smart enough to realize that we needed each other, that the team was bigger than any of us. And, for me, it took a moment of solitude in that trainer's room after Game Seven to figure that out.

That whole series, that entire year, really taught us a lot about ourselves and how to put our personal feelings aside for the greater good. And that reality didn't sink in with anyone deeper than it did with me—the unhappy camper who hid his discontentment much of the season behind a big smile.

I didn't realize the full impact that our championship had on New York City until our ticker-tape parade through the Canyon of Heroes the next day. I've seen parades before, but there is nothing like slowly riding up Broadway past more than two million screaming fans cheering you on, many hanging out of windows, through a blizzard of ticker tape. That is what having the keys to the greatest city in the world means to me. You can't beat it.

For a kid from a small South Carolina town of five hundred people, that victory parade was more exciting to me than Orosco's last pitch or the clubhouse celebration after Game Seven.

How can you compare anything with a party of two million? That parade shut the city down. When I think of all the things we did as a team, that ride through the Canyon of Heroes stuck with me more than anything else.

We were more than a championship team. We were an answer to the prayers of a loyal fan base that had been forced to endure the burden of inferiority cast by the shadow of success of their crosstown rivals, the New York Yankees. While the Yankees may have had the history and the rings to document their dominance, for now, without debate, the town belonged to the New York Mets.

Weeks, months, and even years went by after that crazy postseason of 1986, and I still found myself thinking, *How in the world did we do it? We won it all, but how?!*

12

The Long Hangover

t should have been the start of a dynasty.

If someone had told me after the 1986 World Series that our group of guys would never see the Fall Classic again, I would have looked that person right in the eyes and said, "You're out of your mind!"

We were young enough, talented enough, and the most feared and hated team in all of baseball. With the great core of players we had, we could have won another three world championships. But it wasn't to be.

In an effort to clean up our team's nasty-boy image, Mets management promptly ripped some of the heart and soul out of our ball club by showing two of our key guys the door.

First, it was Kevin Mitchell. Just six weeks after we were crowned champions, he was traded as part of a deal to bring in left fielder Kevin McReynolds from the San Diego Padres. Mitch was made the fall guy by management for Gooden's decline in '86, with the conventional wisdom being that he kept Doc out partying too late drinking, carousing, and who knew what else at that time. Mitch was viewed by management as both a thug and a bad influence on our younger players. But all of those rumors about Mitchell leading guys like Doc, Straw, and Lenny down a bad path were just that—rumors. I never saw or heard about Mitch doing anything other than drink, which everybody was doing anyway. No one in our clubhouse even suggested anything other than that. But what I do know for sure is that we traded away more than just a ballplayer. We traded an imposing figure who gave us the credibility needed to defend our own turf.

What we got in McReynolds was a good ballplayer who, most importantly to management, projected exactly the kind of new attitude the Mets now wanted. Not only did K-Mac not want to rock the boat, he didn't even want to get in the boat! He was a very kind man, the type of person you invite over for dinner every day of the week, but he didn't have that killer instinct that our team was built on. K-Mac was more like, *Okay, whatever happens, happens.* He simply couldn't wait for the game to be over so he could go home. He was just kind of "there."

Next to go was our World Series MVP, Ray Knight, to free agency. Frank Cashen's lowball offer to re-sign him made it clear they didn't want him back. I think the front office wanted to give HoJo a chance to play third every day. As it turned out, HoJo had a big year for us offensively in '87, but the value of Ray as a clutch performer, an enforcer on the field, and a leader in the clubhouse cannot be understated. Platooning the two of them at third base, with HoJo seeing some time at other positions to get his bat in the lineup, would have been a better solution.

People tend to put a lot of emphasis on numbers and less than they should on personalities. The latter is what we sorely missed when we lost Mitchell and Knight. You can't just go and find guys like that on the street. They're a rare breed. And when we lost both of them the same year, it was like a tennis player losing an arm. Forget the strong numbers HoJo and McReynolds put up the next year, because messing with our chemistry hurt the club more than anything else. And to add insult to injury, Mitchell would become a fearsome slugger, winning the NL MVP in 1989 when he led the league in home runs and RBIs and took the San Francisco Giants to the World Series.

But there was nothing that occurred in the off-season that shocked us more than what the Mets announced on April 1, 1987. We all wished it were some kind of bad April Fool's joke, but the reality was that Doc had tested positive for cocaine and would have to enter a six-week rehabilitation program at the Smithers Alcoholism Treatment and Training Center in Manhattan. Gooden wouldn't start a game for us that season until June 5.

I guess I was naive about Doc. I really couldn't see or understand how something like that could happen to such a promising talent. I just didn't see it or maybe subconsciously chose to ignore what was happening to him. I honestly don't know which it was. All I saw was this great talent, the kind that you don't see more than once a decade. I thought that we, as people, were strong enough to say no to any situation that we didn't want to be a part of. I really believed that. But with Doc's situation, I learned that is not always the case. Sometimes we can't say no to some things. We choose to do a lot of things, but even in our choosing we're influenced by some unknown entity, whatever that may be.

This was the beginning of the end for Doc's superstardom and the start of the decline of what would have been a brilliant career.

In retrospect, I never saw the signs. The thing you had to understand about Doc was that physically he looked fine. Using cocaine may have affected his pitching performance, like what we saw in the World Series, but it wasn't a physical injury like a pulled hamstring. While he still had that presence that you wanted to see on the mound, he just wasn't the same guy. You could tell something was different. I didn't know what it was and couldn't put a finger on it, but knew that something special Doc had had was just no longer there.

If I had known that Doc was using drugs, and I had the opportunity to really talk with him, I wouldn't have taken on the role of lecturer by saying, "Doc, don't do this," or "Don't do that." Instead, I would have taken more of a conversational route and tried to make him aware of what was at stake, that he would only get one opportunity for greatness. By staying straight back then, he might not have known where he was going to end up, but at least he would be giving himself the best chance to succeed. I would have also emphasized that his family was counting on him, and that it's not a bad thing to have people depend on you. But I'll never know if that would have worked. Besides, most drug users I've known have always been in denial. They don't want to admit that they need help. They say they're just doing it because it's fun. Yeah, right!

While it's true Keith was our captain, his hands would have been somewhat tied if he had seen the signs and tried to help Gooden. Doc may have told Mex, "Who are you to tell me what to do? Look what you did with the Cardinals and you turned out all right." Then again, Doc may have listened if Keith would have said something like, "I've been through it, and these are the hardships I've endured. You don't need to go through any of that." In that regard, he may have been an excellent person to talk to Doc about his problems. It could have made a difference because Dwight really did respect Keith a great deal.

I think what made Doc especially vulnerable to getting caught up with alcohol and drugs was that he always wanted to please people. I think his being so nice was actually his biggest weakness. I know there is the old saying, "Don't mistake my kindness for weakness," but I think in Doc's case it actually was. He never learned to say no to people. Instead of saying yes to going out all of the time, he should have occasionally just said, "No thanks, I'm going home." But he couldn't.

Plus, he was on the verge of greatness and there were people who desperately wanted to hang out with him. If these people couldn't be great on their own, then they wanted to know someone who was. And Doc was too young to understand or handle that. The one thing I learned quickly in New York was the word "no." I had to get familiar with that word because if I didn't, I would have ended up running myself crazy trying to please people. A young player has to protect himself.

Doc had also developed some associations with certain types of people—people who had questionable values and clearly just wanted to exploit him for his fame and money. I didn't know for sure what kind of influence some of the unsavory people in his life had on him at the time, but it certainly wasn't positive. He was also in a very rocky and toxic relationship with his girlfriend Carline that mercifully ended after the World Series.

I sometimes wonder whether Doc could have benefited by having an in-your-face, tough-guy pitching coach like Bob Gibson when he began using cocaine. Taking absolutely nothing away from Mel Stottlemyre, a great pitching coach for us and an even nicer guy, if Dwight had a guy like Gibson it may have saved him. Because Mel is white, from a social standpoint he wasn't going to grab a young, black pitcher and try to literally shake some sense into him. But a shake-up from a black coach like Gibson, who was our "attitude coach" earlier in my career, might have been better received by Gooden. If nothing else, I believe Gibson would have been able to talk to Doc in ways the more tactful Mel probably would have been hesitant to do. But we'll never know.

So we opened the '87 season with Doc in the drug tank, no Knight or Mitchell, and with our most versatile reliever, McDowell, on the DL after having an operation for appendicitis. Plus, management was getting ready to move Raffy out so they could hand the shortstop duties over to Kevin Elster. Sure, we still had Keith. We still had Gary. Straw was still there. Lenny was still there. Wally was still there. I was still there. But losing the guys we did was a *really* big hit, man! The rest of the league, which hated us so deeply, was smelling blood in the water.

But despite the ill-advised player personnel moves, coming off the dominant season we had the year before, I was still anticipating a strong '87 campaign. However, it was clear to me that our clubhouse needed to be corralled somewhat. It was simply too volatile to last long-term. Eventually, the club was going to self-destruct and not really learn from some of the things that happened the year before—the partying, the fighting, and the egos. We began to lose track of what made us *really* good and needed to put a stop to some things that may not have hindered us before, but certainly would catch up with us later. We were showing signs of being less gritty and had started to bathe in our own glory a little too much.

However, unlike what many people think, there wasn't a discipline issue on the Mets at that time. There may have been some personal issues, like Doc's, we had to deal with, but that had nothing to do with discipline. Davey had the respect of the players. He never lost the team or the clubhouse by being too lax. And as much as we disagreed with some of the things he did, we respected him for being his own man. He always did what he thought was right and didn't point any fingers. The difference was that in '86, we were just too talented and arrogant not to be great. Anything that even remotely resembled adversity was quickly overshadowed by our performance on the field. But now our handling of our own adversity was starting to wane.

While it's true we lost most of our pitchers and some of our position players to injuries at some point during the '87 season, it was the missing swagger and how we no longer intimidated teams that contributed to a complete loss of our identity from just the year before. Every team has injuries over the course of a season, but we had enough talent to rise above them. Our problem was that when we lost enforcers like Mitchell and Knight, two guys who fit in perfectly with the spirit of our championship team, and replaced them with less intense players that were still feeling their way around, we were lost as a baseball club. In the meantime, management spent too much time assessing what we had, what they wanted, and what they didn't want. For as great as Cashen was at building us into a champion, he was beginning to do just as good a job at tearing us down. The front office had no clue when it came to understanding the team's chemistry and what truly made us so great in the first place.

Think about it. Talent-wise, Howard Johnson's numbers were much better in '87 than Ray Knight *ever* had. And Kevin McReynolds, at that time, was the superior defensive outfielder, base runner, and hitter over Kevin Mitchell. But talent isn't everything.

The front office was losing their grip on what made us so dominating the year before. They were just losing control and grasping at whatever they thought could rein in our team. They felt that many of the players were not displaying the image the front office desired and they wanted to get a better handle on the players off the field. One of their ideas was to name Keith the captain at the start of the '87 season—the first in Mets history. They thought this move would solve some of the issues that existed. Needless to say, Gary didn't care too much for the decision and, taking into account his sensitive psyche, it may have contributed to his drastic decline in power numbers that season. I simply didn't understand the reasoning behind the decision, unless there was some psychological or symbolic meaning management was after. That team had demonstrated that it didn't need a captain. That role was already being played by Keith, so there was no need to formally name him one.

We didn't make the playoffs in '87, finishing with a respectable but very non-dominating 92 wins, three games behind the Cardinals. But as disappointing as the season was, things only got stranger in '88.

We came to camp the next spring and management named Gary co-captain. That was even more puzzling than naming one the previous year. Kid was apparently *still* bothered by the fact the club made Keith the captain despite his past involvement with cocaine and the embarrassment of his testimony in the Pittsburgh drug trial. But if that was the reason they named Gary a co-captain, simply to appease him, it was definitely another mistake. In an effort to fix what they didn't even know was wrong, they actually screwed up even more. I had no idea what they were thinking, but it didn't work. The players didn't care.

By all accounts, it would appear to someone on the outside that we were back to our dominating ways in '88, winning 100 regular season games and taking the division by 15 games. But the reality was the team was pulling apart from within. Lenny and I were growing more and more unhappy with the platoon system we were in, guys weren't getting along as was well as they once did, and that killer instinct we once had was all but gone. Publicly, I kept quiet about my discontent. I kept my troubles behind closed doors. But I didn't like the way things were going. I was getting considerably less playing time, as moves were being made that weren't conducive to my becoming a better ballplayer or in helping my career progress to the level I felt it should have reached.

I understand that management's first obligation was to the organization. But I felt that there should have been some room in there to do what was best for me as well—even if that meant trading me somewhere else. But Frank and Davey were adamantly opposed to that idea, with Cashen saying he didn't think he could get enough in return for me. It was very upsetting because I really believed that I had earned a certain amount of respect from the organization. And since I made sure I wasn't a distraction to the success of the team, I was hoping they would have done what they could to accommodate me. It was bad enough that I hadn't done anything to cause me to lose my job as an everyday player, but even worse that I wasn't being given the opportunity to win it back. Management was satisfied with the way things were with the platoon system. They must have thought, *Don't worry about Mookie. He loves the Mets. He'll never rock the boat!*

We also had another uncomfortable platoon situation with two very good ballplayers at second base in Wally and Teuf. But none of my teammates were really speaking out about their respective displeasures, either. We just had a ton of talent on that team and something had to give in terms of getting us more playing time. It was a major issue.

But there was something else going on that I thought I would never see in a Davey Johnson clubhouse—a player getting special privileges.

Gregg Jefferies was the poster boy for resentment on our team from the first day he showed up in spring training. Although he was just a rookie, the club allowed him to do things that no player would even think about requesting. For example, a common rule during spring training is if you're injured, you come to the ballpark anyway and check in with the medical staff. If they feel you are unfit to play, they give you permission to go back home. That rule didn't apply to Jefferies. He made his own program and came to the park when he wanted to. Players really disliked that. Here he was, just a twenty-year-old rookie, a guy that hadn't done anything yet, and he was given special treatment.

Jefferies was Mets management's golden boy, viewed by them as the second coming of Pete Rose. He was treated in a hands-off way. *Stay away from him! Don't touch him! Leave him alone!* They even allowed his father to coach him. Just crazy stuff that you simply couldn't believe. And Davey was allowing this to happen! It's possible Johnson was being told by Cashen to allow this to go on, but the players were really upset about it. Based on how our team had always operated, we expected that Jefferies would come in and toe the line. But instead, this kid was making his own rules. He also gave the impression he was squeaky clean, like a "junior Gary Carter."

Gregg was a big part of the reason the clubhouse was now so divided. Most of the team really didn't like him because, even though we had guys who had their own individual ways and quirks, they *always* respected the other players and the rules of the team. But I don't think Mets management trusted us with their coveted number one draft pick from 1985. Perhaps they feared a repeat of what happened to Doc as a young player.

Another issue we saw right away was how management over-estimated Gregg's potential. While he showed some promise, Jefferies would never perform with the Mets the way they thought he would. While Jefferies was a good player, his talents were limited. He could swing the bat, could run a little bit, but was not particularly strong defensively at any one position.

Three years later, he was shipped off to Kansas City.

In fairness, it wasn't entirely Gregg's fault that some of our clubhouse issues centered around him. Some of the blame was squarely on Davey for allowing it to go on and alienating his other players by catering to Jefferies's every whim.

By contrast, our other bright young star, pitcher David Cone, fit right in and was quickly accepted into the Scum Bunch. His love of the nightlife may have been one of the reasons Kansas City traded him to us, but that made him great for New York. Plus, his 20-3 record that year certainly didn't hurt. Cone would go on to have a tremendous career, highlighted by the perfect game he pitched as a Yankee years later.

Despite the internal turmoil in 1988, we found ourselves one win away from taking the NLCS over the Dodgers and returning to the World Series.

There was no question we had a better team than Los Angeles. We had beaten up on them all year, winning ten of 11 games and outscoring them by nearly a three-to-one margin. The only major threat in their lineup was their really banged-up, hobbling leader Kirk Gibson—playing despite two badly injured legs. LA had perhaps the weakest offensive team ever to make it to the postseason. The only thing they did have going for them was pretty good starting pitching—Hershiser, Valenzuela, Tim Leary, and Tim Belcher—which we felt would need to pitch shutouts to beat us.

But I think we miscalculated how hungry they were and took them for granted when it really counted the most. We were cruising along, up two games to one, and had a 4–2 lead in Game Four heading into the top of the ninth inning at Shea. This was when Davey and Mel didn't make an obvious pitching change and that would turn the series around in the Dodgers' favor.

Doc was pitching his heart out and, like most pitchers back then, wanted to finish what he started. But Dwight didn't have anything left, having thrown well over a hundred pitches through eight innings, and Davey never should have sent him out to the mound to start the ninth. After the leadoff batter walked, up came a left-handed hitter with some power in Mike Scioscia. Our excellent, hard-throwing, lefty closer Randy Myers was warmed up and ready to come in. But Davey didn't move from the dugout and Scioscia promptly drove Doc's first offering deep over the right field fence to tie the game. We were in a state of shock. The whole stadium was. The general feeling was, *How did that happen? They weren't supposed to do that.*

Now we would be tested. We had won ball games all year long because we were just more talented than everyone else. Scioscia's home run would check the character of a much different crew of

Mets from that gritty '86 team. I thought, *Are we going to be able to stand up and show what it takes to be a champion?*

After the home run, Davey still left Doc in there to face two more batters before Myers mercifully came in to pitch. I couldn't believe it. Doc was left out there to throw 133 pitches in that game. To no one's surprise, when Myers finally did come in, he was outstanding, shutting down the Dodgers over the next 2⅓ innings. Randy should have started the ninth and recorded the save, and we should have been up 3 games to 1.

But it wasn't to be.

Gibson homered in the top of the twelfth off of McDowell to give the Dodgers a 5–4 lead. We battled back, loading the bases in the bottom of that inning with just one out and Straw and McReynolds coming up. Jesse Orosco, our former warrior of a closer now pitching for the Dodgers, would get Straw to pop out to second before Orel Hershiser came in to get McReynolds on a short fly to center to end the game. It was a gut-wrenching defeat. We just weren't the same team from two years before. The '86 team would never have lost a game like that. The '88 edition couldn't regroup from Scioscia's blast and never recovered from it.

With Lenny playing center against three straight right-handed Dodger starting pitchers, I watched from the bench as we split the next two games before losing Game Seven in LA, 6–0. In that final game, the Dodgers scored all their runs in the contest off of Darling in just one-plus innings. Hershiser was outstanding, shutting us out on just five hits.

In the series, Hershiser started three games and appeared in four, and gave up only three earned runs in 24⅔ innings against us. He had great control and was very smart at evaluating hitters' swings and getting them to hit balls to his fielders. He could be overpowering, but his greatest attribute was a lot of movement on his fastball and great command over three different pitches. He made you hit his pitch. You never squared it up really well against Hershiser. He understood the game and studied the weaknesses of hitters as well as any pitcher I ever saw.

But for as great as Hershiser was in that series, he still didn't approach the dominance and genuine fear that Mike Scott put into us in '86. Still, without Orel, there was no way the Dodgers would have beaten us. It just goes to show that anything can happen in a short series in October, especially when a team has a hot pitcher.

After beating us, Los Angeles went on to defeat the mighty Oakland A's in the World Series in five games, another major upset. Maybe the Dodgers were just destined to win it all that year.

The next season, 1989, saw two events that really exemplified how the Mets had gone from a superpower to a team on the verge of self-destruction.

With the first one, we had barely unpacked our bags at Port St. Lucie for spring training when, on team picture day, years of tension between Darryl and Keith finally boiled over. On this particular day, Straw refused to stand next to Mex for the picture because he said he was tired of Keith lecturing him about different things. Keith called him a crybaby, all hell broke loose, and the two of them had to be separated by some of the guys.

It was only March 3. I thought, *Man, this could be a long season!*

Darryl could be moody and temperamental. It's hard to say how much those characteristics derived from, as we know now, his drug use back then, or from his natural disposition. Either way, I never had a problem with his behavior. The only issue I ever had with him was with his attitude toward the game. It was, well, different. He sometimes didn't respect the game or utilize his God-given talents to the fullest.

As for Straw's volatile side, like he displayed on photo day, it was never far from the surface. Straw also liked to pick on certain guys on the club. For example, he was merciless with Teufel at times, even coming up with the nickname Mr. Richard Head for him. For Darryl, Teuf—a quiet and not very outspoken guy—was like that one kid in high school everybody picked on. Straw just liked to needle Teuf and see how many buttons he could push. I don't think Straw actually disliked Teuf, but he enjoyed using him as a punching bag. Tim was also a privileged white kid from Greenwich, Connecticut, as well as an outsider, coming to us in a trade. That made him a pretty easy target for Darryl's wrath.

So while Darryl taking on Keith was not entirely surprising, it was a bad omen for the season.

The other event was stunning.

We had just finished a weekend series in Philadelphia on June 18 when the Mets announced they had traded Lenny Dykstra and Roger McDowell to the Phillies for Juan Samuel. I was floored. Samuel was basically a .240 hitter with little power by that stage of his career and had recently led the league in strikeouts four straight years. Lenny's All-Star career was about to take off and Roger was in his prime. It didn't make any sense for us to unload two players of that caliber when we were only two games out of first place. I didn't know what Cashen was thinking from a talent perspective. Maybe he felt like he couldn't control Lenny and Roger anymore. I thought it was just another major step by Frank to distance the organization from our crazy, yet wildly successful, '86 team. We still had some guys on the team who he felt were detrimental to the image of the Mets. It forced him to make some terrible decisions. With this latest trade, he had basically dismantled most of what remained from the heart of that championship club.

Samuel was a career second baseman whom the Phillies used in center field for the first two months of the '89 season. He was still learning the position. So for as bad as I thought the trade to get him was, at least now I would have my full-time job in center field back.

Or so I thought.

Nothing could have prepared me for the shock I would have the next night at Shea when I checked the lineup card. *Leading off and playing center field, Juan Samuel.*

The writing was on the wall. It was the beginning of the end of my Mets career.

13

The Press Conference

t was the ultimate humiliation.

In the two weeks since Lenny and Roger were traded for Juan Samuel, I watched in disbelief as Davey penciled Samuel into the lineup game after game in center field. While Samuel had some talent, he was no center fielder. I was very upset and didn't understand how the Mets would think he was capable of doing a better job there than I could.

It was the tipping point. I had finally come to grips with the fact that the Mets no longer saw me as a significant part of their present or future plans. My facade of being a happy camper had gone on long enough. While I was upset with the organization for not showing me the level of respect I had earned, I was even more frustrated with myself for allowing it to go on for all the years that it did.

Meetings with Frank and Davey weren't giving me clarity. I would ask them, "What is my role? What do you expect of me?" But they never had an answer. I pleaded with them to trade me. They refused, still contending they couldn't get equal value in a trade. But what value were they talking about? After all, they just went out and got Juan Samuel to play center field. I thought, *What value do I have to them if I'm not playing?*

With nowhere else to turn in the organization, I decided to hold my own impromptu press conference after batting practice before our July 2 game in Cincinnati. Not in the lineup for the third straight game, I had reached my boiling point. I concluded that if I didn't speak up and say something, people would think I didn't care about not playing. I was very concerned that my teammates, the media, and the fans would just think, *You can do anything with Mookie. He just takes it and doesn't say a word.*

Sitting in the dugout, a band of curious reporters assembled in front of me. I shared with them my disenchantment with the Mets and how I wanted to be traded. I explained why I could no longer live with the current situation and that I didn't understand why the Mets no longer appreciated my value to the team.

I honestly don't know if any of them took my declaration seriously at the time because it was so out of character for me to show that kind of frustration. To be clear, I wasn't under the illusion that Mookie Wilson wanting to be traded was front-page news nor did I expect it to be, but my goal with the press conference was to let everyone know that I was an unhappy camper and hoped that management would come to the realization that I no longer would accept whatever role they dished out to me. I was truly concerned about my future as a professional ballplayer and had put behind me the notion that I would always be a New York Met.

I can't say I was bitter at ownership and management, but I was very disappointed. I had enjoyed a decade filled with many great moments as both a Mets player and an adopted New Yorker. I thought that my long-standing relationship with team owners Fred Wilpon and Nelson Doubleday had grown beyond an employer/employee relationship. And while Frank Cashen and Davey Johnson are good men who accomplished a lot, it was obvious from their actions that they thought less of my abilities than I did. In the end, I was treated as just another paid employee forced to accept whatever was decided. It made me feel so under-appreciated.

I also felt my loyalty to the team was a personal missed opportunity. Although I had good career numbers, I truly believe I was shortchanged because of management's decisions. The years 1985 through 1989 were troubling and confusing times for me regarding my place and value to the team. People say the Mookie/Dykstra platoon was great because it made the Mets stronger. While I tend to agree, I would also add that the only reason it worked was because I thought more of the team than myself. You see, while it benefitted the club, the loss of playing time made me a weaker player with fewer opportunities to maximize my performance and value. Who knows how much being in a platoon and later as a role player adversely affected me financially? I guess I'll never know.

But as troubled as I was, I took pride in my playing ability and didn't let my emotions affect my efforts on or off the field. I continued to play whenever and wherever I was told. But if I had perhaps spoken up back in '85 and remained a starter as I thought I should have for what became a very successful Mets team, I could have looked back at a very different kind of career than the one I had. To this day, I'm still a little bitter and angry about how my career ultimately turned out.

I'm no different from most athletes who want to make their mark in their respective sport. I devoted my life to baseball. And I understand that when it's taken away from you, whether justly or unjustly, there are always going to be some what-ifs and resentment. But in my case, my bitterness stems from my belief that I was very good at what I did but could have been a lot better and done much more if given the opportunity that was not extended to me. It would have been easier to accept if I didn't earn that chance but, fortunately or unfortunately, I did. And that's what hurts the most—the feeling that I earned the opportunity.

Maybe they didn't owe me or any of the players an explanation for why they made the moves they did, but I didn't think it was fair to the guys who stayed to have to try to continue with another group of players when the basis for what we had in '86 was good enough. I just don't know what they saw or didn't see in those players they either traded or let go. But I've learned one thing and that's that we will never see a mixture of guys like we had in the mid-eighties ever again. And that's on any team. The days of teams seeing half their roster go out partying all night are over. Nowadays, they want a team of complete ballplayers that lead squeaky-clean lives, exactly the type of club the Mets were trying to put together after we won the World Series. But those teams never win championships. They just don't.

I at last got my wish and was traded to the Toronto Blue Jays on July 31 for pitcher Jeff Musselman and a minor leaguer. My playing career with the Mets was over. It felt like an end of an era. I left the Mets as their all-time leader in runs scored, triples, and stolen bases. While I was sad about leaving New York, I would finally have an opportunity to play regularly again.

On reflection, for as magical as the Mets' rise from the depths was in the early eighties to reaching the ultimate in '86, in the final analysis our club was the ultimate underachiever. While management is responsible for systematically disassembling the great team they put together, I'm also saddened by and even angry with the "poster boys of underachievement," Doc and Straw, for wasting so much of their tremendous natural talents. Putting aside what they could have meant to our ball club's success, I'm angry at what they let slip through their fingers and what they could have represented not only to New York and baseball, but also to the African American player. What those two young superstars represented was much bigger than themselves.

Personally, I had to go down a much different path than Doc and Straw. I went through spring trainings where I couldn't get a house to stay in because of my color. By contrast, those two guys signed out of high school, never had to experience that kind of racism, and had a golden opportunity to be an inspiration to a lot of kids. Sadly, I don't think they saw it that way. I believe they thought their lives were just theirs and theirs alone. A lot of people may think that way, but with athletes, how they live their lives becomes just as important as what they've accomplished on the field or all the money they've made. The reality is that an athlete's life, especially one like Doc's or Straw's, can have a profound impact on other people's lives. And Doc and Straw didn't stand up and become the players they should have been to represent the Mets, the city, their families, and their race as well as they could have because of their involvement in drugs. I thought they really shortchanged everybody, including themselves.

I realize all of that might sound harsh, that I'm singling out those two guys, but it's a lesson learned for other aspiring athletes not to fall into the same trap. Doc and Straw are actually good friends of mine and have always treated me with a lot of respect. And I'm very proud of them both in their efforts to straighten out their lives. In recent years, Doc put on a lot of weight, but has since lost most of it and now looks really good. He's trying hard to get his life back in order and I pray that he does. As for Straw, he opened his own ministry a few years ago and is remorseful for the pain he caused others. Both of them are lucky to be alive and have been given a unique opportunity to help others.

Knowing full well the Mets would trade me out of the National League for public relations purposes, my move to Toronto was as good a landing spot as any in the AL. There were some guys I knew over there, players I had played against way back in the minor leagues. And as fate would have it, Mazzilli was selected off waivers by the Blue Jays the same day as the trade that sent me there, making the transition a little easier on me.

The Blue Jays were a team on the brink of greatness. They had a very young and talented club with power, speed, and pitching, but were missing one last ingredient to take them to the next level: grit. That was where I would come in. Toronto manager Cito Gaston made that very clear. In my first meeting with him, he told me exactly what my role would be on the ball club, a welcomed difference from my existence with Davey and Frank.

Cito said, "Mookie, we have the talent, but we need a little fire. We need you to show these kids your aggressive style of play. Tell me when you want to play and when you don't want to play. But set an example for these kids."

I said, "That's fine with me. I'll do the best I can."

I loved playing for Cito. There were no ifs, ands, or buts. It was like, "Here is what we want from you. This is why we brought you here."

I was reinvigorated. I helped the Blue Jays make the playoffs that year, playing in almost all of their remaining games the final two months of the regular season, and batted .298 for them. In the American League Championship Series, we lost to the Oakland A's, an extraordinarily talented team that would go on to sweep the Giants in the World Series. But it was obvious to me that our club was getting stronger.

I really loved living in Toronto. It's a great sports town, but also one where a player can go unrecognized in public. That hardly ever happened in New York. There is nothing greater than being a successful athlete in the Big Apple. I don't know what reaction singers and actors get from people there, but for me it was amazing. While it sometimes got annoying because people often wanted a piece of you or wanted to buy you dinner or a drink, at least I never had to wait in line at a crowded restaurant!

Even today when I'm in New York, I can walk into a place, get recognized, and a restaurant staff goes overboard to make sure I have whatever I want. I may not get freebies like I used to get, but I'm still well taken care of. It's something I never take for granted. Even though I've been out of the game for a long time now, it still amazes me how often I get recognized and the fuss New Yorkers make over me. I talk to ballplayers in other cities and tell them there's nothing like playing in New York. I don't understand why a lot of players don't want to play there.

The other difference I noticed in Toronto was with the media. Sometimes the New York media makes you feel like you have a bull's-eye on you. Because of the competition for a scoop, the New York papers were always looking for an angle they could write about. While they could give a player a pass in certain areas, you might be that one ballplayer that sneezed the wrong way and reporters would write that you didn't wipe your nose the right way. The *New York Post* frequently ran gossipy stories about our guys on the front page, back page, and Page Six. Enough already! The Toronto press was much more tame.

We finished in second place in the AL East in 1990, but were back in the ALCS the following year, again falling short, this time against the eventual world champion Minnesota Twins. But the fact that we were losing to teams that would go on to win the World Series made getting eliminated a little easier to swallow because we knew we were getting beaten by the best.

The Blue Jays didn't exercise their option to bring me back for the third year of my contract in 1992. While I was disappointed with their decision, I understood the reasons given and was impressed that their general manager, Pat Gillick, took the time to fly to my home in South Carolina to deliver the news. I did have an opportunity to sign a minor league contract with the San Francisco Giants and compete for a job on their big league roster, but my right shoulder was shot and I would have needed another surgery on it to have a legitimate chance of making the club. I decided against that option and retired. I had played through the pain the previous year and didn't want to go through that agony again.

The Blue Jays would go on to sign free agent Dave Winfield, a perfect final piece to putting them over the top. Toronto would win the World Series that year, and then repeat in 1993, replacing the veteran presence of Winfield with that of Paul Molitor and Ricky Henderson. Starting with me, Toronto added seasoned leaders almost every year to help their young team grow and show the rest of baseball just how serious the organization was about winning. I was proud to be the first of that distinguished group and, in some way, feel that I helped that organization on their path to becoming a world championship team.

It was a good two and a half years in Toronto. They had a few rowdy personalities—Pat Borders, George Bell, Rob Ducey, and Dave Stieb—who might have made the cut into the Scum Bunch, but as a team they were a good bunch of guys that weren't nearly as radical as the Mets were in their heyday.

I retired as a player that didn't complete a career in the fashion I would have liked. I left the game, but not on my own terms and with plenty of regrets—the biggest not speaking up much earlier about my playing time with the Mets. And there was plenty I was going to miss as well, like the camaraderie of my teammates, the excitement of a pennant race, and the roar of the crowd when I raced around the bases or chased down a fly ball in the outfield. Playing baseball was my passion and, while I had other interests in my life, would always be my first love.

I knew I would miss it dearly.

14

Life After Baseball

There was nothing that could have prepared me for the restlessness, emptiness, boredom, and feeling of worthlessness that came after hanging up my spikes for the last time. Playing baseball had always been as important to me as the air I breathed. And now it was over. It felt like a part of me had died.

The void in my life was haunting me. As much as I enjoyed having more family time and the opportunity to lower my golf score, it just wasn't cutting it. I needed something to do.

Oh sure, I tried a number of interesting jobs I thought I would be good at, like selling insurance and securities, but my heart wasn't in those kinds of things. I lacked the drive, commitment, and, perhaps, even the desire to succeed at them. After a couple of years, it all became clear to me: baseball was my passion and I wouldn't be as happy or fulfilled in any other business.

I actually gave serious thought to attempting a comeback a couple of years after retirement. But then reality set in. My only realistic option to get back into the game I loved was by becoming a coach.

It's funny, but during my playing days, I never envisioned myself as a future coach. I took notice of the insane number of hours they put in each week, the uncertainty of job security, the sometimes lack of respect from the players, and their modest salaries. But now I understood why they put up with it all. Baseball was where they belonged and the challenge of coaching had replaced the thrill of competition.

My first post-playing-career job in baseball was as a roving instructor, specializing in outfield and baserunning skills in the Mets' minor league development department. It was a good platform for me. I quickly gained confidence in my ability to instruct and soon developed my own coaching techniques and drills.

But my first real opportunity to coach came in 1997, Bobby Valentine's first full season as manager of the Mets, when he asked me to be a part of his coaching staff. I would not only stay in the familiar role of outfield and baserunning instructor, but would also be the first base coach. Bobby remembered my aggressive style of play from the days when he served as the Mets third base coach. I accepted the position not knowing if I was ready, but it was evident that Bobby thought enough of my abilities to hire me for his staff. What also helped were our common philosophies in outfield and baserunning instruction, making the transition a lot easier for me.

I have always admired Bobby V as a baseball man. He has succeeded in the sport because of his intellect. He understands the game as well as anyone I've ever been around and knows how to manipulate it in his favor.

But some of the same things that made him successful were also his undoing. Many of his players and even front office executives have been very intimidated by Bobby and what they perceived as his dual-personality. They feel that he tried to manipulate them to do what he wanted them to do and that everything Bobby does has an ulterior motive behind it. It's that belief held by so many that has hurt Bobby in a lot of ways through the years.

Even umpires didn't like him because he's not afraid to break out the rule book on them, not to mention the infamous fake mustache after being ejected from a game one time. Man, that mustache was funny. But many umpires, as well as players and front office personnel for that matter, didn't have an appreciation for his humor. To them, it wasn't one of Bobby's best attributes.

But to his credit, Bobby V is one of the most prepared managers and baseball people I've ever met. He was very demanding on his coaches and some of them didn't like it, saying they had their own way of doing things. But Bobby would always hold his ground and shoot right back at them the fact that they weren't the manager—he was.

A lot of players felt the same way about him as the coaches did. They took issue with him because they liked their individuality and didn't want to change the way they went about their business. In this regard, Valentine was perceived as a micromanager. But no one can argue with his getting the most out of his players. In our six years together, from 1997 through 2002, the Mets were a team with limited talent. In fact, in many a pregame coaches' meeting, one of us would ask, "How are we going to win this ball game today?" The answer was always, "With smoke and mirrors." It was a running joke, but with some truth to it.

Bobby recognized the limitations of the players on the team and that's where his managerial skills really came into play. One example of his expertise was the way he kept opposing teams on edge by having all these defensive trick plays ready to go. One of them was Bobby's unique variation of the "shortstop wheel play" to defend against the bunt. Typically, the third baseman charges home toward the bunter with the shortstop covering the vacated third base. The opposing hitter will sometimes try to take advantage of the opening at shortstop by slashing at the ball instead of bunting it. But Bobby would sometimes defend against the slash by having the shortstop fake going to third and holding his ground, and having the first baseman also fake charging toward the hitter and holding his ground at first. It drove other teams crazy and really would catch them off guard. We may have only used these tricks once or twice each year, but once you have the other team aware of what you're capable of pulling off, they look at you a little differently. Bobby V wrote the book on manipulation, and it was a good thing, because with the lack of raw talent on the club, we couldn't rely strictly on traditional plays. Bobby's success in creating distraction under the illusion that we were going to attempt trick plays, which he always ran through our phenomenal defensive shortstop Rey Ordonez, became a huge headache for other teams.

So while people are free to not like Bobby's personality and massive ego, they have to respect his ability to manage. He helped turn around the franchise and led the Mets to the playoffs in 1999 and then the World Series in 2000. With our roster, it was amazing we made it so far in either year. In my mind, those seasons were Exhibits A and B on why Bobby was such a great manager with the Mets.

But after a disappointing fifth place finish in the 2002 season, Bobby V had worn out his welcome with GM Steve Phillips. The two of them had a relationship that started off well when they were both working together in the Mets' minor league system, but that later developed into a bitter power struggle. Whereas Bobby was an excellent evaluator of talent, Phillips was lacking in that area. I saw this firsthand during my time in player development prior to becoming a Mets coach. During that period, I had a few disagreements with Steve regarding personnel decisions.

One time, when Steve was still a minor league coordinator in 1996, I was invited into a meeting he scheduled with some of his coaches to evaluate young players a couple of weeks into spring training. The goal was to come up with the names of the guys we felt had the potential to one day reach the major leagues. To me, one of them we saw that spring was a no-brainer. While he didn't have an athletic-looking body and had a below-average throwing arm from the outfield, he ran well and, boy, could he *hit*. But most importantly, he seemed to have an intangible that you can't teach—he was a "gamer." He was the type of player that rose above his limitations. I listened to Steve and some of those coaches rattle off a few names but none of them was the one I was thinking of.

After the meeting ended, I went into Phillips's office and said, "Steve, I just want to know what you and your guys are looking for when you say a player is major league–ready. Please explain this to me because I'm hearing all these guys' names and not one person mentioned *Benny Agbayani*. That kid is going to play in the big leagues one day."

Steve disagreed and would do everything in the world to keep him in the minors.

But two years later, Agbayani was in the big leagues with the Mets. There was just no keeping him down. By this time, Phillips was our general manager and sometimes sent Benny back to the minors just to make his point. Bobby fumed over this because he loved the way Agbayani played. But Phillips held his ground, preferring to keep a one-dimensional guy like Matt Franco in Agbayani's place. Benny was a much better player, but Steve, for whatever reason, didn't see it that way.

As it turned out, Agbayani, despite playing just parts of four seasons with the Mets, had two of the their biggest home runs in team history. The first was what remains the only major league grand slam ever hit in Japan, an eleventh-inning shot that gave the Mets their first win of 2000. Then, later that year, he hit a game-winning home run in the thirteenth inning of Game Three of the NLCS against the Giants. But despite being a solid player with a flair for the dramatic, Phillips sent Benny packing in a three-team trade following the 2001 season. Steve wouldn't allow Bobby to keep one of his favorite players.

Phillips was just waiting for a down season to show Bobby the door. And soon after the '02 season, a last place finish for the Mets, Bobby was gone and so was his coaching staff.

There is no question in my mind that the main reason Bobby V would have to wait ten years before getting another major league managing job was because of the way he challenged and intimidated front office executives. He would have made most of them look bad with his baseball intellect and they knew it. The long wait certainly had nothing to do with his ability to manage, teach, and get the most out of his ballplayers.

When he finally did get another chance to manage in the big leagues with Boston in 2012, he was set up to fail. Bobby simply never had a chance. The Red Sox brass put him in the impossible situation of tightening up a laid-back clubhouse where the inmates were running the asylum. The guys they had were still loyal to the player-manager style of Terry Francona, who was practically canonized in Boston for delivering two world championships after an eighty-six-year drought. Bobby's "my way or the highway" reputation had preceded him, and those players weren't going to have any of that. They were used to doing things their own way.

My theory is that the Red Sox front office used Bobby as a one-year rental. The manager they really wanted in the first place was John Farrell. The problem was he was under contract with Toronto through the 2012 campaign. Once the season ended, Bobby was fired and Farrell was hired. The Red Sox pretty much just used Bobby V and, after a 93-loss season, likely destroyed any chances of his ever getting another manager's job in the major leagues.

One of the things that surprised me when I coached under Bobby in the late nineties through 2002 was how much the game had changed from the time I played. No longer was speed and defense as important as the power game. In fact, Nike at that time ran a popular commercial with the catchphrase "Chicks Dig the Long Ball." It was very well done and really captured that period of baseball. Of course, as we know now, there was a reason balls were flying out of ballparks at a record pace at that time. It was the height of the steroid era. And hypocrisy at its finest.

Today, of course, baseball is making a concerted effort to rid the sport of performance-enhancing drugs (PEDs). A player really needs to think twice now before putting anything in his body. But in the aftermath of the long baseball strike that wiped out the end of the 1994 season, the World Series, and the start of the 1995 campaign, the owners needed the long ball to save the game in the same manner that Babe Ruth's power surge did in the years immediately following the Black Sox Scandal of 1919. Make no mistake—major league baseball and the owners didn't care about steroids back then. Instead, they embraced how the long ball was bringing fans back in record numbers. Forget the game—guys like Mark McGwire, Barry Bonds, and Sammy Sosa were filling the stadiums for *batting practice!* It became an event all its own that was worth the price of admission.

With steroids, it was a "don't ask, don't tell" environment in baseball. Teams suspected what was going on. But the use of steroids by countless players wasn't important to the owners until the politicians threatened to take away baseball's exemption from the Sherman Antitrust Act unless they cleaned up their sport. It was only when baseball got its hand caught in the cookie jar that Commissioner Bud Selig and the owners got serious about ridding PEDs from baseball.

Many of the fans I've talked to care deeply about how steroids adversely affected the one blessed thing in baseball that is unique from other sports—the record book.

And it's so true. To even a casual fan, when they hear the

number "61," Roger Maris's single-season home run record comes immediately to mind. "714?" Right away, you'll hear someone say, "Babe Ruth's home run total." "755?" "Hank Aaron!" "56?" "Joe DiMaggio's hitting streak!"

Sadly, the Steroid Era, and the bloated offensive numbers created, made a mockery of it all.

As for the players who used PEDs? Well, I don't agree with what they did, but I can certainly understand why they did it. Players saw who was making money. If I played baseball during that time, I would have been viewed differently compared to when I played because stealing bases was no longer seen as much of an asset. So someone like me would have needed to find a way to get bigger and stronger to stay in the game. And when I coached during that era, guys were always looking at their stats and saying stuff like, "I've got to hit for more power. I've got to keep up." Even today to an extent, young players think it doesn't matter if they strike out 250 times in a season as long as they hit 30 home runs. Their feeling is that a strikeout is a reasonable price to pay as long as they hit home runs.

Baseball needs to get even tougher on guys who use PEDs. There are still players out there using them by evidence of how many are still getting caught. As it stands today, you have to wonder if the benefits of using PEDs outweigh the risks. After all, what's the worst thing that can happen to a player if he gets caught? Well, they get a fifty-game suspension and don't do it anymore. But even if they do get suspended, their teams usually welcome them back with open arms. They're like, "Okay, let's go. Get back out there and play."

The reality is if a player can get away with using PEDs for a number of years, they've made their money. Nobody can take it back. All they need is that one big contract to set them and their family up for life. And for the marginal player on the cusp of making the majors or staying in the minors, you can understand the allure. Some of them might be thinking, *I'm not going anywhere without them.*

As for the fans, they tend to play both sides of the PED argument. On one hand, they are quick to call the guys that get caught "cheaters" who are destroying the game they love. But they also have to take some of the blame as well. Fans demand a winner. They don't come out to the games for the sheer joy of watching their team play no matter what product is put on the field. For example, Mets fans right now are saying the team doesn't spend enough money. They don't want us to build a winner through our farm system and astute trades—nobody wants to hear that. If the Mets, or any team for that matter, has the money, the fans want it spent on the first free agent who can hit 40 home runs. Don't ask why or how he hit all those dingers, just bring him in!

The Baseball Writers Association of America (BBWAA) made a major statement against the Steroid Era in 2013 by not electing any player into the Hall of Fame. And I think that's great. But I will say this: if I had a vote for the Hall of Fame, there is still one player from that tainted era that would have gotten mine—Barry Bonds. That's because I saw him play before the accusations about him came out and everybody knows the "demarcation line" with Barry—he was clean prior to 1999. And during those first thirteen years of his career, he was exceptional and refined in every phase of the game. Barry, unlike those one-dimensional sluggers of his era, was a perennial MVP that could do it all. He was a first-ballot Hall of Famer well before he got involved with steroids.

Bonds made a huge error in judgment by juicing. Clearly he was affected by and perhaps even jealous of all of the attention McGwire and Sosa were receiving in their friendly rivalry to break Maris's single-season home run record in the summer of '98. But one thing's for sure. Once Barry went on whatever steroid he was using, knowingly or unknowingly, he was phenomenal—perhaps the most feared hitter who ever played the game.

———

After Bobby and our coaching staff were dismissed by the Mets following the '02 season, I was reassigned and made manager of the Kingsport Mets of the Appalachian Rookie League. But I was confused as to why I needed to leave my coaching job in New York. I thought, *Didn't I do my job well enough? And if I didn't and that was why they replaced me, then why am I still in the organization?*

Maybe Steve believed I was a Bobby Valentine guy and thought it was best to move me. Or I was transitioned to let the incoming manager—Art Howe in this case—pick his own staff.

In any case, managing was my new job. But while I appreciated the opportunity, the Rookie League was hardly a true testing ground of what being a skipper was all about. At Kingsport, my lineup, pitching rotation, and daily available players were dictated to me by others in the organization. I understand and mostly agree with this process because protecting and developing these young players is the organization's first concern. Wins and losses are secondary. But the process does very little in developing managers.

After managing my second year at Kingsport, the Mets flew me up to New York to interview for the first base coach position, the same job I had for six years under Bobby V. Willie Randolph had just accepted the manager position after they fired Art Howe. I thought, *Now, why in the world would I need to fly up to New York to interview for a job they knew I had done for them before?* But I interviewed anyway and, lo and behold, didn't get the job. Incredible.

The Mets bumped me up to manage the Brooklyn Cyclones, a higher-level team in the Short-Season A-Ball New York–Penn League, in 2005. But there really was little distinction between the Appalachian and New York–Penn leagues in terms of managing. My hands were still tied from making most personnel decisions on the team. While I enjoyed managing and felt I had the baseball knowledge and experience necessary to possibly do it at the big league level one day, it didn't appear likely that it was ever going to happen. I was so disappointed that, despite having paid my dues at the lower levels of the minor leagues for several years, I was never given any feedback on what I needed to do to become a better manager. There was simply no career path.

After the season in Brooklyn, with no indication from the Mets on how I was doing or where I was headed, I decided to explore other options outside of baseball. Dejected and disappointed, I saw there was no room for me or intent within the organization to make me a big league manager. I realize that not everyone who wants to be a manager is managerial material. But that determination can only be made when a candidate is given a legitimate opportunity, which I was not.

It was around this time that I had an epiphany. I suddenly

realized the inconvenient truth that within the Mets organization there was an ongoing trend of not tapping into the knowledge, experience, and winning attitude of our 1986 championship team. The Mets have shied away from that iconic club because they haven't wanted their current one exposed to that hard-partying culture which, while well documented, has also been somewhat exaggerated at times. They don't want the players to walk into the manager's office or the executive suite and think, *We're associated with the '86 Mets because we've got them in positions of authority.* It's not the image the Mets' ownership and front office want to cultivate.

I really don't understand this way of thinking at all. Guys from our '86 team should be represented in positions of development all throughout the dugout, in the bullpen, and upstairs in the front office. You want people to help the young kids coming up to understand what it means to play and win in New York, and what the Mets fans expect and want out of their players. Sure, some of our guys got mixed up in some bad situations, but if nothing else, the guys from that championship team are older and more mature now and can warn the current Mets about some of the pitfalls of fame. All of this has value, not to mention how their great baseball minds can help make the current team become better and smarter ballplayers.

The Mets have been distancing themselves from the image of our '86 team for quite some time. You can trace its beginnings all the way back to when they traded away Kevin Mitchell almost immediately after winning the '86 World Series. I don't think young fans have a sense of how the Mets ruled New York City during the mid to late eighties. The team may have an occasional day when they'll bring in a guy from the '86 team and have them throw out a ceremonial first pitch, but there's no true constant reminder of the team's past successes.

It just defies common logic. That team had so many astute players who have never been extended any decision-making positions within the club. Three of our brightest baseball guys—Mex, Ronnie, and Ojeda—are team broadcasters. Teufel is currently the third base coach.

Where's everybody else?

Well, Roger McDowell is a pitching coach with the Atlanta Braves. Rafael Santana is a scouting and player-development supervisor for the Chicago White Sox. Howard Johnson is a batting coach in the Seattle Mariners organization. John Gibbons managed in the Mets' minor league system for seven years, including three at the AAA level, but when Bobby V got fired, Gibby didn't even get a chance to interview for the top job. Toronto snatched him up and three years later he was the AL Manager of the Year with Toronto. Ray Knight managed the Reds for a while and is now a Washington Nationals broadcaster. Lee Mazzilli was a Yankees coach and later managed in Baltimore. Dwight Gooden once had a front office job with the Yankees. Danny Heep is coaching at the college level despite wanting a shot at a professional baseball position. Doug Sisk can't get back in. Neither can Jesse Orosco. We'll wait and see what happens with Wally, who is currently the Mets' AAA manager in Las Vegas. I hope he gets his shot one day at managing the Mets, but I'm not holding my breath.

It's just a shame that the Mets have such a great pool of resources from the eighties that they choose not to take advantage of. If it's because of what happened with Doc, Straw, and Lenny, then it still doesn't explain why they wouldn't hire some of the others.

Say what you will about how tyrannical late Yankees owner George Steinbrenner could be with his managers, players, and staff. But he was famous for bringing back former Yankees and putting them in high-, mid-, and low-level positions. Once a Yankee, always a Yankee. In that sense, our crosstown rival shows more loyalty and has closer ties to their former players than the Mets do.

If I was ever a general manager, knowing what I've experienced at the highest of highs and lowest of lows, while taking into account my own personal convictions, I would try with all my heart to pick the best human beings I could find to field a team. However, I would not let anything overshadow my choosing the players with the most talent and intangibles. So, if all things were equal between two players, I would pick the more model citizen. But if you've got one guy who you know drinks a little bit, fools around a little bit, but is just a head-and-shoulders bigger "gamer" over the other guy, guess who I'm going to battle with? The guy that drinks and fools around every time. That's because if you have a job like the general manager, you're not only representing yourself, but also the person who employs you and the city the team plays in. They want to win. That's the thing that matters most to them. Now, what does that say about me? Well, I guess in a sense you can say I am selling my soul. Who knows?

But take the 2012 World Series as an example. There's no doubt in my mind, player for player, top to bottom, that the

Detroit Tigers had a better team than the San Francisco Giants. Not even close. But the Tigers didn't have the intangibles, the "gamers," that the Giants had. The '86 Mets had the best of both worlds—the talent and the intangibles. The attitude and desire to win and to rise above whatever was in the way was too great to lose. What weakness did our team have? Well, a lot of our guys partied too much. But that wasn't a weakness because the next day they were ready to go. Whatever it took to win, we did.

I stayed away from baseball for four years through 2009, living my life back in South Carolina, wondering if I had a place either back in the Mets organization or somewhere else in baseball. To my surprise, and a real knock to my ego, no one seemed to be aware of why I left baseball and nobody called to find out. It was a humbling experience.

Missing the competition and excitement of baseball, I swallowed my pride and contacted the Mets. They invited me to interview with the team's minor league director Adam Wogan and his assistant John Miller. I was soon hired for the position of outfield/baserunning coordinator. I really enjoyed coaching and evaluating players again and believed I had found my rightful place in baseball at that stage of my life. And just as important, I felt like I had reestablished my relationship with the Mets organization, which is what I always wanted in the first place.

But just as I had become comfortable in my new role, the Mets' new manager for 2011, Terry Collins, approached me about being his first base coach. Terry was the minor league field coordinator the previous year when I took over the outfield/baserunning duties and told me he liked the job I was doing with the kids. I never campaigned for the first base coaching position when it opened up because, quite frankly, I loved what I was already doing. But when Collins offered me the job, I somewhat reluctantly agreed, saying, "Okay, Terry, for you, I'll do it."

Coming back to coach for the Mets was much different than my first go-around. I now felt like an outsider. I really wasn't given any information about what was going on with the club and was kept entirely out of the loop on important matters. On more than one occasion, I would stand in the outfield before a game, look around, and think how crazy it all was. It's obvious that they hired me for a reason, but they left me wondering what that reason was.

That season, the Mets were pretty mediocre, though there were some signs of progress. Despite our fourth place finish, Terry had done a pretty good job with what he had to work with. Following the season, Collins, as well as his pitching and hitting coaches, was retained, but GM Sandy Alderson fired me along with bench coach Ken Oberkfell and bullpen coach Jon Debus. I guess the brass pinned some of our relief pitchers' subpar performance on Debus, but who knows why they canned Oberkfell and me? And by getting rid of the three of us, was it really going to make the team any better?

I was pretty confused. I initially got wind of all of this a few days after the season ended when Terry called to say I would be getting a call that the Mets weren't bringing me back. This was just several days after the last time I saw Terry and we were talking team strategy for the upcoming spring.

I said to Terry, "Why would you take me away from a job I

loved, make me your first base coach, but then not bring me back? I have a problem with that. I don't get it."

Terry said, "Mookie, it's not my call."

I thought, *Well, it was your call when you hired me. What happened between January and October?*

I knew I wasn't going to win this argument, so I let it go.

It was a strange season coaching under that new regime. I felt like I was watching the deterioration of the Mets organization. They seemed to have no identity. They kept mixing and matching and trying to do this or do that. They were making trades and signing free agents to long-term contracts instead of developing their own identity by investing in the farm system. While I believed they had a direction they wanted to go in, I questioned whether reaching it was truly obtainable. My concern was that the character of the players they were looking for superseded the talent they brought to the table. Character on a team is important, but you've got to have the horses to win.

A few months after firing me from my first base coaching duties, Sandy made me the team ambassador, a role I still play today for the ball club. As ambassador, I make appearances here and there in the corporate suites at Citi Field among other venues. I also work as an extra minor league coach, visiting each club—AAA Las Vegas, AA Binghamton, and A-Ball teams in Port St. Lucie, Savannah, Kingsport, and Brooklyn—for three days a season. I make myself useful by helping to coach and pitching batting practice. But I don't have the authority to instruct or teach on anything other than what those managers want taught. I have to do what they ask, even if I disagree with the methods being used with the players.

It's sad to admit this, but I have basically become a hood ornament for the Mets. I have no decision-making role at all in my job
description. I would have liked an explanation as to why I was
moved from first base coach to the ambassadorship, but none was
ever given. I feel that I deserve to hear just some words to justify
the actions of an organization that I have honored and promoted
every day of my nearly thirty-year existence in it. I understand that
jobs come and go in the baseball business, but sometimes management loses sight of how these moves play with people's lives. When
you have no stability and don't know what you're doing from one
year to the next, it's very difficult to do anything. One year you're
making $100,000, the next year just $40,000. Where's the reasoning? How can people live under those circumstances? For as difficult as it is, I don't think it really bothers team management, and
that troubles me. I don't care about not having a job. If they fire me
because they have a better replacement, that's fine. But when no
information is given as to why a move is made, it's much worse
than getting an explanation I might disagree with. They just dictated my career as a player and a coach and it wasn't right.

I suppose the reason I get so emotional about all of this is
because I *really* love the city of New York, the fans, and the Mets
organization—the only one I really know. It bothers me that the
Mets trust me enough to stand before the cameras, sponsors, and
fans, to say and do all the right things, yet feel that I'm not worthy
to be a vital part of helping this organization become a championship team again. It's depressing to think that I only represent a
moment in history and a visible, recognizable face of a great memory fading into the mist of an ensuing generation of disappointment

and change. I have spent many restless moments trying to figure out if there was something I should have done that would have changed the team's opinion or perception of my leadership skills. I thought that perhaps my feelings were the musings of an aging athlete whose time had passed, fueled by ego. However, I have grown to understand the difference between my ego-based feelings and the facts.

The reality is that I was a successful major league ballplayer that helped turn a perennial losing ball club into a champion by leading with an aggressive style of play. I gained a wealth of leadership experience and an ability to teach and manage through my work in player development and coaching, all while under the tutelage of some of the truly gifted baseball minds of our time. Because of this, I never wanted a token job, but rather one with purpose and value to the Mets organization. I wanted to be remembered as one of the people responsible for restoring the Mets to the great and proud organization it once was—and can be again.

But despite my knowledge and passion for the game, the Mets have never viewed me as a "baseball guy." The club has demonstrated a lack of respect for my abilities in the area of leadership. While I love interacting with fans in my current role as team ambassador, I desperately don't want this to be my last chapter in baseball. I still have too much to offer.

If I have a legacy, I don't want it to be about hitting a slow roller up the first base line. I would rather it be that there isn't a person alive today with more passion and love for the game of baseball than yours truly.

15

Entering the Ministry

I must live by the words and virtues of Christ.
My life must be an example to others, a display
of how God can work in their lives, and a
testimony of God's grace and mercy in me.

—Mookie Wilson

As a Christian, I had a strong sense a few years ago that there should be more to my life than just being a former major league baseball player. I wondered what exactly my calling should be to please God. My family had been members of the Zion Mill Creek Baptist Church in Columbia, South Carolina, for more than a decade by this point, and I was already quite active in the church, helping out here and there. But I just felt compelled to do more. It gave me an uneasy feeling.

After talking with our pastor, Bishop Wendell Sumter, about how I felt, he asked that I consider becoming a deacon. My father had been a church leader, the equivalent of a deacon in the

United Methodist denomination, and my brother Phillip was on his way to becoming a deacon, so serving God runs in the family. After attending some classes with the senior deacons, finding out as much about that role as I could, I became one.

One of the first things I did as a deacon was initiate a Future Leaders program. I would mentor a dozen or so young men, mostly in their early teens, on a host of social, financial, and spiritual topics each Saturday morning. Some of them had attended our church, others had not. The goal of the program was to help them become better and more responsible young men, allowing them to accept who they were and understand how to grow into effective leaders.

To mix things up a little bit, we would sometimes have outings, like attending sporting events in Atlanta and other places. The one thing I found in dealing with young people is that you can't pound the gospel into them. So I wanted to make it more educational and fun, then kind of ease them into learning the virtues of Christ as we went along.

I really enjoyed interacting with these young men and answering the interesting questions they posed. While I didn't talk about my professional career too often because I didn't want it to be a distraction to what the group's goals were, some of them wanted to hear my take on the challenges of being a Christian athlete. It's an interesting topic because of the way displaying one's Christian beliefs on the playing field has evolved since my days in professional ball.

Back when I played, particularly in the minors, where players had to argue with a manager just to get five minutes of baseball chapel on Sundays, it wasn't easy being a Christian and it was often easier to just keep it to yourself. Today, of course, is very different. I sometimes get asked about sports' most famous Christian athlete, Tim Tebow, and how he gets down on one knee and gives thanks to God after scoring touchdowns—commonly referred to in the American lexicon as "Tebowing."

I love the idea of what Tebow does because I came up in a time in sports when that would never have been accepted. He has brought a greater awareness to the Christian athlete than anybody else.

There is, however, one thing about Tebowing that I have an issue with. My concern is whether what he does is used to glorify God or to bring more attention to himself. I realize a person's relationship with God is personal and, not knowing Tebow at all, I don't really know why he does what he does after *every* single touchdown he scores. But if you're going to be vocal and display your faith as often as he does, then you have to do it with the good *and* the bad. So if he throws an interception, he's got to thank God for that, too. I know that sounds a bit extreme, and I'm not saying he should do it, but I would just hope he at least thinks to himself, *I threw an interception, but Lord, I thank you for what it is.*

It's the same thing with the guy who crosses home plate after hitting a home run, points to the heavens, and thanks God. Okay, that's fine, but why not do it after popping one up?

As Christian athletes, we have to be careful not to mislead people into thinking that we only praise God when good things are happening to us. You want to be happy and show your faith in God *all* the time, even when things are not going the way you want them to go. First Thessalonians 5:18 in the Bible tells us, "In everything give thanks; for this is the will of God in Christ Jesus concerning you."

A lot of people in the secular world criticize Christian athletes for praying before and during games because they feel that God doesn't choose sides. What many people don't realize is that what most athletes are doing, or should be doing, isn't asking God to help them win, but rather they are giving thanks to Him for the opportunity and ability they've received to become professional athletes. When Tebow played in New York, the Lord wasn't rooting for the Jets because he was playing for them. And their losing record *clearly* proved that.

Another religious issue came up during the 2013 Super Bowl. Ray Lewis made a comment using a very powerful scripture that said, "No weapon formed against me shall prosper." Hey, Ray, you were just playing a *football* game. It's a competitive sport. The team on the other side of the field isn't your enemy. They're your competitor. I thought it was very inappropriate to use that scripture in the context he did. In the secular world, it was interpreted to mean that the 49ers and their fans were evil. And he said it twice!

Since being connected with a double murder during Super Bowl weekend in 2000, Lewis wears his religion on his sleeve. I think after that experience, reality may have hit him hard. Redemption and finding God after something like what Lewis was involved in can happen. In fact, it happens a lot. Sometimes you have to get to the lowest point in your life before you realize there's something more to life than what you're living at the time. I've seen a lot of players have bad seasons and come back the next year saying they found Christ. Something dramatic usually happened in their lives that pushed them to search for something that's emotional, not physical. And that's when they often turn over their lives to Christ.

In addition to the Future Leaders group, Rosa and I help sponsor what we call the Golden Society, an organization for senior citizens. Rosa really spearheads that, but I am actively involved. It's about giving seniors "a day." They can come in, have a nice meal, get catered to, and listen to speakers we bring in to talk about health, security, financial, and social issues. Every one of them who comes gets a gift basket and we set up a bingo game for them. It's just a wonderful thing for the seniors. It's a time when they can voice their feelings about what they need. In turn, we try to meet those needs. We make sure they feel like it's *their* day.

Rosa and I have always felt that seniors sometimes get overlooked in churches. We don't tap into their wisdom as much as we should. In the Golden Society, we want them to feel like they're a part of our church and to never underestimate their value to it. I have learned so much just by talking with them. It can be an awesome experience.

After a year or so of being a deacon, I called Pastor Sumter and said I needed to talk with him again. This time, I told him I thought I needed to go a step further and become a minister.

His first question was, "Now, Mookie, do you want to be a preacher or do you want to be a speaker?" He explained that people who are not ministers speak all the time at church.

Initially, I didn't really know how to answer the pastor's question. I thought of myself as more of a speaker and less of a preacher. His recommendation was that I start taking some ministerial classes to see where the Lord would lead and place His spirit in me to do what I was called to do. It was in these classes that I learned the proper etiquette in writing and reading sermons and getting critiqued by other ministers to make sure what I prepared was God-given and inspired. The ministers did a great job at making sure I knew what was involved and what the duties entailed.

I soon reached the conclusion that I did, in fact, want to become a minister. To be effective, I needed to try even harder than ever before to be as Christlike in my daily life as I could. Anybody can quote the Bible, but to preach the gospel, you have to live by your words. I was committed to doing just that, because without displaying it, my words would be rendered worthless.

Pastor Sumter was a big help in preparing me mentally for my task, because I had some concerns. My style of preaching, while full of energy, is somewhat different from many other black preachers. I didn't think I fit into the mold of ministers I enjoyed. Since I wasn't like them at all, I thought that maybe preaching was something more than what God wanted me to do. I wondered if that was a problem, so I addressed my concern to Pastor Sumter, who said, "Mookie, be who God calls you to be. Everyone's not meant to have Joel Olsteen's soft-spoken delivery or T. D. Jakes's theatrical techniques. Your own style is going to reach somebody. There will be people in that congregation who will receive your message."

Pastor Sumter's message was clear. He was telling me to be who I am and not try to change. If God gives someone a gift, He will make room for it. Once I understood that I needed to be myself, I was much more comfortable in my approach to preaching. You don't have to run across the pulpit or jump up and down on the pews to get the message across. You just have to be comfortable in your own skin.

And it's so true. Sometimes a congregation gets too caught up with what a preacher is doing and not enough with what they're saying. I had a friend who was blown away by a sermon at another church. He came up to me practically giddy about it and said, "This preacher was wonderful! He was brilliant!" I said, "That's really great. I'm glad you enjoyed it. What was his message that you were so impressed with?" He had no idea.

It just goes to show that a preacher's theatrics can sometimes drown out the actual message of the sermon.

One of the challenges that I have as a preacher is getting some people to focus more on my message and pay less attention to the fact I played professional ball. I want people to see *Mookie the Preacher*, not *Mookie the Center Fielder*. I've had people come to the church and say, "I heard you were here and I just had to see you." Don't get me wrong, I understand it. And if it brings even one more person to the church who might not have come if I wasn't there, and they feel God's grace through one of my sermons, then it's a very good thing. I would just prefer that people come to believe that if I had never played ball that being a minister would have been my true calling.

Anyone who knows me knows I love to have fun. And I think

church should be uplifting and people should enjoy the experience of being there on Sunday mornings. As such, I always try to interject some of my sense of humor into my sermons and have been told by some people that I could make a living as a stand-up comedian. But really all that I'm doing is sharing my life experiences in my preaching. I may jot down a few notes to make sure I cover certain topics or biblical stories, but a lot of what I say just comes to me in the moment, so I can be somewhat unpredictable or even politically incorrect with some of the humorous things I come out with at times.

Something I never do is rehearse a sermon. I have always tried to avoid sounding too scripted like other speakers I have heard. And to keep the congregation's attention, I try to come up with parables, like Jesus did, that are related to subject matters people can easily understand and relate to. My very first sermon was titled "Batteries Not Included." In it, I was trying to give a message that would encourage people to have faith because it is the power source that enables us to utilize the gifts of God. In another that I called "Can You Hear Me Now?" I used the famous catchphrase from the Verizon commercials to talk about how God warns us about the consequences of sin before we are tempted to commit one. So far, my technique of keeping things current has worked well in keeping the congregation engaged.

While I truly enjoy discussing the Bible with others, one of my pet peeves is when people say the good book is outdated. My feeling is that scripture is never outdated. While I understand that the stories in the Bible were sometimes written several hundred years after the event actually happened, people need to stop taking the Bible literally all the time. Nowadays, we've got cars and trains, and our society and laws have changed dramatically from biblical times. And the Bible covers that by stating in Romans 13 to "Obey the laws of the land as well as the laws of God." Life changes and you have to live within the structure of the society you're living in. But that's no reason for compromising your Christian virtues. It's not that hard.

We get in trouble when we try to rewrite the Bible. You simply have to try to keep the spirit of its message. It is what it is. No matter how much you try to change it, the scripture is the scripture. But when we try to change what it says to conform to the rules of what is socially acceptable today, that's where a lot of issues come up. People try to justify what they're doing now and what they believe. In Deuteronomy 4:2, the Bible says, "Do not add to what I command you and do not subtract from it, but keep the commands of the Lord your God that I give you."

I was born and raised in the church environment—my first exposure to it was at St. Luke's United Methodist Church in Ehrhardt, South Carolina, from childhood through my time playing professional ball. But after moving to the Columbia area fifteen years ago, the two-hour drive each way just became too much and Rosa and I began looking for a church that was closer to us. That's when we were introduced to the Zion Mill Creek Baptist Church by my youngest brother, Phillip, and his wife, Natalie. Even though it was a little different from what we were used to, I never got wrapped up in denominations. If it's a Bible-based church, it's a church. Plain and simple. And in a stroke of luck, Pastor Sumter also acted as the principal at our daughters' middle school, so the girls really felt comfortable and enjoyed going there to listen to him preach.

The first aspect that I liked about the Creek, as we sometimes call our church, was the energy. Both the congregation and chorus are so alive and the pastor is full of energy. And that's the way it should be. My father always told me to make a joyful noise unto the Lord. In fact, the O'Jays made a song titled "Make a Joyful Noise" in 1976 that he absolutely loved. Like any church, we have our issues, but the love, the caring, and the concern that people have for one another make it a truly wonderful place for praise and worship. Like Pastor Sumter once said, "It's the kind of church that pulls people in and the spirit of the Lord moves in your heart and mind." Before we even knew anyone at the Creek, we had a great feeling about the place.

I guess you can say that Rosa and I are a husband-and-wife ministry team. Rosa, who had already been a lay speaker at St. Luke's, joined the ministry two years before I did and is already ordained. I expect to be ordained anytime now.

Being ordained is a long and sometimes difficult process, which is a good thing. It keeps me from being complacent and gives incentive to study scripture whenever I have the opportunity. The Watery Association, comprising hundreds of churches, includes senior pastors who will test and basically put me through the ringer in its own kind of final exam. I've heard that when the Watery Association panel of ministers gets through with you, you are completely spent. But that's fine with me and the way it should be. Becoming an ordained minister should be difficult. If you want to be a minister just to say you are one, or for the glamour of the position, you're doing it for the wrong reasons. The sole purpose of entering the ministry should be about working for God's kingdom and supporting the gospel of Christ.

I haven't been this content since the end of my baseball career. As has been the case throughout most of my life, I'm not certain what the future holds. Should Rosa and I move to Florida in five or six years as we plan, I like the idea of being a pastor at my own church. I will be in my early sixties then and will have a lifetime of experiences to tap into when preaching to a congregation. I think there is something to be said for the wisdom of age. Nothing beats experience. I'm convinced that all the book knowledge in the world doesn't meet what is gained in life's journey. Even when you're talking about the gospel, the scripture, or the Bible, it doesn't matter. Until you experience certain things, it is very difficult to help others with the challenges and hardships they encounter in their own travails.

I can talk to people about rejection. I can talk to people about financial struggles. I can talk to people about abuse. I can talk to people about bigotry. I can talk on and on and on because I've lived it all. On the flip side, I've also experienced prosperity. So I've been at both ends of the spectrum and everything in the middle. But I've never been happier than I am right now.

Even though I would have loved the opportunity and still have the desire to manage the Mets—guess what?—I can take it or leave it now. I couldn't say that three years ago when I realized the chance to manage them was never going to happen. I was, in all honesty, a pretty bitter person. I thought that everything I worked very hard for was taken away. But sometimes people have to reach their lowest point to understand God's plan. Maybe that was my low point.

But I'm really at peace with it all now. I had a great run in baseball and while I'm not going to lie and pretend there aren't some regrets, there comes a point when you have to move on. You can't live in the past. You can't stew over missed opportunities. Maybe I'm doing what I'm supposed to be doing right now.

With props to the Stephen Stills song "Love the One You're With," the same goes for one's occupation. If you can't have the job you want, love the job you've got.

And right now, I love what I'm doing by serving the Lord.

AFTERWORD

The venue was the National Baseball Hall of Fame in Cooperstown, New York, a place that holds everything that's dear to the game. I haven't met a ballplayer yet that doesn't respect the institution and doesn't want to spend a day just walking through it to see how far the game has evolved.

How appropriate and what an honor it was to wrap up nearly two months of media events and book signings by promoting my autobiography, *Mookie*, before an enthusiastic crowd in the hallowed museum's Grandstand Theater.

The Hall of Fame is one of those places where you have to be invited. It's like the White House for ballplayers. It was well worth the effort of waking up at 6 a.m., driving the four-hour roundtrip with my co-author Erik Sherman from Binghamton, New York, where I was helping instruct the Mets' Double A team that week, and making sure I was back at the ballpark by 2:30 p.m. My only regrets were that I was unable to spend the rest of the day walking around that beautiful upstate hamlet and taking up Hall of Fame president Jeff Idelson on his generous lunch invitation. But I plan to make it a point to return there at the earliest opportunity.

The entire book tour, not to mention the writing and publishing process in general, was more than I expected. I had anticipated the volume of work involved, but I think I learned more about what authors go through, what publishers endure, and the tremendous amount of effort behind the scenes to get a book published. I was pleasantly surprised by it all and thrilled I had the opportunity to experience it.

Although I enjoyed each of the media events and interviews I did since the release of the book, some of them definitely stood out as favorites of mine. Aside from the Hall of Fame, I really enjoyed another Q&A that Erik and I did at the Yogi Berra Museum. What's great about this format is that I got to give answers as long and detailed as I wanted, much better than the fifteen-second sound bites preferred by the media. And I loved the fact that the questions came from a savvy baseball audience, a great way to interact with the fans.

A similar event was held at LaGuardia Community College in Queens, New York—"Mets Country!" Upon arrival, I was invited into the office of Dr. Gail O. Mellon, LaGuardia's president, and I presented her with a signed copy of the book. Dr. Mellon later introduced me to an audience of mostly inner-city and immigrant student-athletes in the school's theater in such a way that made me proud. An educator first and foremost, Dr. Mellon said I was one of her heroes more for the fact that I wrote a book than for my playing career. That made me feel really good because we are so sports-conscious in this country that sometimes it's easy to forget about the person that's inside the uniform and what they accomplish off the playing field.

Once on stage, not only did I once again get to answer questions, this time from moderator and professor Dr. Habiba Boumlik, but I was also permitted time to give a lecture on the topic of "Race and Sports," a subject that is near and dear to my heart.

It's scenarios like these when I'm at my best. Giving lectures to students may very well be a part of the next phase of my life, particularly when I feel that by sharing my experiences and challenges from my humble beginnings as a sharecropper's son to where I am today can make a difference in their lives. I've experienced a lot in my life and have not just survived, but thrived. I have defied the odds and that's a message of encouragement and hope that needs to be told. Kids need to know that success is not about numbers or dollar signs, but rather about being happy.

I get so frustrated when people say, "Oh, he makes millions of dollars playing ball. He's got to be *so* happy." No! A rich player is a human being, just like you and me. People have this perception that money solves everything. But in reality, money causes problems as often as it solves them. Most athletes just want to be accepted as human beings. That's why when ballplayers get together they never talk about money or the material things they own. Instead, they often discuss things like how many deer they got when they went hunting, or how big a fish they caught on a fishing trip, or how their daughter is driving them crazy! The conversations center around real life events like most other people's.

The LaGuardia event was one of the most energetic settings I've taken part in to date. I was honored to speak where governors, mayors, congressmen, and captains of industry have delivered speeches. I sensed the energy from the young people, and by watching their faces and reading their body language, I felt I was really getting through to them. By reminding the students that I wasn't *always* a preacher, I believed they could sense I could relate to many of the challenges and temptations they face each day. And despite the many different races and cultures in the audience, I emphasized how, as a people, we're all looking for the same two things—the freedom of opportunity and respect. I encouraged them to forget about what people look like, or what they sound like, and to pay attention to the contribution and value they can give to their community and country. It's like what Jackie Robinson said, "A life is not important except in the impact it has on other lives."

I would like to continue giving lectures to young people, to make them aware that the assistance they need to succeed is there if they put themselves in the position to grasp it. It may not be everything they want, but it's a start. If people saw where I came from, they would understand that anything is possible with perseverance and the right attitude.

Perhaps the most high-profile and enjoyable experience of the media tour was my appearance on *The Daily Show*. It was unforgettable because I've watched Jon Stewart for years and enjoyed how comical he can be on the issues of the day. He made it clear that he was a fan of mine and the Mets, which definitely put me more at ease. And by going on his show, I got some major kudos from my children, who are huge fans. When I initially told Preston about it, he said, "Of all the opportunities you have with promoting the book, if you do nothing else, you *have* to do Jon Stewart!"

Afterwards, Preston called to say I did a good job and looked great. But my son, ever-fashionable, questioned my choice of wardrobe. Hey, what's wrong with a long, white jacket?

My children are my biggest critics, so it felt good knowing they supported me so overwhelmingly in this project, and everything I have done and tried to achieve over the years.

The book signings were a trip. It felt as if the fans were walking up to my table like they were visiting a dear old friend. It was a *hundred percent* positive. There is no questioning the bond that I have with the New York fans. It has always been more than just a player-fan relationship. These people have allowed me to come into their homes, to be a part of their families. Many have named their pets or even their children after me! I mean, that's *closeness*! Not every ballplayer can say they have this kind of special bond with their fans so I don't take it for granted. And I think because it still exists all these years since I retired makes me appreciate it even more.

I signed over 2,200 books for fans in the eight-day period following the release. I enjoyed every minute of it, speaking with every one of them, writing personalized inscriptions, and having my picture taken with whoever asked. I do the extras as much for me as I do for them. I have always felt that doing the little extras for my fans, especially if they are willing to wait in line to meet me, is the least I can do for them. They deserve my respect and acknowledgment.

From my regular autograph signings at card shows, I am fully aware that my speaking with the fans means more than my signature ever will. That's why I fully engage myself with them. I can relate to what they're feeling, because I felt that way when speaking with Jon Stewart. Thus, I think it's important to, at the very least, say hello, ask how they're doing or talk about a hat or T-shirt they may be wearing. It's really meaningless chatter, but for the average fan it's a really big deal. I guarantee they'll remember the conversation I had with them even more than reading the book. They'll read it and then go buy another one, but the memory of our brief conversation will endure.

I honestly wish, had time permitted, that I could have had a five-minute conversation with all of them because many had interesting stories.

And, *oh*, some of those stories!

There were three anecdotes from fans at the book signings that really stood out as the most amusing to me. My favorite was from a Brooklyn woman who said she went into labor as the bottom of the tenth inning of Game Six of the '86 World Series began. Her husband asked her to hold on until after the Mets finished hitting. Of course, we rallied to win and at the book signing she *thanked me* for hitting the game-winning ground ball that ended the game so she could get to the hospital and deliver her baby! I mean, *that's* a fan!

Another good one was from a twenty-seven-year-old man who said that for nearly the entire nine months of his mother's pregnancy, his parents were going to name him Mookie. But then, with a touch of gallows humor, he revealed how just days before he was born, his grandfather William died, so he was named Bill instead.

And then there was another gentleman who, as a young boy in the eighties, told his mother his favorite Met was Mookie Wilson. For months, his mother repeatedly corrected him, telling the youngster he must mean "Mikey" Wilson. But then she took him to Shea Stadium one afternoon and was set straight when the lineups were announced and she realized the boy was correct all along.

But of all the stories I heard from the fans, there was one at the very first book signing in a Manhattan Barnes & Noble which meant the most to me. A man who appeared to be in his late fifties told me that after reading my book he felt inspired to go back to college and get his degree like I did well after my playing days were over. It was hearing nuggets like that one that made me feel I fulfilled my true purpose of writing this book. I understand how people wanted to read about my views on the '86 World Series and Game Six and all of that—and that's great—but for someone to tell me that I inspired them to improve as a person is more important to me than inspiring someone to be a better Mets fan.

There was another element of the book signings that was an unexpected bonus for me—some of the people that showed up.

When you do a book tour, you meet so many interesting folks, but the last thing I expected was to meet a relative I had never met before, which is exactly what happened at the Words

Bookstore in Maplewood, New Jersey. Perhaps if a chance encounter like this one had occurred in New York, that would have been a different story because I have relatives there, but I didn't know I had any in the Garden State. In this case, the charming young lady was my mother's sister's granddaughter.

I truly wish I'd had the time to speak with her more than just the minute or so I had at the book signing. I would have asked her more about her grandmother—my aunt Cora—about her parents, and how she ended up in New Jersey. Thankfully, my wife, Rosa, got her phone number so we can stay in touch.

Another fortuitous encounter was at a Long Island book signing where I met Joe Diecedue's sister. She was so touched that I named one of the chapters in the book after her family's restaurant, Joe's Seafood, a chapter in which I reflected on my time working there as a maître d'. With tears in her eyes, she hugged me and didn't want to let go. Her brother, Joe, and her father, who ran the restaurant, have long passed away and their place has been closed for years, so it was heartwarming to see a member of that family again. I had a very rare player-fan relationship with the Diecedues and we were as close as people from opposite cultures could be.

I suppose if I had one wish that would have enhanced the media and book signing tour and made it even more wonderful than it already was, it would have been to have my father at my side to experience it all. A day didn't go by when I didn't think about him so, in a sense, I guess he was with me the whole time. But when I consider how my family came from a small town in South Carolina and how we went through the things we did

together—the civil rights movement, segregation, and bigotry—
and then to end up in the "big city" doing a book tour, I can't
help but think my discussing the lessons he taught me and the
impact he had on my life would have made him proud.

I also think he would have really loved the book because he
always embraced "truth." And while he believed some things
were better left unsaid, whether positive or negative, in the case
of my autobiography the truth makes a difference because I'm
telling people about my life and feelings. Thus, despite his being
a private person, I think he would have had an appreciation for
everything I wrote.

However, my father probably would have thought the media
hype for the book was a bit overdone, primarily because he was
a very simple person who didn't like attracting attention. So in
that respect, the press may have turned him off just a little bit.
But overall I think he would have been pleased and would have
enjoyed the whole experience. There is no question in my mind
that if my father were alive and well enough to travel, I would
have made it a point to get him to New York for the tour, just as
I made a point of flying him up for the 1986 World Series. I
would have insisted he joined Rosa and me.

As for the media's immediate response to the book, I can't
say I was surprised that much of it focused on some of the more
controversial aspects of it. Honesty always has a way of raising
eyebrows and I expected that to happen here. But I think some
of what I wrote was misunderstood. Some of the terms I used
made it seem like I was angry or furious with the Mets. But
there's a big difference between being disappointed and being

angry, and I was glad I was given numerous opportunities to clarify my feelings about the Mets organization.

Not surprisingly, the catchphrase "hood ornament" that I used in the book to describe how I saw my current role with the Mets received the most attention. I knew that phrase was a bit ambiguous, but I liked the fact it was a bit mysterious. I wanted people to say, "Oh, what does Mookie mean by that? A hood ornament?"

I must admit it got a lot more play than I expected, but that was fine with me.

So what's behind my "hood ornament" comment? Its meaning is something I picked up from my truck driving days. While a hood ornament identifies what kind of vehicle you're driving, it has nothing to do with the actual operation of it. So while people identify me with the Mets, as the team ambassador, I currently have no input in the decision-making processes in helping run the team. I was hoping people would get that point without my actually spelling it out for them, but I was happy to explain it. Of everything I wrote in the book, the "hood ornament" phrase is one of the things I love the most because it perfectly described the state I am currently in with the Mets.

I haven't received any comment or feedback from Mets management since the release of the book and, to be honest, I didn't seek or expect anything. I have, however, heard from a few longtime Mets employees who told me they loved it.

It was really no surprise to me that some of what was written in the New York tabloids or aired on talk radio and television was formulated by commentators before they even read a single page of my book. It was obvious they just trolled through the bullet points the publisher sent out looking for anything with a hint of controversy or negativity. And, hey, I understand it. The media has a job to do, whether it's to get ratings or sell newspapers. I have enjoyed a very good rapport with the media for the more than three decades I have been in New York and I think it's my understanding of how they do their jobs that has helped me weather any storm that may come up. Rule number one is not to take what's said or written too seriously. And rule number two is to not believe everything you read. If a player can't deal with these realities, than they shouldn't read the papers at all.

A lot of media focused on what I wrote about how Darryl Strawberry and Doc Gooden never realized their full potential, disappointing both their fan base and themselves because of their drug and alcohol dependencies.

Well, guess what?

I have since bumped into each of them and their responses to what I wrote were overwhelmingly positive. They both gave me high fives and said they really enjoyed reading the whole book, particularly the chapters dealing with the eighties Mets. They both said it was the "absolute" truth and they had an appreciation of how everything was addressed and how nothing was left out. They knew that anything I wrote about them was not meant to be malicious, but rather just part of a story I was telling. It made me feel good that they took it the right way because they truly are dear friends of mine.

From the very beginning of this writing project five years ago, when I began putting my notes together, I felt I needed to be completely forthright to those who were going to spend their hard-earned money to buy the book and take the time to read it. And the feedback from them has been great. They seem to understand what I was trying to achieve through my writing, that nothing was dressed up or tailored to make everything rosy. In the simplest of terms, they appreciated my honesty.

As hard as it is to believe, I think I received more attention from this book than at any time when I roamed center field at Shea because people were accustomed to seeing me play baseball. But to actually write a book, and to be on national television promoting it, attracted people to me as a person and gave them a much better sense about what makes me tick and how my experiences have shaped who I am today. And some of those readers weren't just fans, but friends and even family I've known for years.

One of the first public places I went to after coming home from the book signings and media tour was my church. People there congratulated me and some told me how they were regularly texting Rosa during the tour to find out which television or radio show I was going to be on next. With satellite today, it's not difficult to find most any program on TV or the Internet.

Even though I have been a member of my church for well over a decade, many of the members viewed me more as a celebrity rather than as a regular person. But now that many of them have read the book, they've found out new things about me—like my challenging upbringing—that they really didn't know much about. They now know another side to me, which I think is great. It has already facilitated much conversation which I am quite sure will continue for a long time to come.

Prior to the start of the service, all of the ministers—myself included—met in Bishop Wendell Sumter's office to get our assignments for the morning. After the conclusion of the meeting, as everyone was walking out, I presented a signed copy of my book to the bishop with a special note thanking him for all the help he has given me over the years. The bishop took the book with him to the pulpit and, during a segment of the service called "From the Pastor's Desk," a time used to give the congregation news about the church, he said, "Mookie, we want to welcome you back and congratulate you on the book."

The bishop then pointed out references in my autobiography regarding my involvement, dedication, and commitment to the church. He proceeded to read a few paragraphs from various pages and then stopped, telling the congregation with a smile, "That's all I'm going to read now, because I want you to go out and buy the book!"

When he later realized that the testimony he gave about me was printed on the back cover, he was pretty shocked and told me how much he appreciated the gesture and how it made him feel like a celebrity. It was awesome.

As for my family, most of my siblings and in-laws have read the book. But I know for a fact that my sister, Dorothy, and sister-in-law, Merdestine, have already read it *twice*! But neither they nor my other siblings were surprised by the contents of the book because those family members are, of course, quite aware of how I grew up. But I think there might have been some relief because before the book came out, some of them worried about whether or not I was going to write too much about them. But while I promised them I wouldn't reveal any family secrets, the reality was we could never *afford* to have any family secrets, anyway!

I think a way in which this book could prove to be a valuable family heirloom for us is how it will pass along our history to the younger members of the family, like my thirteen-year-old nephew, Brian, who, after reading a couple of chapters, was surprised with what he learned about the struggles endured in our family's past. Up until now, I think the kids thought they were all just a bunch of fairy tales.

Those same recollections also flooded the collective memories of my brothers. After publication, a few of us talked about some of the other bad things we experienced in the South during the sixties. What was already in the book was pretty powerful, but there was another frightening experience we discussed that none of us will ever forget.

My older brother, Richard, two of our younger brothers, and I were walking home after a day of fishing when some white guys in their late teens pulled over alongside of us in a pickup truck. There were more of them than there were of us. Richard knew these young men to be real bad news and let's just say they started saying some really awful , racist things to us—to put it mildly. Night had fallen and we didn't know what they were going to do to us. I was only eleven years old at the time and we were all really scared. Richard, who was about fifteen at the time, was very concerned and kind of pleading with them to leave us alone. We didn't know for sure what they had in the back of their truck, but there was a realistic concern that they might be armed.

Somehow, Richard convinced them to leave us unharmed, but the fear of an experience like that stays with you forever.

Two or three years later, after we moved into town from the farm, Richard noticed one of guys that was in that pickup truck, walked up to him, and knocked him out cold.

There were other stories like that, of course. It was a different world back then. However, I didn't want the book to be flooded with too many of these stories. Maybe I'll write about more of them in my next book!

And that brings me to another point. I've been told that almost every author looks back at a completed book they've written and thinks, *Uhh, I wish I would have mentioned this or that.* In my case, I may have included more faith-based content, perhaps even another chapter on the topic. And while I gave readers a taste of what it was like growing up African American in the South during the sixties and seventies, I might have added more of my experiences that would have enhanced people's understanding of what it was like during the civil rights era in a small town.

Don't get me wrong, I don't wake up in the middle of the night or anything like that and regret any omissions that may have made the book better. I am really pleased with the product as it is.

Perhaps the best thing for me in writing this book is how it has changed the way I think about things. I needed to write it because it enabled me to come to grips with my feelings about certain things that maybe I wanted to ignore or push to the side. For example, I didn't want to admit to myself that I was angry with the Mets for a while. *Very* angry. But writing about it brought all of that angst to the forefront. It's not healthy to keep negative feelings inside. Thus, the experience of writing a book was very therapeutic and I likely saved myself a couple hundred thousand dollars in therapy!

So what's next for me?

I will always remain involved in baseball at some level. Once the game gets in your blood, you can't just throw it away. So I will probably be instructing or coaching baseball right up until my very last day on this earth because I love the game that much.

I guess the ultimate question, which I've been asked numerous times since the book release, would be *where* I will be doing this. Unfortunately, that's not entirely up to me. I love the Mets but, without question, I would be willing to coach in another organization. But I wouldn't want a coaching job just for the sake of having one. That's not in my plans—never was, never will be. I have made that perfectly clear to everyone, including the Mets. I have a wealth of experience and a knowledge of the game that I believe would be a valuable asset to any organization.

Aside from baseball, I have many other aspirations as I enter the next phase in my life. I will continue to preach and I look forward to becoming an ordained minister. I also enjoy lecturing and have actually thought about becoming a teacher one day. And I'm serious about writing more books and am, in fact, well into two new writing projects.

In looking back at my past, I have a lot to say that can have a positive influence on people's lives. I have an appreciation for where I came from—even some of the unpleasantness. After all, you can't grow if everything is always good. In other words, it's impossible to understand what sweetness tastes like if you have never tasted bitterness.

Rosa and I talk all the time about what we used to eat and drink in the early days of our marriage. For example, if there were some sardines and grits in the house, we made a meal out of it. We couldn't always afford Kool-Aid or soda, so we mixed syrup and water together to make "sweet water." But by reflecting on the tough times, we remind ourselves of how blessed we are now. It's funny, but sometimes I look back on my youth and think to myself, *Those were the good old days. I miss doing some of the things we had to do to get by.*

You're probably wondering why in the world I would want to relive my beginnings. But a couple of years ago, I actually looked into purchasing a two-hundred-acre farm close to where my mother lives in South Carolina. I know it sounds crazy, but that area is where I'm from—it's home and will always be home. The purchase of the farm never materialized, but a part of me wishes it had.

I get asked all the time, especially when in New York, how the book is doing. I'm tickled to death to tell them that it's selling well not just in the Big Apple, but in cities across the country I never anticipated, like Chicago, Seattle, and Los Angeles. And, of course, it was gratifying to see the book named by the *New York Times* as one of the bestselling sports books of June 2014.

I've also been asked my thoughts about a possible movie adaption of the book one day. Well, Rosa and I had some fun with who would play my part. I like Omar Epps, but my wife's choice was Denzel. I told her, "Let's be realistic, he's *too tall* to play me!"

But more important than the book sales or any dreams of a movie being made is how this experience was more fulfilling than I ever thought it could be. A book is a part of you, it's something you created. It's something that you leave behind well after you're gone. Perhaps fifty years from now, someone will pick up my book and buy it.

The idea of such a thing is truly very special to me.

—Mookie Wilson
Eastover, South Carolina
July 2014

ACKNOWLEDGMENTS

We would like to thank the following for their contributions to this book: Bill Buckner, Gary Cohen, Ron Darling, Bud Harrelson, Dan Hart, Keith Hernandez, Jay Horwitz, Marc Levine, Roy Markell, Tim McCarver, Bobby Ojeda, Howie Rose, Bishop Wendell B. Sumter, Jim Trdinich, John Tully, and Rosa Wilson.

Denise Silvestro did a terrific job as our editor and the enthusiasm she showed for the project throughout the entire process made her a joy to work with. Special thanks, as well, to managing editor Jennifer Eck and assistant editor Allison Janice, for their tireless contributions to the success of this project.

Sally O'Leary was invaluable as our proofreader. And her wealth of historical knowledge of the National League from her many years as the Pirates' public relations director also enabled her to provide us with insightful feedback on the book's content.

Rob Wilson is not just a literary agent, but a caring friend who always gives spot-on advice.

Recognition should be given to several books, newspapers, and websites that proved to be valuable sources of facts during our research. They include *If at First . . .* by Keith Hernandez and Mike Bryan, *The Bad Guys Won!* by Jeff Pearlman, *The Greatest Game Ever Played* by Jerry Izenberg, the *New York Daily News*, the *Wall Street Journal*, the *New York Post*, the *Boston Globe*, and the websites BaseballReference .com and NewYorkTimes.com.

—Mookie Wilson and Erik Sherman

I can hardly thank Erik Sherman enough for all of his hard work in developing questions that made it easier for me to recall the various periods of my life. Erik helped make writing this book one of my greatest experiences—second only to my baseball career. He demonstrated to me through this project that there is more to my life than what I knew about myself. He brought back distant memories that seemed like they happened just yesterday—not only things in the book, but even things that aren't in the book. He has been a great asset and there is no way I could have done this without him.

—Mookie Wilson